Understanding Social Inequality

Understanding Social Inequality

Tim Butler and Paul Watt

SAGE Publications
London ● Thousand Oaks ● New Delhi

First published 2007

SAGE Publications Ltd
1 Oliver's Yard
55 City Road
London EC1Y 1SP

SAGE Publications Inc
2455 Teller Road
Thousand Oaks, California 91320

SAGE Publications India Pvt Ltd
B-42 Panchsheel Enclave
Post Box 4109
New Delhi 110 017

British Library Cataloguing in Publication data

A catalogue record for this book is available
from the British Library

ISBN 0 7619 6369 3   978 0 7619 6369 1
ISBN 0 7619 6370 7   978 0 7619 6370 7

Library of Congress control number available

Typeset by C&M Digitals (P) Ltd., Chennai, India
Printed on paper from sustainable resources
Printed and bound in Great Britain by Athenaeum Press, Gateshead

Contents

• • • • • • • •

List of Figures and Tables

Acknowledgements

●●●●●●●●

This book has, like many if not most academic books, been long in the making – arguably the combined half century that we have both been teaching sociology and particularly social class to often skeptical students. Our first debt must therefore be to those students who expressed, on the one hand, their concern and even anger at the various forms of inequality they observed and in many cases experienced in their lives but, on the other, their doubts as to whether sociological approaches to social class could adequately describe let alone explain it. We have both been heavily influenced by Mike Savage's project to make class a central part of the sociological account of contemporary life. We also both acknowledge a debt to Chris Hamnett who, at different times and in different institutions, supervised our doctoral theses, and has continued to influence our thinking. Thanks to the following for reading and commenting on sections of the book: Judith Burnett, Anne Chappell, Wayne Clark, Rosie Cox, Chris Gifford, Shirley Koster, Robert MacDonald and Ian Roper. We are very grateful to the anonymous reader who made a number of extremely helpful suggestions about how we might restructure the book, almost all of which we have adopted. Finally, we would like to thank Chris Rojek and Mila Steele, our Editors at Sage, for their patience in the face of an annual succession of excuses about why the book was not yet written.

Tim Butler and Paul Watt
December 2005

CHAPTER ONE

Introduction

- Rationale
- Structure of the book

Rationale

Socio-economic inequality is massive and in many parts of the world is getting wider. According to Kerbo (2003), income inequality in the United States, the richest society on earth, has widened in every year since the 1980s. By 2000, nearly three per cent of American households were living on less than $5,000 a year while over 13 per cent had incomes of $100,000 and over. The net wealth for black households in 1991 was just $4,604, whilst Bill Gates, the richest man in the world, had assets of $54 billion in 2001. Levels of income inequality are widest in the United States out of all the major industrial nations and the gap between it and the others has itself grown since the 1970s (Kerbo, 2003). Western European countries have also experienced greater income inequality, especially Britain during the 1980s and 1990s (Hills, 1995; Walker and Walker, 1997; Flaherty et al., 2004; Hills and Stewart, 2005). In Britain the median income of the richest tenth of the population increased by over 60 per cent in real terms between 1979 and 1996/97, whereas that of the poorest tenth rose by only 11 per cent (and even fell by 13 per cent if income is measured after housing costs!) (Sefton and Sutherland, 2005: 231). Poverty also increased dramatically in Britain from 7.1 million (13 per cent of the population) in 1979 to 12.5 million people (22 per cent) in 2001/02 – poverty in this sense means below 60 per cent of median household income after housing costs (Flaherty et al., 2004: 31).

Such statistical evidence indicates the scale of inequality, but it does not by itself allow us to understand its social nature and impact. In particular, it does not show how ordinary people struggle to get by, or in some cases fail to get by, on limited means. In order to understand such social processes, other sources must be referred to. These include social scientific studies based on qualitative research methods, such as interviews or participant observation, with those eking out a living on various combinations of welfare benefits and low-paid work (Newman, 1999; Chamberlayne et al., 2002; MacDonald and Marsh, 2005; Smith, 2005). Another source is a number of books by committed journalists who have temporarily taken the jobs that provide the permanent source of income for the millions of the 'working poor' in both Britain (Abrams, 2002 – see Box 1.1; Toynbee, 2003) and the United States (Ehrenreich, 2002).[1]

Box 1.1   AGENCY CLEANING IN LONDON

Fran Abrams worked at three minimum wage jobs, as an agency cleaner in London, as an agency worker on the bottling line at a pickle factor in Yorkshire, and as a care assistant at an old people's home in Scotland. For her first job, she attended the Casna agency 'training session' at a hotel near central London. The session, which was due to start at 11 p.m., actually began at quarter to midnight:

'Samuel [manager] sits down and launches into a 20-minute lecture about reliability. This is obviously a key Casna Thing. More interesting, though, is the brief summary of our pay and conditions. Tonight will be an unpaid training night, though we will be reimbursed if we stay six weeks. There will also be a one-off £10 deduction for setting up a bank transfer facility. No one gets paid unless they have a bank account. If we leave without proper notice – he doesn't say how long this is – our pay will be cut to £3.60 per hour'.

Fran's first job was on the night shift at a hotel. Most of her workmates were immigrants, many of whom were also students. Fran had to clean the staff changing rooms:

'The men's are filthy. There are pools of urine all over the floor, dotted with bits of sodden toilet paper. There's obscene graffiti all over the walls of the cubicles, and several of the toilets are blocked. [...] I must empty the bins, pick up the rubbish from the floor before sweeping and mopping, then clean all the sinks, mirrors and toilets. Then I have to do the same thing all over again in the ladies'. It's incredibly hot down here, but even if it wasn't I'm sure I'd still be sweating copiously'.

After four weeks Fran left and calculated whether it's possible to live on the minimum wage in London:

'I just about manage to break even on my budget, but only after living for the best part of a week on a single bag of pasta. Then my payslip arrives, and I find I haven't been paid for most of the scheduled extra hours I spent doing offices or for my overtime. I've worked almost 119 hours, not including breaks, and I've been paid £418. ... After tax and other deductions, I take home a grand total of £363. My expenses, which consist of rent, transport ... and food, come to £474. ... No, I'm sure you can't live on these wages in London. And yet somehow, by staying with relatives or living in hopelessly overcrowded housing, by always walking or catching the bus, by juggling two jobs or even three as well as studying, tens of thousands of people in London do just that'.

Source: Abrams (2002: 11–13 and 60–1).

While there is ample statistical and experiential evidence on the nature and effects of inequality, it is also paradoxically the case that the study of social class, which is centrally concerned with describing and explaining socio-economic inequality, is no longer central to academic sociology. Indeed, some sociologists have claimed that the study of class is no longer relevant to understanding contemporary society at all, if it ever was (Pakulski and Waters, 1996). Why do they think this? The main answer is the argument that society has changed in ways that mean that the old class divisions are no longer important. Class is ultimately derived from economic distinctions bound up with the social relations of production ('you are what job you do') which dominated what Ransome (2005) calls the 'work-based society'. In the contemporary affluent 'consumption-based society' (2005), the social relations of consumption ('you are what you buy') are more significant. Another possibility is that spatial relations ('you are where you live') have grown in social importance to supplant those derived from social class (Savage et al., 2004, 2005a, 2005b).

This shift in the significance of class can be illustrated by the career of Ray Pahl, a prominent British sociologist. During the 1960s, Pahl was one of the major advocates of the utility of class as a way of describing, understanding and explaining patterns of social and spatial interaction. This was seen in his highly influential class-based critique of the newcomer/local divide in rural commuter villages (Pahl, 1965). By the late 1980s, Pahl had published a controversial paper in a major urban studies journal that amounted to a personal volte-face, as well as a challenge to the dominant class paradigm: 'class as a concept is ceasing to do any useful work for sociology' (1989: 710). For Pahl, the old class categories made less and less sense as a way of explaining social patterns of behaviour. His radical change of mind sparked off a series of chain reactions within the discipline of sociology (Lee and Turner, 1996).

This book broadly takes issue with the substance of Pahl's influential pronouncement, but is nevertheless very well aware that the usefulness of class for sociology is something that has to be demonstrated to those sociologists *outside* the somewhat rarefied confines of what has become known as 'class analysis' (Crompton et al., 2000; Savage, 2000; Wright, 2005). Class is simply too important to be left to the already convinced established specialists. This book is therefore aimed, at least partly, at the non-specialists within sociology who may agree with Pahl and who feel that class is no longer relevant. The book is also aimed at those more generally trying to 'place' (spatially and socially) social deprivation and inequality in a society seemingly divided between the 'have lots' and the 'have nots' yet one in which many people in the global North feel that they have grown steadily better- if not well-off.

Until the 1980s, post-war British sociology was dominated by a concern with stratification and especially class. Although the intellectual underpinnings of this concern were diverse, as we discuss below, the result was a rich seam of sociological research which placed socio-economic inequality centre-stage within the discipline. The major sub-branches within sociology demonstrated a fundamental concern with social class, as seen in the following 'classic' texts which still repay reading today:

- Family – *Family and Class in a London Suburb* by Peter Willmott and Michael Young (1960).
- Education – *Learning to Labour: How Working Class Kids Get Working Class Jobs* by Paul Willis (1977).
- Employment (or what used to be called 'industrial sociology') – *Working for Ford* by Huw Beynon (1984, first published in 1973).

As well as making a serious contribution towards a sociological understanding of the structures and processes governing social inequality, these kinds of books were often written in a highly readable style which could not only grab the imagination of the average sociology undergraduate but could even appeal to the lay reader.

Five major developments have occurred within the social sciences during the last 30 years that have had a profound impact on academic sociology in relation to the analysis of social inequality.

- The introduction of new theoretical approaches and perspectives, notably feminism, poststructuralism and postmodernism, as well as the work of the French sociologist Pierre Bourdieu.
- The 'cultural turn' has led away from understanding social inequality through economics and politics towards symbolic representations of cultural difference (Devine and Savage, 2005), as exemplified by the influential and expanding field of cultural studies (Munt, 2000).
- Class is no longer 'king' – there has been a progressive expansion of the domain of inequality to incorporate elements previously marginalized by a monolithic class paradigm. Gender, ethnicity, age and their associated identities have steadily moved up the sociological agenda with the consequence that class has become just one among several sources of inequality (Bradley, 1996).
- A renewed interest in space and place, topics traditionally associated with the discipline of geography. This has led to a certain rapprochement between sociologists and human geographers which has been particularly fruitful in the field of urban studies (Savage et al., 2003).
- Globalization – however real or imagined its impacts – has undermined the perceived national experience of systems of class inequality and so led to its increasing marginalization in sociological discourses.

As a result of these developments, class no longer acts as *the* bridge across the various sub-specialisms within the discipline of sociology. Instead, the study of social class, or class analysis, has effectively become a sub-specialism in itself. This academic specialization and division of labour can be regarded as an inevitable result of disciplinary expansion with far more sociology departments and sociologists in existence now in comparison to the 1960s and 1970s. However, we also think that it can lead in directions, both theoretical and methodological, which ironically mean that the study of inequality becomes removed from providing a clear connection between the 'private troubles' and 'public issues' which constitutes what C. Wright Mills (1970) called 'the sociological imagination'. Having taught stratification to sociology undergraduates for several years, many of whom have come from working-class, poor and otherwise disadvantaged backgrounds, we are aware that some of the established approaches and debates in the field of class analysis have not connected up with their own 'private' worldviews and experiences, for example, as in debates over the 'best' occupational class scheme to use; see below.[2]

Our aim in this book is to offer a path through some of the debates and issues that are pertinent to the analysis of social inequality, especially class inequality. We aim to do so in an accessible manner that stimulates students' sociological imaginations and prompts them to question how the study of inequality can link up private troubles (including their own) with public issues. This book makes no apology for being centrally concerned with social class, but in a manner which does not ignore 'other' aspects of inequality, for example ethnicity, age and gender. Careful readers will have spotted that we referred above to covering only 'some' of the issues and debates relevant to class analysis. We are not claiming to be comprehensive and it is therefore important to indicate the boundaries and biases of the book.

Traditionally, sociology was taught as a series of trinities – first between social theory, social structure and methods, and second within theory between Marx, Weber and Durkheim. The third trinity was the 'holy grail' of sociological analysis – finding the synthesis between structure and action. We believe that these trinities are no longer as apposite as they once were, given the way that a series of writers, notably Pierre Bourdieu (see Chapter 8), have developed a sociological approach which transgresses many, if not all, of these boundaries borrowing (at least in the UK) from a number of traditions. This has contributed towards a cessation in the traditional divisions within sociology and to a more synthetic approach which has also seen a blurring of boundaries with cognate disciplines and fields, notably human geography, cultural studies and social policy. Thus, although we make reference to social theory and theoretical debates, we do not claim to offer either a particular theoretical approach or a comprehensive theoretical overview of the terrain of class analysis. Examples of the former include the neo-Marxism of Erik Olin Wright (1997), whilst examples of the latter include Crompton (1998), Savage (2000) and most recently Wright (2005); readers are encouraged to refer to these sources.

In relation to methodology, we are not centrally concerned with the question of exactly how one operationalizes the concept of social class in survey research, typically via the employment of occupational schemes which are often hierarchically arranged (Duke and Edgell, 1987). Crompton (1998: 55) has referred to the 'employment aggregate approach' to class analysis which uses occupation as the best indicator of class in survey-based research and aims to find out what impact the class scheme has on a range of dependent variables, for example rates of mortality or ill health (Townsend et al., 1988). The official Registrar General's (RG) social class scheme, which groups a large number of occupations into a smaller number of hierarchically organized classes, has historically been the major way that this employment aggregate approach has been conducted in Britain, not least by government agencies (Reid, 1998; see Table 1.1 below).[3] As Reid demonstrates, occupationally based class schemes, like the RG's, can then be correlated with a large number of other variables, such as rates of illness or the proportion of young people going to university, and this allows the measurement of

Table 1.1   Registrar General's Social Class scheme

Social Class	Occupations	Examples
I	Professional	Solicitor, doctor
II	Managerial and technical	Manager, nurse
IIIN	Skilled non-manual	Secretary, receptionist
IIIM	Skilled manual	Electrician, hairdresser
IV	Partly skilled	Caretaker, hospital porter
V	Unskilled	Cleaner, labourer

Source: adapted from OPCS (1991:12)

statistical correlations between occupational class and differences in health, education, income, etc. Research on health inequalities has shown that mortality rates follow a 'class gradient'; in other words that the percentages of the population dying and being ill are highest among social class V (unskilled occupations) and they decrease as one moves 'up' the class scheme to their lowest level in class I (professionals) (Townsend et al., 1988).

Despite its utility in correlating with and predicting life chances, such as mortality rates or chances of attending university, the RG class scheme has been subject to various criticisms including its uncertain theoretical basis (Rose and O'Reilly, 1997; Crompton, 1998). Such criticisms have meant that the RG scheme was replaced from 2001 by an alternative more complex scheme, the National Statistics Socio-Economic Classification (NS-SEC); see Rose and O'Reilly (1997) for a rationale and discussion of the new scheme. The eight-fold NS-SEC is effectively a modified version of the neo-Weberian class scheme originally devised by John Goldthorpe (1980) to measure social mobility in Britain (see also Erikson and Goldthorpe, 1993). Table 1.2 shows the NS-SEC and Goldthorpe equivalents.

As Breen (2005) has pointed out, there has been a slight shift in the conceptual principles underpinning the Goldthorpe class scheme. Initially it was based on clustering occupations according to their market situation and work situation along Weberian lines (Goldthorpe, 1980). Market situation refers not only to the range of immediate rewards that accrue to an occupation, for example salary/wage levels, occupational pension schemes and access to perks such as company cars, but also 'prospective rewards' such as promotion opportunities and incremental salary increases. Work situation refers to the occupation's location within a system of authority and control and the degree of autonomy that people within that occupation have in undertaking their work tasks. The principles underlying the Goldthorpe scheme later shifted to employment relations, notably whether employment is regulated by a 'labour contract' as in the case of the working class, or a 'service relationship' as in the case of the service class (Erikson and Goldthorpe, 1993). Those in the service class (salaried managers and professionals) are advantaged relative to both the intermediate and working classes by possessing higher rewards, including 'prospective rewards' in the form of career opportunities, as well as greater levels of authority and autonomy within organizational hierarchies.

Table 1.2 National Statistics Socio-Economic Classification and equivalent Goldthorpe class names

NS-SEC classes	Goldthorpe class names
1 Higher managerial and professional occupations	Service
2 Lower managerial and professional occupations	Service
3 Intermediate occupations	Intermediate
4 Small employers and own account workers	Intermediate
5 Lower supervisory and technical occupations	Intermediate
6 Semi-routine occupations	Working
7 Routine occupations	Working
8 Never worked and long-term unemployed	–

Sources: adapted from: http://www.statisitics.gov.uk/methods-quality/ns_sec/default.asp (23 March 2005), and Roberts, 2001: 25.

The employment aggregate approach has involved some of the most protracted debates within sociology, for example between neo-Marxists and neo-Weberians (Marshall et al., 1988; Erikson and Goldthorpe, 1993; Wright, 1997), as well as the acrimonious 'women and class' debate over the role of female employment and whether the household or individual constitutes the best 'unit' for measuring occupational class (H Roberts, 1993). Summaries of these debates and alternative class schemes are available elsewhere (Crompton, 1998; Roberts, 2001; Bottero, 2005) and again interested readers are referred to these (see Further reading at the end of this chapter).

Crompton (1998: 122) has suggested that a fruitful methodological alternative to the employment aggregate approach in class analysis is the case study 'which views the social unit (the neighbourhood, the trade union, the workgroup, the political party) as a whole'. Hence the emphasis moves away from the multivariate analysis of large survey data sets based upon occupational clusters, towards an understanding of the processes of class formation whereby the dynamics of action and consciousness are explored within specific contexts of unequal rewards and life chances. The case-study approach also highlights the intersection of class with 'other' axes of inequality:

> Such studies invariably reveal the complexities of group formation, and in particular, the interpenetration of the 'economic' with the social or cultural. Thus they have focused not only on 'class' factors – that is, economic power as reflected in production and market relationships – but also on ascriptive (status) factors associated with gender, race and age, as well as cultural and normative assumptions, and the influence of contextual factors such as locality and community. (1998: 203–4)

Although case studies are often thought to be synonymous with qualitative data, they can also embrace quantitative data, and Crompton points to the use of the latter in the 'critical case study' of affluent workers in Luton by Goldthorpe et al. (1969), discussed in Chapter 3. In this book, we make frequent use of case studies to illuminate the dynamic nature of class processes and also the complexities of contemporary class relations. Many of these case studies are furthermore attentive to the spatial context of social action and again this is something that we wish to emphasize.

Our main source of reference for much of the material in this book is Britain. Nevertheless, where appropriate, we discuss material drawn from North American and European societies in many chapters. In this manner, we are trying to engage with the increasingly globalized nature of social inequality. Our approach is to indicate something of the broad contours of class as they apply across the Western world, but within the context of globalization which means that similar processes of inequality-generating mechanisms are taking place. This is not to say that these processes are having the same effect everywhere; they don't. Considerable differences arise in each nation-state context, especially in relation to the circumstances of those at the bottom of the socio-economic hierarchy partially at least as a consequence of differences between 'welfare regimes', as we discuss in Chapter 6.

Finally, as mentioned above, our primary focus in this book is with socio-economic or class inequalities. In this sense we agree with Harriet Bradley (1996) in her book *Fragmented Identities* who suggests that class is still extremely important, not least because of the unquestionable 'social fact' that contemporary societies are massively unequal in material terms, as we highlighted above. To abandon 'class' altogether in the face of overwhelming evidence for the growth of socio-economic inequalities seems sociologically perverse. In her book, Bradley offers a 'synthetic approach' to class analysis that we are sympathetic to, even if it ultimately raises as many questions as it solves (Walby, 1992; Crompton, 1998). Bradley concedes that any singular 'return to class' is weakened by its reliance on a form of 'grand narrative', associated with Marxism, and that other forms of inequality, such as gender, ethnicity and age, have their own dynamics which cannot be reduced to class. Instead, she suggests that one potential way forward for class analysis is to understand the ways in which the various dynamics of inequality intersect and interweave. In other words, class analysis can only proceed by abandoning its hegemonic pretensions and embracing the multidimensional nature of social inequality. Whilst we broadly endorse this position, we also think that achieving the comprehensiveness that Bradley advocates is beyond a text like ours. Therefore, while we make reference to 'other' aspects of inequality, notably ethnicity, gender and – to a lesser extent – age, we accept that specialists in these areas will undoubtedly find our book deficient.

Structure of the book

There are two main themes to this book. Firstly, that the social world has changed immensely over the last 50 years and that the 1970s/1980s marked a tipping point between an old industrial society whose origins lay in the Enlightenment and Industrial Revolution and a new one which has arisen out of a post-industrial information led economy. The restructuring from one to another, a process which is far from complete in 2006, is the subject matter of contemporary sociology and this book. The second main theme is that what were once mainly social processes, which were associated with particular places, are now ones which are truly socio-spatial in which place cannot simply be 'read off' from changes that were essentially social in origin. This reflects in the structure of the book which is organized roughly according to these two themes which, of course, are incomplete, inchoate and interbred but nevertheless, we argue, are at the heart of the changing object of sociological study over the last half century.

Chapter 2 goes on to examine two main intellectual frameworks, postmodernity and globalization, that have challenged many of the central claims of class analysis. Chapter 3 focuses on the 'collar line' in differentiating classes, paying attention in particular to the changing relevance of occupation and how this was manifested in the industrial city and the slow move towards the suburbs in the context of afflu-ence. Chapter 4 develops this argument by focusing on how scholars working in Marxist and Weberian traditions attempted to come to terms with these intra-class divisions against the background of increasing social and economic crisis in the 1970s and how the inner city developed as a metaphor for the nature of the changes taking place. In essence we argue, both groups had to throw away the sociological rulebook in order to comprehend the restructuring of national class systems and space economies.

In Chapter 5 we examine the consequences of this in terms of the new and emerg-ing spatial and social divisions: the emergence of global cities, gentrification of the inner city and – controversially – of an urban underclass. Chapter 6 focuses on the notion that, despite increased aggregate affluence, advanced capitalist societies during the last 30 years have increasingly generated high and sustained levels of poverty and also what has come to be termed 'social exclusion'. We discuss these issues in relation to debates around how welfare states are organized in Western societies. Until the col-lapse of the Soviet Union and East European state socialist societies in the late 1980s and early 1990s, the comparative analysis of stratification in advanced societies tended to focus upon differences between such 'second world' societies and 'first world' Western capitalist societies (Giddens, 1973; Hamilton and Hirszowicz, 1993). Since the demise of the state socialist societies there has been renewed interest in the differences between Western capitalist societies (Crow, 1997). Chapter 7 examines processes of class formation among post-industrial service workers, examining the new work created by this restructuring as well as those who undertake these jobs.

Finally, in Chapter 8 we pull these debates together to suggest that an emerging sociology of stratification drawing heavily, yet eclectically, from the work of Pierre Bourdieu and others, based in a broad range of empirical methodologies, is begin-ning to paint a very different sociological picture from that of the sociological ortho-doxies of the past half century. It is one which recognizes the place (literally) of choice and belonging in the context of new economic and occupational divisions in which sociological subjects play a very active role in painting the picture of their surrounding society.

———————————————————— **Further reading** ————————————————————

Crompton (1998) remains probably the best single overview of the terrain of class analysis. Wright (2005) provides an outline of the theoretical foundations to six major perspectives on class, including Wright's own neo-Marxism, Goldthorpe's neo-Weberian approach, and Bourdieu. Wright (1997) is a somewhat neglected, but extremely rich comparative neo-Marxist study of class structure and consciousness. Bradley (1996) offers an exceptionally clear overview of the postmodernist challenge to the analysis of social inequality across the four dimensions of class, gender, race/ethnicity and age. Gibson-Graham et al. (2000) present an eclectic collection of stimulating essays that draw upon poststructural theory and Marxism. Bottero (2005) is an excellent account of the debates over class that largely complements our own, but coming at it very much from the perspective of the 'Cambridge School';· she places more emphasis than we have on issues of gender, sexuality and arguably ethnicity, but says less about issues of place and space. Marshall et al. (1988) is based on a large-scale survey of the British class structure in the 'employment aggregate' tradition. Devine (1997) is a detailed comparison of class stratification between the United States and Britain.

The history and operationalization of the National Statistics Socio-Economic Classification (NS-SEC) can be found at http://www.statistics.gov.uk/methods_quality/ns_sec/default.asp

Modernity, Postmodernity and Globalization

CHAPTER TWO

- ◼ Introduction: the end of certainty
- ◼ The Enlightenment 'project', modernity and postmodernity
- ◼ Globalization
- ◼ Models of globalization
- ◼ Globalization and migration
- ◼ Conclusion

Introduction: the end of certainty

In this chapter, we focus on two linked discussions that, over the past quarter of a century, have unsettled the ways that we had come to understand the nature of social stratification in advanced industrial nations. The discussions are those about the nature of postmodernity and of globalization, terms that have been highly contested both from within and outside the academic sociological community. What was once clearly in the academic domain of sociology – the nature of social stratification – has become generalized across the broad fields of the humanities and social sciences as well as a more public intellectual milieu.

We begin the chapter by attempting to unravel what is meant by 'postmodern' through a discussion of the rise and fall of the concept of 'modernity' whose origins we trace back to the Enlightenment. The development of sociology, and particularly the sociology of social stratification and industrial society, is similarly traced back to the Enlightenment. We suggest that it was a combination of Enlightenment philosophy and the development of capitalist modernity that gave rise to the particular certainties and structural imperatives that characterized sociological thinking for much of the twentieth century. In particular, classes were seen as the natural flora and fauna of this habitat and they determined the broad patterns of social behaviour. The implosion of this relatively stable socio-economic environment in the late 1970s and early

1980s has given rise to a plethora of ways of thinking about how we understand and explain the relationship between individuals and their social settings. These are all characterized by a far greater degree of disconnectedness between social structure and individual behaviour and a notable victim of this has been the pre-eminent status enjoyed by social class and the associated concerns about socio-economic inequality. Whilst no consensus has emerged, it is clear that sociology now pays far greater attention to 'other' aspects of social inequality and difference, notably gender, ethnicity and age (Bradley, 1996), and the role played by cultural factors as seen in the 'cultural turn' (Devine and Savage, 2005). By way of illustration, it can be argued that the politics of class identification have been replaced by a politics in which constructions of identity are now far more complex than the relatively simple formulations of even 30 years ago (Devine et al., 2005; Ransome, 2005). We conclude our discussion about postmodernity by identifying how 'it' was something that emerged from the crisis of modernity.

The second great unsettling movement in recent decades also emerged from the crisis of the post-war socio-economic settlement that had begun to develop in the late 1970s. This has come to be known as globalization, a concept whose origins lay in the nature of the particular economic crisis of the period and whose resolution – 'automate, emigrate or evaporate' as Thrift (1988: 9) put it – called into question the nature of the national economy, the nation state and the settled notions of class structure. Despite the great Empires (notably those of, first, the United Kingdom and then the United States) that had characterized the nineteenth and twentieth centuries, nation states and national cultures had acted as the main economic, cultural and social containers for Enlightenment thinking and capitalist modernity (Hardt and Negri, 2000). Quite how far this has been broken down by the apparent rise of globalization is unclear.[4] Despite record flows of money, culture, information and populations across national borders and the rise of the internet, satellite broadcasting, transnational corporations and the European Union, there has been a sustained disagreement about the significance of the nature and extent of these changes. Even those who have argued most strongly for the rise of a more global set of political and economic relations have conceded that there has also been an increased sense of localism in many spheres of social, political and cultural life. It is, however, clear we can no longer rely on a sociology that operates within a largely *national* concept of a 'society', as happened for much of the twentieth century – in which statements about the '*British* working class' went largely unchallenged (Urry, 2000).

The generations that were born in the immediate aftermath of the Second World War and the subsequent decade (the baby boomers) have witnessed probably far greater changes in the technological and social organization of their lives than any generation since the Industrial Revolution transformed the household economy in the late eighteenth and early nineteenth centuries. This has happened across the social spectrum, encompassing the winners as well as the losers in the massive changes that have taken place.

Undoubtedly, across the globe, there have been more losers than winners in the restructuring of the last quarter century but, sometimes, we can gain a better insight of general processes by studying those who are not the 'usual suspects'. Studying social class simply from the perspective of the working class, for example, has, it has been argued, blinded many to its continuing possibilities (Savage, 1995). Moreover, there is much to be learned from the intensive, small-scale qualitative study in understanding how social processes work. We are currently witnessing another iteration of capitalism and the ways in which it works through the lives of individuals whether they be technology consultants or 'nickel and dimed' service workers (Sennett, 1998; Ehrenreich, 2002; Toynbee, 2003). All of these people, not just the advantaged, are reflexive beings who are aware of how the processes of socio-economic restructuring – a term unheard of until 20 years ago – have become embodied in their lives yet feel, for the most part, largely powerless to do anything about it.[5]

Our aim in this chapter is to consider *postmodernity* and *globalization* as the two over-arching, over-egged yet over-simplified terms that frame much contemporary discussion about the relationship between people and their place in the social structure. In *The Condition of Postmodernity*, David Harvey (1989) introduces the notion of 'time-space compression' (see Box 2.1) which provided one of the first specific links between the changes that were happening at the level of the economic system and that of cultural representation. His approach informs much of the remainder of this chapter. Harvey's book makes a powerful critique of the concept of postmodernism whilst locating its causes and consequences in more conventional Marxist political economy.

Box 2.1 TIME-SPACE COMPRESSION

Harvey (1989) argues that postmodernism is a cultural construct of the flexible accumulation of the economy, or what others have called globalization. To make his argument Harvey discusses the phenomena of what he calls 'time-space compression'. Harvey claims that ever since the increased mobility and internationalization of capital in the early 1970s, society has undergone another round of 'time-space compression' which is the likely root of the postmodern condition. According to Harvey, 'the general effect is for capitalist modernization to be very much about speed-up and acceleration in the pace of economic processes and, hence, social life' (1989: 230). The goal of this speed-up is to accelerate 'the turnover time of capital' which is composed of the 'time of production together with the time of circulation of exchange' (1989: 229). In this process, the rapidity of time annihilates the barriers of space. As Harvey puts it, 'innovations dedicated to the removal of spatial barriers ... have been of immense significance in the history of capitalism, turning that history into a very geographical affair – the railroad and the telegraph, the automobile, radio and telephone, the jet aircraft and television, and the recent telecommunications revolution are cases in point' (1989: 232). All these modernizations have served to make the world a smaller place, and have in the last quarter of the twentieth century connected disparate markets together in the creation of a world market with global producers and global consumers. For example, the world from 1500 to 1960 got 70 times smaller as the average speed in 1500 of horse-drawn carriages or boats was 10 mph versus planes in 1960 which could fly 700 mph. The

---

Fordist economy, however, with its spatial 'rigidities' in which capital was held to be loyal to a place, to a nation, ended up becoming a bottleneck, a spatial barrier to be overcome. Coupled with the advent of new global communications technology, like telephones, satellites, TV, and the fax, it has become increasingly feasible for corporations to become transnational, to transcend spatial bottlenecks like the nation. It was thus the dismantling of the Fordist economy, which became too 'rigid' and constraining to capital in the early 1970s with the emergent onset of a flexible regime of accumulation, which marked a 'new round' of time-space compression.

Source: http://it.stlawu.edu/~pomo/mike/timespac.html (accessed 22 February 2005)

Both terms – postmodernity and globalization – represent not just the nature of the social and economic world at the turn of the millennium but also the period that immediately preceded it – the long post-war boom *and* the massive neo-liberal restructuring that followed. In the long term, neither of these periods will probably be seen as typical but the way in which one has followed the other has made the present and future seem particularly uncertain and conjectural – whether as citizens, non-citizens like asylum seekers, or even as social scientists such as ourselves. It is therefore perhaps unsurprising that the concept of 'risk' has achieved such a high profile both in the management of public and private enterprises and in the explanation of social and corporate behaviour, notably in the work of Ulrick Beck (1992). The identification of risk has now become an explicit strategy for managing the uncertainty that is once more central to capitalist society. Risk can only be managed if it can first be identified: this applies as much to organizations as to individuals. The Higher Education Funding Council for England (HEFCE) requires all universities to undertake a risk analysis identifying the major risks to their 'business' and to develop strategies to deal with them; these might range from a collapse in students taking sociology programmes, to an accident 'taking out' their teaching facilities, or facing a legal action for 'poor' supervision on a PhD programme. Likewise, individuals are increasingly encouraged to identify the main risks in their lives and develop strategies to offset the unthinkable – whether it is ensuring that both partners in a household don't work in the same employment sector or taking out critical illness insurance.

-------- **The Enlightenment 'project', modernity and postmodernity** --------

Box 2.2 MODERNITY AND DEAD WHITE MEN

Modernity stands at the end of a long line of philosophical footnotes to Plato – who first imagined a rational state (no poets allowed) in his *The Republic*. From the 1920s onwards a series of philosophers tried to break with what is known as Western metaphysics, among them Martin Heidegger (1889–1976), Emmanuel Levinas (1906–95), Michel Foucault (1926–84) and Jacques Derrida (1930–2004). Between them these thinkers questioned the old binary that something was either here or not here (especially Derrida), the relation of the individual as a unified individual, the ethical relation of the observer to the rest of the universe (Levinas, more problematically Heidegger) and the notion that there was something universal called human nature (Foucault). (Butler and Ford, 2003: 12)

The Enlightenment is associated with the period in the late eighteenth century when the history of ideas took a huge new step. At approximately the same time, the Industrial Revolution began to transform the relations of production in the north of England and the French Revolution did the same for the divine right of kings and absolutist political ideas. It marked the beginning of the end of the era in which, as the well known hymn *All Things Bright and Beautiful* composed in 1848 put it:

> The rich man in his castle,
> The poor man at his gate,
> He made them, high or lowly,
> And ordered their estate.

The Industrial Revolution – encapsulated in the Hymn Book once again by William Blake's poem *Jerusalem* as the dark satanic mill – posed a threat to the existing order equal to that of the Guillotine of the French revolutionaries except that it was rather more drawn out. Industrial revolutions take time to come to pass, unlike an iconic event such as the storming of the Bastille in 1789 by the 'sans culottes' of Paris which set in train the French Revolution and embodied the ideas of the Enlightenment into concepts of governance.[6] As the term 'the Enlightenment' suggests, it symbolized a belief that the understanding for events in this world lay either in science or the actions of human beings, and that in principle 'all men are born equal before God'. The French Revolution, although subsequently degenerating into terror, was founded on the trinity of 'liberty, fraternity and equality'. The constitution of the newly liberated United States of America became the living embodiment of Enlightenment principles with its separation of Church and State, separation of powers between executive, judiciary and legislature and the principle of 'one man, one vote'.

Box 2.3   THE ENLIGHTENMENT COURSE AT THE UNIVERSITY OF ESSEX

By 'The Enlightenment' we mean the modern currents of ideas and attitudes, in thought and culture, that surfaced in Europe in the late 17th and 18th centuries. These ideas and attitudes are not harmonious, simple and unified, or totally new, but they do share a determination to break from dogmatic religion, feudal social relationships, and political absolutism. Intellectually, this movement was influenced by the new science associated with Galileo and Newton; culturally, by a turn from religion to interest in nature, especially human nature; politically, by the development of liberal thought associated with the bourgeois revolution; and socio-economically, by the growing importance of the commercial middle class and entrepreneurial capitalism. These developments are studied in this course, not only as key documents of 'the modern world view', but also as current problems in all areas of Comparative Studies.

There are two compelling reasons why the Enlightenment is the subject of a common course for students in the School of Humanities and Comparative Studies. The first is that it was such a comprehensive movement, embracing philosophy, art, literature, music; social, cultural, linguistic and political theory; differing conceptions of human nature and our place in the universe; and profound economic, social and political changes. The second reason is that the Enlightenment period left a rich legacy of ideas and problems. To study the Enlightenment is an important part of our understanding of our own historical situation, in Europe and globally.

The course begins by examining some of the factors that led to a crisis in the medieval social system and the Christian worldview. Concentrating initially on the work of Descartes, who is often seen as the founding author of 'The Enlightenment'. We then consider the efforts, prompted by social, political and intellectual upheaval in England, to secure legitimacy for knowledge and government. The Spring Term focuses on crisis and revolution by the mid-eighteenth century, provoked in part by wars and natural catastrophe, the Enlightenment had already entered upon a moment of self-scrutiny and crisis – evident in the work of Rousseau, Voltaire and Diderot. The latter part of the same century witnessed an increasing number of political, social and economic tensions which were to come to a climax in the American and French Revolutions – though whether the philosophes 'led to' Revolution or whether Revolution retrospectively bestowed a coherence upon the programme of the philosophes is still a matter for debate.

Source: http://www2.essex.ac.uk/courses/result.asp?coursecode=CS101& level= 1&period=FY&yearofcourse=04 (accessed 28 July 2004).

Sociology can therefore be seen as a direct creation of the Enlightenment leading to the rise of a new class of what Saint Simon termed 'secular priests' – whose so-called founding fathers also included writers such as Comte, Spencer, Durkheim, Marx and Weber. Sociology was never and can never be a discipline that agrees on much – that too is part of its Enlightenment heritage. According to Mann, 'Sociology can only be a society's understanding of itself and this is constantly in flux and contested' (1983: v). Whilst this claim is hardly open to contestation, it might be argued that, for part of the second half of the twentieth century, sociology was able to achieve a measure of consensus as the study of industrial society and the nature of social inequality. Even the Parsonian structural functionalists who focused on the normative order of the social system, to the exclusion of the underlying structures of inequality (Lockwood, 1956), drew a basic contrast between 'traditional' (pre-industrial) and 'modern' (industrial) societies (Parsons, 1970). Sociology was essentially about understanding the functioning of modern society.

The Enlightenment dominated Western thought throughout the nineteenth and much of the twentieth century. It became associated with the rise of mass societies, which were the outcome of systems of industrial, factory production and the slow growth of democracy as its system of governance. From the beginning of the twentieth century, mass consumption spread from North America into some areas of Europe before coming to a shuddering halt with the economic depression and political instability in the late 1920s. The subsequent experience of extremism together with the widespread social cohesion of wartime existence during the Second World War led many to hope that the previous shortcomings of capitalism had been transcended. The belief in scientific and technological progress combined with the willingness of capital, labour and the state to work together led to what was seen as a historic settlement between the realities of the market economy and the aspiration for social justice (Hobsbawm, 1994).

Ultimately this long wave of capitalist economic development manifested itself in a crisis of profitability in the late 1970s (Massey and Allen, 1988). The result was increased unemployment, factory closures, falling stock markets and rising inflation until a new and very different economy emerged, hesitantly at first, in the late 1980s and then more strongly in the early 1990s. In this 'new economy', neo-liberalism had become the emerging consensus and relations between the state, capital and labour changed once again. It is against this background, that the notion of postmodernity emerged.

Modernity

A search through a leading dictionary of sociology published 20 years ago does not reveal an entry for modernity (Mann, 1983). It is only comparatively recently that the term has come to such prominence in sociology courses and textbooks.

Box 2.4 MODERNITY

Modernity: A term describing the particular attribute of modern societies. A good deal of sociological work is based on the assumption of a sharp divide between pre-modern and modern societies. There is considerable debate as to the qualities of the two kinds of society as well as to when Western societies became modern. Modernity is distinguished on economic, political, social and cultural grounds. For example, modern societies typically have industrial, capitalist economies, democratic political organization and a social structure founded on a division into social classes. There is less agreement on cultural features, which are said to include a tendency to the fragmentation of experience, a commodification and rationalization of all aspects of life, and a speeding up of the pace of daily life. Modernity has required new systems of individual surveillance, discipline and control. It has emphasized regularity and measurement in everyday life. The values of modernity include activism, universalism and affective neutrality. There is disagreement about the periodization of modernity,

---

some writers associating it with the appearance and spread of capitalism from the fourteenth to the eighteenth centuries, some with religious changes of the fifteenth century onwards, which provided the basis for rationalization, others with the onset of industrialization in the late eighteenth and nineteenth centuries, and still others with the cultural transformations of the end of the nineteenth and the beginning of the twentieth century which coincide with modernism. Recently it has been argued that contemporary societies are no longer modern but postmodern. (Abercrombie et al., 2000: 229)

Modernity emerged from a coming together of Enlightenment ideas and the experience of industrialization which found expression in many fields of life from the mid-nineteenth century onwards, but notably in the process of urbanization. Savage et al. (2003: 3–4) argue that 'a coherent programme for urban sociology would be concerned with the mutual impact of two analytically separate entities, *capitalism* and *modernity.*' They draw on the work of Berman for whom modernity was an essentially dualistic concept, which simultaneously promises excitement, adventure, joy etc. whilst threatening danger and destruction. Berman sees being modern as being 'part of a universe in which, as Marx said "all that is solid melts into air"' (cited in Savage et al., 2003: 4). For Savage and colleagues, the city has often equated with modernity – the most famous example being Wirth's essay *Urbanism as a Way of Life* (1938). Sociologists have, they suggest, taken a 'wrong turn' here because the behaviour which Wirth identified as being primarily urban (such as disorganization and the predominance of segmented and secondary relationships), was in truth an outcome of modernity. Modernity, Savage et al. point out, in the early years of the twentieth century was only solidly gathered in the larger metropolises which they believe explained the incorrect elision between modernity and urbanism. Urbanism was the site for the coming together, in an often dysfunctional relationship, of modernity and capitalism. Interestingly, Savage et al. (2003) suggest that Marxists in the 1970s made the same mistake of attributing all the experience of modernity to capitalist economic organization. In their view, capitalism and modernity are irreducible to each other since, 'the social inequalities of capitalism and the social disorganisation of modernity are symbiotic. A precise and adequate formulation of the dialectic of capitalism and modernity has yet to be devised' (2003: 201).

Capitalism and modernity have had a tendency to consummate their relationship in ways that, whilst illustrating this symbiosis, point to the contradictory nature in both – particularly in the relationship between individualism and mass behaviour. In art and architecture, for example, there was nearly a century of what might be seen as 'high modernism' beginning in the middle of the nineteenth century. This marked the great optimism of the early Victorian period that coincided with the seemingly unstoppable global expansion of the British economy. The technological achievements of the train and the telegraph were reflected in the Great Exhibition of 1851. The Victoria and Albert, the Science and the Natural History Museums are the leading examples of this period. They were built in South Kensington out of the profits of the 1851 Great Exhibition and formed the nearest London ever got to a neo-imperialist exercise in city planning.

The next 100 years marked the rise and fall of not only the British Empire and its economic and geo-political hegemony but also the belief in 'progress'. Progressive and rational men [sic] such as Charles Dickens' Mr Thomas Gradgrind believed that scientific progress and rational behaviour would lead to increasing wealth and well-being (Box 2.5).

Box 2.5 *HARD TIMES*, CHARLES DICKENS

'Now, what I want is, Facts. Teach these boys and girls nothing but Facts. Facts alone are what are wanted in life. Plant nothing else, and root out everything else. You can only form the minds of reasoning animals upon Facts: nothing else will ever be of any service to them. This is the principle on which I bring up my own children, and this the principle on which I bring up these children. Stick to Facts, Sir!'...Thomas Gradgrind, Sir. A man of realities. A man of facts and calculations. A man who proceeds upon the principle that two and two are four, and nothing over, and who is not talked into allowing for anything over. Thomas Gradgrind, Sir – peremptorily Thomas – Thomas Gradgrind. With a rule and a pair of scales, and the multiplication table always in his pocket, Sir, ready to measure any parcel of human nature, and tell you exactly what it comes to. It is a mere question of figures, a case of simple arithmetic. (Dickens, 1994 [1854]: 1–2)

An alternative reading of course, might argue that this led to a century that culminated in two world wars having experienced countless minor wars and at least two large economic depressions. The Second World War ended with the dropping of two atomic bombs which obliterated two Japanese cities in 1945. This event marked the absolute end of the age of innocence about science – the power of humankind was now such that it could destroy the world many times over (Hobsbawm 1994).

In many other, more creative and less harmful, respects however, the modernism of the nineteenth and twentieth centuries demonstrated the power of humankind to defy the accepted limits of what was considered 'natural'. In music, for example, Shostakovich reinvented the notion of what was musical and melodious – and, in so doing, was celebrated, denounced (as a petit bourgeois) and finally rehabilitated as a great socialist figure by Joseph Stalin – thereby illustrating the somewhat fragile relationship between the individual and the mass incarnation of the working class. In art, the early Victorian love affair with representation symbolized by the Pre-Raphaelites gave way to a number of different artistic movements that challenged the notion of 'what you get is what you see'. The Cubists, for example, challenged the idea that the head is really the head you see and drew it many times in many different ways thus indicating the power of thought and the complex relationships between time and space. This same concern with representation was also at the heart of such movements as Surrealism and Impressionism that developed in the late nineteenth and early twentieth centuries. Similar movements took place in literature (James Joyce), sculpture (Marcel Duchamps) and other artistic fields.

Box 2.6   HIGH RISE LIVING

My father was a Modernist; my mother still is. I was a Modern baby, my sisters (planned) followed at 18 month intervals. At the time of my birth my father had put us down for a flat in the new Barbican development. Fate intervened; dad won £500 on the Premium Bonds and put a deposit on a SPAN house in Blackheath. I often wonder what would have happened had we grown up in the parts of London my dad casually tortured my imagination with later. He would say 'We thought about living here,' as we drove down the Abbey Road or along London Wall. I wasn't really convinced that Blackheath was London at all, whereas these glances of North London were the London of my imagination. The Barbican development interests me because it is part of my past and part of my present reassessment of that past. I remember it as fragments: the Moorgate disaster; my father pointing out the towers; visiting the new London Museum; taking students to the Barbican arts centre; trying to find the arts centre. More recently, I remember being depressed at the way my students unthinkingly dismissed Modern housing projects as failed social engineering, as if this were a universally applicable, deep thought. They, of course, are simply repeating what they have been taught ...

... As recently as October 2000 the London *Evening Standard* commented, under the headline 'It's awful but I like it' – 'The Barbican is like Mr Potato Head in *Toy Story*, its ear is where its mouth should be, its arm is in its eye socket, its nose upside down. It's a garbled sentence'. These comments, and most of the next two columns, reflect an almost continual bad press for the Barbican since the early 1970s, cursed by being completed during a period when the certainties of post-war planning and architecture were first questioned then rejected. Reviled when the acceptance of large public-funded projects ran counter to the new political consensus of the 1980s. Forgotten in the 1990s ... The Barbican has endured decades of critical abuse that has created a habit of deprecation in the common sense of London – or at least its chatterati. Of course, as Banham, no fan himself, noted in his book *Megastructures*, the wheel of fortune turns every 30 years. Now the Barbican is being reassessed – hopefully for the reconstructive vision that prompted the City and its architects, Chamberlin, Powell and Bon, to challenge a century of suburbanization based on an urbanism that the rest of us are only beginning to catch up with. (Heathcote, 2004: 25–6) (See Figure 2.2 on p. 24.)

Architecture is perhaps the best example of the elisions between modernity, capitalism and the built form of the city. The skyscraper came to represent the dominance of corporate capitalism more clearly than anything since the adoption of the classical style by imperialist powers in the mid-nineteenth century. The skyscraper brought together a number of factors: technological, ideological, artistic and economic. Essentially, it represented a desire on behalf of both modernism (the architect) and capital (the corporation or in some instances the state) to show that it could transcend nature. It depended however on the maturation of two crucial engineering technologies – building with stressed concrete and developing high speed lifts. Modernist architecture showed the ability of humans to transcend the rules of what was natural – for example, that pitched roofs were necessary in order to deal with rainwater and external gutters and drainpipes to take it away. More significantly, it demonstrated that you could build in dimensions that apparently defied the laws of gravity and the thing stayed up – even in earthquake zones. The alliance between modernism and corporate capital was consummated in Manhattan during the 1930s. It was elsewhere, however, that the familiar skyscraper design – tall, slab sided and undecorated – was born. Oscar Niemeyer's building for the Ministry of Education and Science (MES) in Rio (in 1936) is generally held to be the first modernist skyscraper and much of the influence can be traced to Le Corbusier whose ideas for a city in the sky found more favour in Brazil and Argentina than in Europe or North America (Fraser, 2000). Niemeyer had to import the steel and concrete from Belgium to complete the building, but in many ways it represented much of what was important about modernism in the context of an ex-colonial country beginning to assert its position in a world which had seen it solely as somewhere that produced coffee and rubber. 35 years later, Niemeyer was the lead architect of many of the buildings in Brazil's modernist capital city away from the coast in the uncharted centre of the country. Brasilia came to represent what Brazil aspired to and, in Lucio Costa's master design, its overall conception (as a bird, or an airplane or whatever you choose), as much as Niemeyer's individual buildings, marked a break with the colonial past of Brazil's other cities and symbolized its new forms of governance (Holston, 1989). The three powers (executive, legislature and judiciary) are grouped together in, yet separated by, a huge plaza and each has its own symbolically rich architecture; the legislature, for example, is a skyscraper consisting of twin towers joined half way up, thus forming a capital H for 'humanity' (Holston, 1989). Kubitschek, who authorized and built much of Brasilia in the four years of his presidency between 1956 and 1960, was forced into exile by a military government in 1960, marking perhaps the end of the bold bid for national identity and the re-imposition of North American hegemony. However, the modernist buildings of Brazil and Venezuela during these years – during a period in which the US eye was off the ball with problems elsewhere – is indicative of some of the contradictory nature of the relationship between capitalism and modernism (Fraser, 2000). Traditionally, modernist skyscrapers are seen as the iconography of the power of North American corporate capital and are symbolized by the Empire State building and its slab faced successors. This was epitomized by the destruction of the World Trade Center on 11 September 2001. What started off as the expression of a communist architect in a resurgent Brazil in the 1930s had become established as *the* symbol of global capitalism 70 years later.

We will return to the theme of cities in much of this book (Chapters 3, 4 and 5) to highlight the continuing tension between capitalism and modernism and to develop the idea that we are now a predominantly urban society globally. Films, such as *Metropolis* or *Modern Times* and novels such as George Orwell's *1984* or *Animal Farm*

Figure 2.1 MES building in Rio de Janeiro

and those of Franz Kafka, illustrated the ways in which mass society and, by association, the ideas of modernity helped to sow the seeds which ultimately led to the destruction of the Enlightenment project.

Postmodernism

Postmodernism cannot be seen to be simply all that modernism is not, nor can postmodernity be seen as the antithesis to modernity. However, postmodernism *is* a reaction to the hegemonizing project of the Enlightenment. In architecture, this can be illustrated by the pastiche of styles that marks much contemporary architecture in financial centres or corporate edge cities that have become increasingly prevalent in the 'information age' (McNeill, 2005). This borrows promiscuously from a range of styles and traditions whilst meeting the technical requirements for large load bearing trading floors with plenty of ducting and cooling for the massive computing power now required in such buildings. This can be illustrated in London by comparing the iconic office building of the early 1970s – Centrepoint – which was controversially built at the bottom of Tottenham Court Road in London's West End, and the Broadgate Centre which was constructed in the City in the 1980s to compete with the loss of business to Canary Wharf at the time of financial liberalization. Centrepoint (Figure 2.2), built by the developer Harry Hyams, was a building typical of its period in which major corporations wanted a significant building at the centre of the city to mark their presence. The tall, thin multi-floored structure was ideal because it allowed each department to have a floor and was also easily subdivided into suitable offices for the hierarchy with prestigious corner offices for departmental heads and the like. The top officers would have even showier offices on the top executive floors with express lifts to get them there quickly and with minimum contact with their subordinates. Centrepoint represented the time: a hierarchical building, lots of sub-divisions and much status differentiation; perhaps not surprisingly, by the late 1980s it had become difficult to let. Many of the corporations that had built such buildings have gone into liquidation (the Pan Am building in Manhattan being a good example) but, even if they haven't, their structure and needs had changed out of all recognition. As companies have downsized, delayered and restructured, their organizational needs have also changed. Out went departmental hierarchies and in came flexible and functional team working which required large floors with flexible dividers. Managers now emphasized their role as team players and did not wish to be seen as cutting themselves off from their teams. The introduction of ICT meant that buildings like Centrepoint were now largely redundant: they simply could not be plumbed for the new requirements – lots of cabling and the need to get rid of the heat generated by the electronics. Perhaps most significantly, corporate restructuring meant that only the command and control functions were to be based in the city and these functions were increasingly strategic and essentially financial with a need for access to the financial services offered by the City of London with its lawyers, bankers and other financial engineering specialists. Hence the rise (literally) of the so-called groundscraper building which would meet the needs of the new industrial structure and the City of London had to change its planning guidance to enable such developments to take place or face a critical haemorrhaging of business to Frankfurt or Docklands. Hence, Broad Street station was demolished and Liverpool Street Station was built into the basement of the new Broadgate Centre in order to retain many of the new big US banks. The 1960s high rises on London Wall are now being replaced with newer buildings – such as the building designed by Terry Farrell on London Wall (see Figure 2.2). These buildings exhibited a common style in which function still dominates form – the usual description of modernist architecture, but – unlike some of the buildings they replaced from the 1960s – they were built from the highest quality 'traditional' materials to witness the power and cultural capital of their new occupants. The 'big

Figure 2.2   The West End and the City – Centrepoint, J.P. Morgan building on London Wall and The Barbican

six' law firms either located to Canary Wharf or built themselves new postmodern offices around the City, as have the big merchant banks and other financial intermediaries (Hamnett, 2003).

This trend is also reflected in similar tendencies in music, art, books and politics where 'everything seems to be double-coded, paradoxical, winking at us that it shouldn't be taken too seriously, while of course it *is* too serious' (Butler and Ford, 2003: 14). Butler and Ford go on to argue that the alienation of industrial production which was inherent in modernism is deepened in a situation where, 'we may not know our neighbours anymore but we can have email conversations with friends we've never met in Los Angeles and Melbourne and prefer to text message a mate than have a conversation with the person sitting next to us on the train' (2003: 14). What postmodernism marks in all these areas is the end of certainty. Butler and Ford argue that this came of age in the events of September 11th in which the War on Terror became the new zeitgeist in that it is a war on an abstraction but, like the assassination of President John Kennedy in 1963, it also marks the end of a form of postmodern relativism (Butler and Ford, 2003: 15).

Lyotard's *Postmodern Condition* (1984) marked the author out as one of the high priests of this end of certainty. The book was originally commissioned as a report for a university and argues that we are moving beyond the traditional metanarratives that have sustained us to date. By this, he means a coherent set of beliefs or knowledges, such as we saw arising out of the Enlightenment or indeed the ones that were displaced by the Enlightenment. 'The Postmodern' is therefore basically questioning the existence of these metanarratives and perhaps, in so doing, has become a metanarrative itself.

Box 2.7 POSTMODERN CULTURE

In contemporary society and culture – post-industrial society, postmodern culture – the question of the legitimation of knowledge is formulated in different terms [from those of the Grand Narratives of the Enlightenment such as science]. The grand narrative has lost its credibility, regardless of what mode of unification it uses, regardless of whether it is a speculative narrative or a narrative of emancipation.

The decline of narrative can be seen as an effect of the blossoming of techniques and technologies since the Second World War, which has shifted emphasis from the ends of action to its means. It can also be seen as an effect of the redeployment of advanced liberal capitalism in retreat under the protection of Keynesianism during the period 1930–60, a renewal that has eliminated the communist lacerative and valorized the individual enjoyment of goods and services. Anytime we go searching for causes in this way we are bound to be disappointed. Even if we adopted one or the other of these hypotheses, we would still have to detail the correlation between the tendencies mentioned and the decline of unifying and legitimating power of the grand narratives of speculation and emancipation. (Lyotard, 1984: 37–8)

The emergence of these ideas coincides with the growth of locally and regionally based forms of identity and, it is claimed, a decline in the importance of the nation state. Individuals appear to act increasingly 'omnivorously', hoovering up a range of different cultures more or less indiscriminately (Longhurst, 1995).

Postmodernism has therefore become associated with the declining importance of the two main navigating points of the post Enlightenment: the nation state and social class. The social certainties that stemmed from this period were those of nationalism and social deference. By contrast, the new watchwords are 'identity' and 'difference' – giving rise, for example, to concerns about 'religious fundamentalism' – which cross national and class boundaries. However, as with modernity, there remains a complex and flirtatious relationship with capitalism; this emerges most clearly in relation to the equally contentious issue of globalization, which we tackle in the next section.

Box 2.8   JACQUES DERRIDA AND DECONSTRUCTION

'Deconstruction', the word he [Derrida] transformed from a rare French term to a common expression in many languages, became part of the vocabulary not only of philosophers and literary theorists but also of architects, theologians, artists, political theorists, educationalists, music critics, filmmakers, lawyers and historians. Resistance to his thinking, too, was widespread and sometimes bitter, as it challenged academic norms and, sometimes, common sense.

Derrida's name has probably been mentioned more frequently in books, journals, lectures, and common-room conversations during the last 30 years than that of any other living thinker. He was the subject of films, cartoons and at least one rock song, by Scritti Politi; he generated both adulatory and vituperative journalism; and he wrote some of the most formidably difficult philosophical works of his time. If he is remembered in future centuries, it is likely to be for contributions to our understanding of language, meaning, identity, ethical decisions and aesthetic values.

Derrida's starting point was his rejection of a common model of knowledge and language, according to which understanding something requires acquaintance with its meaning, ideally a kind of acquaintance in which this meaning is directly present to consciousness. For him, this model involved 'the my of presence', the supposition that we gain our best understanding of something when it – and it alone – is present to our consciousness.

He argued that understanding something requires a grasp of the ways in which it relates to other things, and a capacity to recognize it on other occasions in different contexts – which can never be exhaustively predicted. He coined the term 'difference' (différance in French, combining the meaning of difference and deference) to characterize these aspects of understanding, and proposed that differance is the ur-phenomenon lying at the heart of language and thought, at work in all meaningful activities in a necessarily elusive and provisional way.

The demonstration that this is so largely constituted by the work of deconstruction, in which writers who laid claim to purity of transparency of universality – and this would include most of the significant figures in the philosophical tradition – could be shown, by close and careful reading, to be undoing those very claims in the act of making them by their implicit recognition of the ongoing work of difference.

Source: Obituary to Jacques Derrida, *The Guardian*, 11 October 2004

Globalization

When the unapologetically Blairite sociologist Anthony Giddens was invited to give the BBC Reith Lectures in 1999, he chose as his theme globalization (*Runaway World*) and delivered the lectures from different places around the world: London, Washington, Hong Kong and Delhi in front of an invited audience in each city (Giddens, 2002). There is a clear linkage in Giddens' work, here and elsewhere, between globalization and the themes outlined in the previous section. His various chapters for the lectures are: risk, tradition, family and democracy. In these lectures, Giddens makes an essentially optimistic case for surfing along on the crest of globalization – in this sense he can be regarded as a radical who sees society, at least in principle, now rising above a 'one size fits all' approach to issues of rights, child rearing, the emotions etc. In principle, we now have the possibilities of releasing individual potential and getting away from the stultification of tradition and its guardians which was only partly destroyed by the Enlightenment. This has now given rise, Giddens argues, to a new tradition of 'autonomy and freedom' based around self-identity (but which, as he points out, has its own devils in terms of compulsions and addictions). Therapy, according to this view, has perhaps become the religion of this new age in which there is a clash between 'fundamentalism' and 'cosmopolitanism'. This comes through in the family – that most public of private functions – in which there is an increasing trend towards what he terms 'emotional democracy' particularly in child-rearing practices where it can no longer be the accepted maxim that children should be 'seen and not heard'.

Castells (1996a) offers a somewhat different 'take' on contemporary social and economic processes. He sees in contemporary globalization a shift from *industrial* capitalism, based around *stocks* of physical commodities, to *informational* capitalism based around *flows* of knowledge and information. Industrial capitalism was based in the physical networks of the railway, the telegraph, the telephone and, more recently, the electricity grid, the motorway network and air travel. By contrast, the information age is based around the flow of information through virtual networks (although, as Castells points out, these are rooted in very expensive hardware in physical locations). This dichotomization of the old and new economies became reflected in the so-called 'irrational exuberance' of the world's stock exchanges in the 1990s and the huge valuations that were attached in particular to some communications and dot.com stocks. Castells writing about this so-called 'information age' refers to it as more of a network society than a hierarchical one based around downwardly transmitted power, managed by the state and legitimated by democracy. The transformation of economic relations, associated with the move towards an information-based society, has seen a trend away from industrial production based around armies of workers doing largely repetitive tasks. The role of state has also been under threat because it can no longer guarantee long-term benefits and security to its citizens, in part because it can no longer tie large corporations to its shores. This has serious implications for the state because it cannot make long-term plans about the security of its tax base. Therefore democracy and welfare, which had been the watchwords of legitimation in industrial capitalism, will need to find new equivalents in the information age. Castells has suggested that the European Union might represent, in at least nascent ways, this new form of state in which the state *enables* rather than *provides* social rights for a disparate group of citizens. Castells explores how, in a globalized and networked world, new groups emerge around – for example – identities formed by religion or sexuality (Castells, 1996b).

Giddens, Beck and Castells are all responding, in different ways, to the challenges thrown up by postmodernists about the apparent breakdown of the familiar 'certainties' of industrial society around which much sociological work had been focused. The main transformation has been from a concern with socio-economic inequality to those of cultural and social difference and diversity. For all of these writers, these changes are intimately and intricately bound up with the concept of globalization.

Models of globalization

Held et al. (1999) identify three approaches to contemporary globalization, which they term the 'hyperglobalizers', the 'sceptics' and the 'transformationalists' (see Box 2.9).

Box 2.9 HYPERGLOBALIZERS, SCEPTICS AND TRANSFORMATIONALISTS

The 'hyperglobalizers' believe that there has been a fundamental restructuring of the global economy over recent years in which the nation state has become, as it were, like a subsidiary company to a global corporation. This approach gives much emphasis to the economy and in particular to neo-liberal economics. The development of information and communication technologies (ICT) has enabled these tendencies towards a 'borderless' world in which money and people are able to move in a more or less frictionless manner and in which nation states have little option but to acquiesce. Failure to do so will see them marginalized like those towns in the nineteenth century that failed or refused to come to some form of accommodation with the railway barons and, as a result, were simply by-passed.

The 'sceptics', in contrast to the 'hyperglobalizers', see the death of the nation state as more than somewhat exaggerated and some argue that the level of global interconnectedness is no higher than it was a century ago. National governments, far from being the passive victims of internationalization, are in fact encouraging the process. They argue that the nation state retains considerable amounts of power and still acts as the container for many of the economic enterprises that are globally dominant. They also claim that much of today's global activity is confined to economically advanced regions predominantly in the Northern hemisphere. To a large extent, this has led to the increased marginalization of much of the globe – for example, Africa now is probably more excluded than it has been for the last 100 years.

In a sense, the 'sceptics' argue that what we are seeing is simply a deepening of existing inequalities, rather than a restructuring of the world economic order. Like the 'hyperglobalizers', the 'sceptics' are drawn from across the theoretical and ideological spectrum and include Marxists such as Alex Callinicos (1989) and Paul Hirst (Hirst and Thompson, 1999) and the economist Joseph Stiglitz (2002). Many of the former argue that the discourse of globalization provides a smokescreen to implement anti-welfare and other neo-liberal economic policies.

The third group proposed by Held et al. (amongst which they include themselves) are the 'transformationalists', who share much with the perspectives advanced by Anthony Giddens and Manuel Castells introduced above. They see it as a classic example of one of the periodic 'shakeouts', in which capitalist economies indulge, which forms a 'contingent historical process replete with contradictions' (1999: 7). Some states are becoming more enmeshed in the world economic order whilst others are becoming more marginalized giving rise to a reconfiguration of global power relations. The shape of these power relations has changed and is no longer a hierarchical one but rather forms a set of overlapping circles which penetrate most of the globe. There is no clear distinction between first and third world societies but rather inequality is increasingly nestled together in the major and global cities – which demonstrates the extremes of wealth and poverty. 'Globalization, in this account, is therefore associated with a transformation, or to use Ruggie's term, 'an unbundling of the sovereign relationship between sovereignty, territoriality and state power' (cited in Held et al., 1999: 8). Essentially, to use the language of modern consultancy, what has happened has been the re-engineering of the contemporary state and its relations to social and economic policy so as to adapt to the changes that have been forced by the economic activities of a relatively small number of globalizing corporations and international bodies. In this view, the power of governments is not so much diminished as changed.

Ray (2002) argues that whilst this three-fold categorization is a useful teaching device, it can confuse the often contradictory views held by the various theorists. This is recognized by Held et al. (1999: 2–3) who themselves argue that the debate does not map on to traditional debates in social theory nor is it easily categorized into more political right–left differences. Indeed, they point out that analysts who share broadly common starting points – whether neo-liberal or Marxist – often come to completely different conclusions about globalization. However, they do all appear to conduct the debate in a way that reflects a common set of arguments. In a useful critique of those who argue that globalization has led to at least a partial abrogation of what is termed 'society', Ray (2002) makes the important sociological point that the subjects of many of these processes find themselves deeply embedded in structures of continuing inequality which restricts the transforming possibilities of globalization. There is simply much more 'friction' than the apostles of globalization suggest. In addition, they tend to conflate the consequences for the state with those of their societies. Ray is particularly focused in this critique on the work of John Urry (2000) whose position is probably nearest that of the hyperglobalizers. Urry has however retained a more overtly sociological focus than many other writers by arguing that notions of social structure and relatively unchanging social positions are no longer the dominant characterization of 'our' social world.

In Britain the hyperglobalizing argument can be seen to underlie the accommodation of New Labour to 'big business', because the failure to do so would, it was argued, mean that they missed out on the 'only game in town'. A minor, but nonetheless significant, example of this was the decision by Britain's New Labour Government to delay the implementation of a ban on tobacco advertising in Formula One motor racing because it was feared that Britain might not just lose its Formula One race but also the engineering skills associated with its domination of the construction side of the industry. Another example might be the accommodation with gambling interests on the grounds that gambling would otherwise simply disappear into the ether of the internet. According to the hyperglobalizers therefore, politics is subsumed to the needs of the global economy and systems of welfare and other forms of social politics have to be rethought to reflect a world in which the people and corporations that used to be under the tutelage of the nation state are so no longer. Thus welfare states and social justice are both under threat for a number of inter-related reasons. The increased mobility and volatility of investment and employment means that nation states have to become 'competitive' in relation to taxation – they cannot afford to have tax rates substantially out of line with similar states which, in effect, means there is a long-term downward pressure on taxation. In addition, the instability means, as indicated above, that states have to become much more wary of guaranteeing long-term benefits, many of which may not come into effect for several decades, during which time the tax base is likely to change as industry restructures and workers lose their jobs or move. The increased mobility of workers also raises issues of entitlement: if it cannot be assumed that the same group will stay in employment across the lifecourse, the nation state has to rethink notions of citizenship rights and universal benefits. There is then, it is assumed, a tendency in the hyperglobalization account towards social polarization. This is accentuated by the loss of forms of state intervention to ameliorate tendencies in capitalist economies towards the extremes. Crudely, there is no longer a 'zero sum' game whereby wealth and poverty somehow balance each other out within a nation state and the state can justify moving resources between these groups in the name of social justice and the investment in future human capital. According to this way of thinking, civilization is increasingly based around economic capabilities and the market becomes the basis of a global civilization. There is a 'new world order' and it is one that is essentially based around markets as opposed to politics (Lindblom, 1977). The conflict, as seen by Held et al., is between whether this is seen as a truly global civilization or the basis of a new global oppression. For the elite, it is one in which the jingoism of national difference is being surpassed and is symbolized by an increasing use of English as the *lingua franca* [sic]. These interests are catered for by airline lounges for premium passengers and the global branding of, for example, hotels, which enable them to carry out their business with minimal disruption. For many others, it is seen as the dominance of naked capitalist interest which is symbolized by the conflicts at successive

WTO meetings and the anti-globalization movement more widely. There is a popular literature to support this by a new generation of global activists (Klein, 1999; Monbiot, 2000, 2003).

Globalization and migration

Globalization has meant that the significance of migration and ethnicity for understanding contemporary social inequality has increased. According to Castles and Miller (2003), international migration has occurred in two distinct phases since 1945. The earlier phase lasted until the early 1970s and was associated with the long boom period when the advanced capitalist countries experienced a labour shortage as their economies expanded. Low-skilled workers were sought for the Fordist industries of the period, effectively acting as replacement labour and allowing the indigenous workers to take better paid and less arduous jobs (Castles and Kosack, 1973). Britain, for example, brought in workers from its ex-colonies in the Commonwealth, notably the West Indies, India and Pakistan. Continental European countries either turned to their own ex-colonies, for example, Algeria and Morocco in the case of France, or sought workers from Southern Europe in the case of those without colonies; by 1973, West Germany had imported a total of 2.6 million 'guest workers' from countries such as Turkey and Greece (Castles and Miller, 2003: 72). Migrants tended to cluster in the cheapest housing and poorest inner-city neighbourhoods, not least as a result of racist housing policies and practices (Rex and Moore, 1967).

The second more recent phase of migration associated with globalization has occurred during the last 30 years (Castles and Miller, 2003). Ehrenreich and Hochschild (2003) identify four main contemporary cross-regional flows of persons:

- From Southeast Asian countries, such as Bangladesh, to the oil-producing countries of the Middle East plus the Tiger Economies such as Singapore.
- From the former Soviet bloc to Western Europe.
- The long-established South–North flow from South and Central America to the United States.
- From African countries to Europe.

Reasons for migration involve both economic factors, as migrants seek an improved standard of living, but also increasingly political factors as they flee social turbulence and persecution. This can be seen in the recent flows of migrants to Western Europe from war-torn countries in Eastern Europe, Africa and Asia seeking refuge and asylum (Castles and Miller, 2003). Colatrella (2001) argues that whilst political instability is an important 'push' factor in generating these massive migration shifts, an underlying cause has been the impact of 'Structural Adjustment Programmes' (SAPs) imposed by the International Monetary Fund as part of a structure of neo-liberal governance grafted onto former socialist and developing countries. Colatrella shows how the unprecedented recent arrival of Ghanaians and Senegalese from Africa in the factories and slaughterhouses of North-eastern Italy is intimately connected to the negative impact of SAPs on the Ghanaian cocoa industry and Senegalese peanut production. Moreover, governments in certain developing countries with high levels of emigration, notably, the Philippines and Sri Lanka, have actively developed policies to export labour in order to earn foreign currency and thereby repay debts and reduce unemployment (Parrenas, 2001; Cox, 2006).

The impact of the various waves of migration has meant that the major cities and industrial zones of many North American and European societies are increasingly multi-ethnic in character. Foreign-born residents make up a large minority of the urban population in many Western European cities (Box 2.10).

Box 2.10 FOREIGN-BORN RESIDENTS IN SELECTED EUROPEAN CITIES (%)

France	Germany
Paris >15	Frankfurt >25
Lyons >10	Koln >15
Marseilles >10	Munich >15
Nice >10	Dusseldorf >15
St. Etienne >10	Stuttgart >15
Belgium	*Switzerland*
Brussels > 25	Geneva 35
Antwerp >10	Basel >15
	Lausanne >15
	Zurich >15

Sources: adapted from (De Clercq, 2000 et al., p. 39 and 57; Knox and Pinch 2000, p. 244)

As well as its scale, contemporary migration is also characterized by its diversity: multi-ethnic heterogeneity is a characteristic feature of 'global' or 'world' cities (see Chapter 5). During the last 40 years, London has been transformed from being a white mono-ethnic city to 'one of the most multi-ethnic cities in Europe' (Hamnett, 2003: 126). Despite New York's traditional reputation as the main immigrant city in the United States, Los Angeles has recently become the 'capital of Immigrant America' (Waldinger and Lichter, 2003: 235) as it has experienced a higher rate of migration than anywhere else in the country. Diverse migration flows have also contributed towards the demographic transformation and financial expansion of Toronto, such that it has become 'the major reception area for Canada's immigrant population' (Murdie, 1998: 65). Toronto now effectively represents 'the world in a city' as nearly half of its population is made up of immigrants who are increasingly drawn from a wide range of Asian, African, Central and South American countries (Anisef and Lanphier, 2003).

One important aspect of this recent globalized phase of international migration is its association with the movement of women; Ehrenreich and Hochschild (2003) estimate that women make up half of the 120 million legal and illegal migrants. Feminists have drawn attention to the 'feminization of migration' in Europe whereby an increased number of migrants from outside the EU are female and are subject to specific exclusionary processes as a result of gender inequalities in welfare regimes, labour markets and households (Kofman et al., 2000; Freedman, 2003). As we discuss further in subsequent chapters, many women migrate from less developed countries to service the wants of affluent westerners in the homes, hotels, restaurants and brothels of European and North American cities.

The two phases of post-war migration, but especially the second globalization phase, have effectively rendered traditional modernist hierarchical stratification models more difficult to apply within any one city or society given the resultant complex multi-layering of ethnic and racial advantages and disadvantages found in any one location. This is undoubtedly one of the factors which has prompted the use of the term 'social exclusion' to analyze contemporary patterns of inequality and disadvantage, as we discuss in Chapter 6.

Conclusion

Whilst there has been a seeming disenchantment with class, there has been an underlying deepening of the dominance of capital which has now become increasingly transnational in scope and operations. Despite the growth of the transnational corporation (TNC) and the anti-globalization movement, capitalism has apparently become decoupled from social class. The medium through which much of this has happened has been deindustrialization. This has seen the disappearance into economic marginality of large occupational communities of manual workers in many cities and industrial regions in the economies of the Northern hemisphere. We discuss this phenomenon in depth in later chapters but, at this stage, we should note that the process is also an outcome of the increased feminization of work which has broken the links between gender (maleness) and social class. Ethnicity is a further dimension that has made the issue of occupational inequality and identity far more complex than it was 30 or 40 years ago.

The increased disjuncture between places of work, home and leisure has contributed to the decline of people's sense of 'rootedness' in occupational and residential communities (Blokland, 2003).[7] Class is no longer the source of identity, politics or social behaviour in the ways in which it used to be, but it remains as a kind of benchmark against which individuals 'measure' themselves, often in a sense of what they are not rather than what they are (Skeggs, 1997; Savage, 2000). We return to these themes later in the book but, at this stage, we simply draw attention to how longstanding ways of understanding and drawing attention to social stratification (notably class) have become unsettled both in academic research and amongst the subjects of that research. That unsettling lies at the heart of postmodernism; it also coincides with the dramatic changes that have taken place over the past 30 years in the organization of economy and society. These changes are symptomatic of the transition from an industrial to an information economy: some see this as potentially liberating people from the shackles of industrial capitalism, whilst others see it as a simple transformation in the technical means of production within a yet more capitalistic mode of production (Webster, 1995). Giddens (2002) and Beck (Beck, 1992; Beck et al., 1994) typify the former, with an emphasis on risk and the individual, and Castells (1996a) the latter. Both positions share much in common, but nevertheless their differences are important to our understanding of how the economic and technological changes of the last decades have impacted on our current understanding of the world in which we live. They feature in novels such as William Gibson's *Neuromancer* (1993) and the concept of hyper-reality which finds resonances in the work of the original 1960s pop artist Andy Warhol or more recently the theoretician Baudrillard (Warhol and Baudrillard, 1995).

Giddens and Beck both emphasize the increase in individualism and the importance that people place on risk. Previously industrial economies were seen as transforming nature and increasing wealth, and the issue was the unequal share of the benefits of those transformations of the natural and 'manmade' [*sic*] worlds. Increasingly, however, concerns have arisen not simply about access to wealth but about the very consequences of that wealth transformation. The 'baby boomers', despite being born and raised in the unprecedented plenty and security of the decades after the Second World War, have unlike any previous generation, questioned the *quality* as much as the *quantity* of what the economy can offer (Marcuse, 1964). For the first time, people have had to start making judgements about the likely impacts on them of industrial production – whether it be food, recreational drugs, private transport or industrial processes (Beck, 1992). Advanced capitalist society, having solved for some the problem of scarcity, has now created a problem of excess – in terms of quantity such as obesity – or, more insidiously, of the unknown consequences of technological, scientific or industrial innovation (for example BSE). New means have to be devised for making appropriate, and often individual, 'risk assessments' of social behaviour. The state is no longer trusted to do this; either because it is committed to a particular model of growth (such as a dependency on cheap energy) or because it cannot recognise the problem (such as identifying unadulterated recreational drugs). The internet is the most recent and technologically innovatory of such new sources of information that people are able to draw upon to assess the risk inherent in their everyday lives. The problem is that making all information available on a 'one to many' basis, creates the possibility of allowing what were previously private fears or fantasies to become collective behaviour. The growth of pornography into at least a semi-legitimate industry is one illustration of this trend (Schlosser, 2004).

Held et al. conclude their survey of approaches to globalization with the following definition:

A process or set of processes which embodies a transformation in the spatial organization of social relations and transactions – accessed in terms of their extensity, velocity, and impact – generating transcontinental or interregional flows and networks of activity, interaction and the exercise of power. (1999: 16)

They suggest that this then gives rise to different models of globalization depending on the relationship of intensity/extensity, velocity and impact. In other words, globalization is a 'process or set of processes rather than a singular condition' (1999: 27). It is an emergent phenomenon arising out of the interactions and exchanges of existing national/social systems with a set of wider global processes which give rise to new networks of relations stretching from the global to the local. As such, it is a process of 'structuration' using Giddens' (1976: 120–1) phrase. Few areas of life, they claim, escape this but, on the other hand, one should not read the global across from one area of activity to another – from, for example, the ecological to the cultural – because each tend to have their own dynamics of interconnection. All of this gives rise to processes of deterritorialization and reterritorialization which are so complex that Held et al. conclude that it is wisest to describe globalization as *aterritorial* (1999: 28). All of this means that the ways in which power is distributed and controlled is changing and that disproportionate power concentrates in the hands of elites in the world's major metropolitan centres. This debate is clearly open-ended and forms the background for much of the rest of the book, although our focus is on the sociological as opposed to the political and economic aspects.

Further reading

Harvey (1989) remains the key book for those wishing to read further on the subject matter of this chapter. There are many books on globalization, but Held et al. (1999) remains one of the clearest and most comprehensive. Perrons (2004) offers an excellent detailed historical materialist account of the socio-spatial inequalities arising from globalization. Urry (2000) offers an exciting and provocative account of how sociology has moved beyond the boundaries of the social structures so familiar for much of the twentieth century. Klein (1999) and Monbiot (2003) present critical views of globalization from the standpoint of contemporary activists. Giddens' *The Third Way and its Critics* (2000) is a clear manifesto for a 'transformationalist' perspective on the contemporary globalization debate. There are a number of excellent readers on globalization which provide a broad selection of texts including Beynon and Dunkerley (2000) and Lechner and Boli (2000).

CHAPTER THREE

The Collar Line and Urban Boundaries

───────────────────── **Introduction** ─────────────────────

In Chapter 2 we discussed the rise of modernity and industrial society and how in recent decades these two concepts, which formed the basis for much of the moral, political and economic order during the last 150 years, no longer have the same status at the beginning of the twenty-first century. Much the same can be said about how we account for the social structure of such societies. Until relatively recently, employment and occupation dominated sociological approaches to social stratification. The language of class saturated discussions on how industrial society is stratified and that largely involved the study of a male, white, manual working class. For this reason, industrial sociology lay, for many years, at the core of the discipline as a whole. Whilst this pre-eminence might have been justified by the industrial nature of society, it had two consequences that in the longer term threatened sociological analysis of contemporary societies. Firstly, sociology itself became 'Balkanized' into a hierarchically ranked series of specialisms with little interaction between them. Secondly, with the decline of industrial society, there was a breakdown in the consensus about both the class nature of social stratification and the ways of studying it. In terms of method, industrial sociology had relied, perhaps to an unhealthy extent, on the survey which was developed to study almost any social situation (for example

Lazarsfeld and Rosenberg, 1955). Whilst this approach might have been appropriate for the analysis of large-scale employment situations in which a relatively homogeneous group of workers was employed under broadly similar conditions, as in the factory or coal mine, it was less able to deal with the situation that emerged from this. In post-industrial society, not only is full-time employment declining, but the nature of work and of the working class has also changed. The vertical class divisions of industrial society have become increasingly cross cut by those of gender and ethnicity, for example. This has required new research agendas and methods, as we discuss in later chapters.

This chapter focuses on the two decades following the end of the Second World War and examines the nature of the divide between the blue-collar working class and white-collar non-manual classes. In particular, we look at the key debate that emerged around working-class 'affluence' and its consequences for the relations between the working and middle classes and the changing nature of social class. Most of this debate was conducted by sociologists either working within a neo-Weberian paradigm or a largely atheoretical community studies perspective.

Until the late 1970s, Marxism largely confined itself to a meta-analysis of the economic and social system often conducted from a historical perspective. The problem for Marxism in the immediate post-war decades was to understand the historic failure of the Western working classes to embrace revolutionary socialism, and this required a 'coming to terms' with the successes of welfare capitalism in Europe and, to a lesser extent, North America. Many Marxists found this an intellectually and emotionally difficult reconciliation.

We also examine, in this chapter, the nature of the city and its development in the late nineteenth century as the 'natural container' for the industrial working class. We trace how the sociological study of the city developed in the United States in the early decades of the twentieth century in the work of the Chicago School of Sociology. We argue that just as the nature and indeed existence of the working class began to be called into question in the 1960s, so too did the nature of the city.

Collars and classes

For the first 75 years of the twentieth century, class was dichotomized in both the popular imagination and much of the sociological literature between a manual (blue-collar) working class and a non-manual (white-collar) middle class. The 'collar line' was widely regarded as the backbone of the class structure in the immediate post-war period (Parkin, 1971; Duke and Edgell, 1987; Southern, 2000). This dichotomization was reflected in contemporary discussions about prevailing cultural values (see Box 3.1). Furthermore until its 'rediscovery' in the early 1960s, it was widely assumed that full employment and the welfare state had restricted poverty to that small minority of the population who did not work either because of old age or sickness (Rowntree and Lavers, 1951).

> ### Box 3.1   THE WORKING CLASS AND MASS CULTURE – FROM
> ### RICHARD HOGGART'S *THE USES OF LITERACY*
>
> I have continually stressed the ways in which newer forces are adapting and modify-
> ing elements in what was a fairly distinctive working-class culture. No doubt, some-
> thing similar could be demonstrated in the culture of other classes, if only because
> the newer productions appeal to more than working-class people. This throws further
> light on the claim to an emerging classlessness, which I questioned at the very begin-
> ning of this essay. We may now see that in at least one sense, we are indeed becom-
> ing classless – that is, the great majority of us are being merged into one class. We
> are becoming culturally classless. The newer women's magazines are in this sense
> 'classless' where the older kind belonged to particular social groups. Mass publica-
> tions cannot reach an audience of the size they need by cutting across class bound-
> aries. No doubt many of them have a special warmth for the 'little folk' – the working
> and lower middle classes. This is not because they belong to their audience in the
> way that older working-class publications often did, nor simply because their produc-
> ers subscribe to one of the more flattering democratizing assumptions but because
> that audience forms the majority of their potential readers, because, though they
> would like to attract many others, they must have this group as the basis of their
> sales. (Hoggart, 1958: 342)

Many key sociological research monographs of the post-war period focused on the collar line with a manual working class clearly distinguished from and counterposed to a non-manual middle class (Mills, 1951; Lockwood, 1958; Willmott and Young, 1960). This developed into a growing debate over the usefulness of the manual/ non-manual divide in the form of the so-called embourgeoisement thesis and its more celebrated riposte in the 'Affluent Worker' study undertaken among industrial workers in Luton in Southeast England (Goldthorpe et al., 1969). This developed into a counterfactual debate about the proletarianization of white-collar work and 'deskilling' which continued well into the 1980s. White-collar proletarianization is discussed in the next chapter in the context of the development of a Marxist indus- trial sociology, although its origins lay in debates about class from the 1950s and 1960s (Lockwood, 1958).

───────────── **Work and stratification in post-war Britain** ─────────────

If there was an overarching theme in industrial sociology during the post-war years it concerned the relationship between social structure and the structure of industrial pro- duction; this became known as the 'technostructure'. It was suggested that we were wit- nessing a process of social convergence that was largely determined by the requirement for an educated and socially integrated workforce. This position was argued strongly by

Kerr et al. (1973) in their book *Industrialism and Industrial Man*, but was also reflected in the work of sociologists such as Alain Touraine (1971). This approach was criticized for its 'technological determinism' and failing to identify why a particular production technology should produce a given social structure.

Nevertheless, the nature of the class structure and class convergence was an important concern of both policy makers and sociologists in post-war Britain. Both the Labour and Conservative parties needed to gain votes from the middle and working classes respectively and perhaps more importantly neither wished to see a return to the political extremism of the 1930s, which had done so much to alienate the centre ground over which they were now fighting. In Britain, this process of political convergence is sometimes referred to as 'Butskellism' after RAB Butler and Hugh Gaitskell who were respectively deputy leader and leader of the Conservative and Labour Parties but who both failed to become Prime Minister. Under their influence, both parties aimed to create consensus by signing up to the twin policies of Beveridge (social welfare) and Keynes (economic management) designed to tame the tendency of capitalist economies to economic collapse and consequent widespread social deprivation and political extremism.

A key concern of industrial sociology during the post-war years was 'technological alienation' and the workers' discontent with the job despite real increases in wages. This discontent concerned the nature of the job itself either because it was dirty and/or dangerous or because it was boring and repetitive. It was widely assumed that automation would enable the boring and repetitive parts of the job to be relegated to machines, thus allowing workers to concentrate on the more satisfying and rewarding elements. In *Alienation and Freedom*, Blauner (1964) argued that increasing technological sophistication, particularly automation, had blunted workers' alienation from the industrial system. In part, this was because automation gave workers more time to focus on meaningful tasks and partly because, as the amount of capital invested in technology rose, wages then became less critical to employers who could therefore afford to be more generous. In addition, Blauner argued that, as levels of investment rose, employers needed to keep the machinery running almost continuously in order to make a profit; they needed, so it was argued, to buy workers' consent to ensure that there were no stoppages or breakdowns.[8]

Much of the earliest work in British post-war sociology was concerned simply to understand the nature of working-class life and as such could be quite journalistic or even novelistic in nature. Examples include Zweig (1952) who used qualitative techniques of observation to record what he saw as the attitudes of the 'British worker' in different contexts (see Box 3.2), as well as a variety of community studies which drew upon anthropological concerns (Stacey, 1960; Klein, 1965; Frankenberg, 1966). These community studies often highlighted intra-class status divisions on long-standing lines of 'roughness' and 'respectability' with the former associated with drunkenness, indolence and petty criminality and the latter associated with sobriety, thrift and 'keeping up appearances'.

Box 3.2   THE WORKING CLASSES IN THE **1950S**

Zweig (1952) identified five grades of labour in the working class:

1.   Lowest grade – the disabled, 'unadjusted', handicapped
2.   Labourers
3.   The Semi-skilled
4.   Craftsmen and skilled workers
5.   Supervisory grades.

Zweig claims that, in general, there is little mobility, except for the most skilled craftsmen. Age tends to be a demoting factor (for example, a (coal) face worker will go on to haulage in late middle age). The standard of living, he claims, depends on the wife's skill as a manager. Although Zweig introduced a number of stereotypes of the basic industrial categories, he argued that 'nearly every worker breeds its own type' (1952: 52)

In *Coal is our Life*, Dennis et al. (1956) used the increasingly popular community study method to investigate the interactions between work situations, class situations and social structure in a mining village in the Yorkshire coalfield. The study focused on four major areas of social existence in 'Ashton': work, the union, leisure and the family. The authors demonstrate that it is the strong interactions between the nature of the work – particularly danger and the need to rely on teamwork – and life in the community that help to explain the high degree of class-consciousness and wage militancy. Trade union membership and activity is reinforced by a strong community consciousness in which there is a very low level of female economic activity (less than 15 per cent compared to the norm for the time of approximately 25 per cent). The spheres of work and home were united against a clearly identified common class enemy and this was reinforced by a huge fund of shared experiences. The study reinforced many of Zweig's somewhat impressionistic claims and had an enormous influence in creating, as it were, an ideal type of the English working class against which change was to be measured in the post-war decades. Its Marxist antecedents did little to undermine this broad consensus in British sociology: working-class culture was broadly a reflection of the material conditions of existence. The alienation derived from the dangerous and sometimes violent nature of work was represented in the miner's wage packet that was then reflected in his attitude towards family (with a strict gender division of labour) on the one hand and leisure on the other.[9]

The main point of contention is not the study itself, but the way in which it was then generalized to the working class as a whole, or at least that part of which was characterized as being of a 'traditional proletarian' nature living in occupational communities where there were strong overlaps between work and community. Later work by Richards (1996) has highlighted long-standing inter-regional differences in miners' earnings, working conditions, industrial relations practices and ideologies – see also Moore (1974). These important, yet somewhat random, studies exemplified by the work of Zweig and Dennis et al. highlighted the somewhat chaotic state of sociological thinking about social class which veered between political commitments to an increasingly ideologically compromised Marxism and a culturalist view of working-class affluence and consumerism.

Class theory in British post-war sociology

Post-war sociology was saturated by North American theory, drawing on the structural functionalism of Talcott Parsons (1970) [1951], functionalists such as Davis and Moore (1945), 'middle range' theorists notably Merton (1957), and to a lesser extent conflict theory (Coser, 1956). The development of a sociological understanding of social class during this period was undertaken by a small group of neo-Weberian scholars who seemingly had fewer problems integrating theory and practice than those working in the Marxist tradition. Ralf Dahrendorf (1959), David Lockwood (1958) and John Rex (1961) were the three leading writers responsible for the development of this neo-Weberian approach to sociological work from the late 1950s.[10] All these writers developed a body of theoretical work in the context of empirical studies of industrial change, or in the case of Rex in relation to ethnicity and urban change (Rex and Moore, 1967).[11]

David Lockwood's work in particular was highly theoretically informed. His article in the *British Journal of Sociology* (Lockwood, 1956) remains the single most important critique of Parsonian structural functionalism, the argument being that it entirely ignores the underlying order of structural inequality.[12] This neo-Weberian approach had been developed in his PhD thesis, subsequently published as *The Blackcoated Worker* (Lockwood, 1958), which argued that both market and work situation needed to be taken into account when looking at the class location of groups of workers. A further article, 'System integration and social integration' (Lockwood, 1964), was a key contribution to the later debate about structure and agency in sociological explanation and remains a classic solution to this sociological dilemma (Gough and Olofsson, 1999).

Dahrendorf (1959) explicitly raised questions about the role of conflict in understanding social order and social change which directly challenged the Parsonian orthodoxy. He also challenged Marxist notions about the role of class conflict, arguing that in industrial society (which he suggested had largely transcended capitalist society), conflict had become institutionalized and was a means of tension management rather than an agent of system change. In arguing this, he borrowed some ideas from Coser (1956) who, whilst recognizing the role of conflict, saw it in terms of system maintenance within an essentially Parsonian framework.

Goldthorpe and Lockwood (1963) explored some of Lockwood's ideas regarding class position and changes in the class structure in the context of the debate about working-class affluence. The 'embourgeoisement thesis', as it came to be known, was relatively straightforward. It involved the claim that the increased affluence of manual workers and their families, associated with the high wages earned by semi-skilled male workers in the post-war boom, meant their lifestyles and political attitudes were converging with those of non-manual workers. It was this embourgeoisement process which was routinely wheeled out by psephologists, journalists and political commentators in order to explain the 13 years of unbroken Conservative Governments from 1951 to 1964. There were relatively few sociologists who supported the embourgeoisement thesis wholesale, although Zweig's (1961) book provided limited empirical support for it.

Goldthorpe and Lockwood (1963) hypothesized that such notions were premature in an important paper which was effectively the research design for their later famous 'affluent worker' study undertaken in the mid-1960s. This study examined the work, home and community lives of male workers in three factories in Luton (Goldthorpe et al., 1968a, 1968b, 1969). The factories involved different kinds of modern technology: batch production (Skefco ball bearings), continuous process (Laporte Chemicals) and assembly line (Vauxhall Motors). All three were owned by large foreign corporations and paid 'good' wages. The research constituted a critical case study in the sense that if embourgeoisement was to be found anywhere then it would be amongst such workers in such workplaces.

In their 1963 paper, Goldthorpe and Lockwood had concluded that affluence alone would not be sufficient, even in conceptual terms, to account for a collapse of traditional social-class divisions. Rather, they suggested, there would need to be 'normative' and 'relational' as well as 'economic' explanations for class convergence. In other words, the working class could only be considered to have become 'middle class' if it could be shown to have adopted its norms and behaviour and, crucially, if it was accepted as middle class by the middle class. In the context of post-war Britain, this was manifestly not the case and the cultural and other barriers between the classes remained strong.[13] So at the very least, they would need to find evidence for embourgeoisement at the cutting edge of industrial production, such as in Luton, if there was to be support for the embourgeoisement thesis more generally in the future. They hypothesized that, whereas traditional workers such as coal miners adopted more 'solidaristic' work and political practices rooted in automatic allegiance to both the union and the Labour Party, the affluent workers would be more instrumental in their loyalties and would only support such institutions in so far as they might advance their material interests. However, this did not mean to say that the affluent workers were thereby middle class either, since they were culturally distinct from the non-manual clerks and they continued to demonstrate oppositional attitudes towards their employers. These 'privatized workers' were not middle class, although Goldthorpe et al. (1969) did subsequently detect elements of 'normative convergence' between the manual and non-manual workers in their sample (see Box 3.3 for a summary of the affluent worker findings).

Box 3.3 **FINDINGS FROM THE AFFLUENT WORKER STUDIES**

1. The effect of affluence on the class structure was exaggerated and as such 'embourgeoisement' had not occurred.
2. Some normative convergence between manual and non-manual groups had taken place via economic collectivism by white-collar workers and 'privatization' (or home-centredness) by manual workers.
3. There was evidence of 'instrumentality' where the worker held an essentially 'money model' of society. This instrumentality was reflected in trade union and political attitudes. The affluent workers tended to see the former as a 'service' organization with a high involvement at work (80 per cent voted in shop steward elections), but a low involvement in the more 'political' arena of the trade union branch (60 per cent never attended). Although over 80 per cent voted Labour in general elections, this support was not based on traditional loyalties but was instead conditional on the Labour Party improving their life chances.
4. A 'new' working class had emerged whose work attitudes were instrumental and whose home lives were privatized around the conjugal family.

(See Goldthorpe et al., 1969: 157–95, Chapter 6)

The affluent worker study became a classic of post-war sociology taught to thousands of undergraduates and GCE A' Level students as a prominent exemplar of the best of British empirical sociology (Marshall, 1990). It was, however, not without its critics. In particular, feminists pointed to the fact that it was based on male workers and had nothing to say about their wives (Hart, 1989). As Hart argues, this was of more than theoretical import because other evidence suggests that there was a clear gender dimension to working-class identity and politics with women far less likely to self-identify as working class or vote for the Labour Party. Ironically, as Hart argues, Zweig (1961), the forgotten person in the embourgeoisement debate, was far more attuned to the potential significance of gender since he included female workers in his study and also commented on how they seemed to be less class conscious than their male colleagues.

The affluent worker study argued that the working class had lost some of its collectivist ethos and had become increasingly 'privatized' and home centred, as Lockwood (1966) had suggested; a point of view that provides some support for the subsequent work by Saunders (1990) on home ownership. Lockwood (1966) argued, however, that even if the workers were too busy (in Saunders' words) 'papering the parlour', they had not lost all of their notions of working-class collectivism. They retained, for instance, an affinity for trade union and Labour party affiliation, even if these institutions were now treated more like service organizations, such as the Automobile Association, rather than as part of a class cultural heritage. The working class had become more internally stratified, something which was later to happen with the middle classes, as Lockwood (1995) himself has later pointed out. The affluent worker study, interesting as it was for its substantive findings, was more interesting for the debate that it started around the nature of class and class inequality and how the nature of that inequality varied *within* the working class. This became known as the 'class images' model of social inequality.

Working-class images as the basis for social stratification

The 'class images' model of society, based as it is on the neo-Weberian 'action frame of reference', argues that there is an element of what we might now term 'reflexivity' in how people understand social stratification (Beck et al., 1994). Lockwood (1966) suggested that there is neither simply a stratification or a normative order, but rather that people understand the structuring of inequality depending on where they themselves are located within the structures of inequality (see Box 3.4).

Box 3.4 WORKING-CLASS IMAGES

Goldthorpe and Lockwood (1963) argued that most people have a clearly defined image of the dimensions of inequality in terms of the distribution of wealth, status and power. They argue that this gives rise to two basic types of image of society:

1. A dichotomous or power model – society consists of two contending classes based around the possession or non-possession of power.
2. A hierarchical or prestige model – society consists of a number of strata which are distinguished by prestige.

The first model is seen as a typical working-class view and is essentially collectivistic, whilst the second model is seen as middle class and individualistic. Having articulated these 'ideal types', they were then able to test them empirically with reference to the 'embourgeoisement thesis'. Lockwood (1966) was later able to be more specific, presumably on the basis of the initial findings from the affluent worker research undertaken in 1964. Lockwood argues that people 'view' society from their position within it, and this 'view' or 'image' varies according to how they experience social inequality in their daily lives. He repeats the earlier view that the working class tends to hold an image based on a power model, whilst the middle-class image is based on a hierarchical model. He goes on to argue that there is considerable diversity amongst the working class in terms of their industrial and community milieux. He delineates three types of worker that are all advanced as ideal types:

1. Traditional Proletarian (power model)
2. Traditional Deferential (status hierarchy model)
3. Privatized (pecuniary model).

The differences between the ideal types are summarized in Box 3.5. *Traditional Proletarians* are associated with traditional industries such as mining, ship-building and docking that concentrated workers in solidary communities and isolated them from the wider society. Life was typified by a strong sense of shared occupational experience that spreads over into leisure, and of belonging to a work dominated community as in *Coal is Our Life* (Dennis, et al., 1956). 'Us and Them' was not just against the bosses and white-collar workers, but the whole of the world out there. *Traditional Deferentials*, by contrast, were likely to hold a hierarchical prestige image of social inequality to which he [*sic*] defers, as for example in the case of working-class support for the Conservative Party (McKenzie and Silver 1968). Lockwood (1966) speculates that the 'Deferential' will hold a fourfold view of society based on the idea that there are:

- Genuine leaders
- Misguided leaders (often drawn from the parvenus or nouveau riche)
- Misguided followers
- Himself [*sic*].

Lockwood suggests that most sociological analysis has held the deferential to be an individual – rural, female, elderly – related to occupation (usually service), which brings him into direct association with his boss or middle-class influentials. The work situation will tend to be personal and particularistic. Status for the deferential is 'interactional' and not 'attributional' and there is widespread consensus about status ranking and everybody 'knows their place'. Newby's (1977) study of agricultural workers showed that whilst such 'deferentials' might tug their forelock to the boss's face, they were quite capable of putting two fingers up when his back was turned. In other words, Newby suggested that the situation was a function of the nature of work/power relations and not necessarily of ideology.

For the *Privatized Worker*, the major source of 'cleavage' was seen in terms of material possessions and income. Work relationships were 'instrumental' and community ones were 'privatized'. Work was undertaken in large, automated factories and was seen as a 'necessary evil' to buy goods for consumption – the 'cash nexus' is central. The privatized worker was seen as highly alienated but unlikely to develop a strong class consciousness because his work involvement was too shallow. This is reinforced in the community by life in housing estates which bring together strangers with little in common, so men socialized with their household members in the home rather than with fellow men in the community. Status is based on conspicuous consumption ('keeping up with the Joneses') and, in contrast to the Deferential Worker, it is 'attributional'. Social divisions are de-socialized and reduced to money. The privatized worker sees his world as one of a large band of consumers in which social distinctions are viewed in economic terms.

Box 3.5   WORKER ORIENTATIONS AND CLASS IMAGES

Work Situation

	Job involvement	Identification and interaction with workmates	identification and interaction with employers
Middle Class	+	+	+
Deferential	+	−	+
Proletarian	+	+	−
Privatized	−	−	−

Community Structure

	Interactional status system	Occupational community	Occupational differentiations
Middle Class	+	+	+
Deferential	+	−	+
Proletarian	+	+	−
Privatized	−	−	−

Source: Lockwood (1966: 25)

'Deferentials' and 'proletarians' are located in economic backwaters; they do not think beyond the boundaries of their own communities whilst their community and work relationships are mutually reinforcing. The privatized worker is put forward as a new, alienated and economic man located in the new expanding industries. The conclusion for working-class consciousness is that radicalism is 'a thing of the past'.

There were three reactions to this from outside the neo-Weberian camp. Firstly, the 'twas ever thus' argument advanced by, for example, Westergaard (Westergaard and Resler, 1976) who pointed out that the cash nexus has always been at the heart of Marxist analyses of class. Secondly, there were alternative views of the 'new' working class by writers such as Mallet (1975) who saw these workers in the modern industries of the time as being the new vanguard of the proletariat. This view was given additional credibility by the events that occurred during May 1968 in France. The instigators of the 'May events' were a combination of Marxist-inspired students, young unskilled workers in car plants such as Renault's at Billancourt and the skilled apprentices in Aerospatiale. This fitted with the arguments being advanced by Herbert Marcuse (1964) about a new class coalition of the dispossessed and young workers in high tech industries and students. The third reaction was to hasten the longer-term emergence of an empirically based Marxist industrial sociology based around the concept of labour process; we return to this in the following chapter.

The Marxist response to sociology

Marxism maintained an uneasy relationship with sociology for much of the immediate post-war period. This largely reflected the turmoil within the Communist Parties and between them and non-Stalinist Marxists, but it also reflected the very real discrimination and harassment experienced by Marxist academics in general and members of the Communist Party in particular.[14] In Britain, much of this debate (or rather lack of it) focused around the Hungarian uprising in 1956. Khrushchev's so-called 'secret' speech, in the same year, officially acknowledged, for the first time, that there had been 'excesses' under Stalin and this opened up debates within the Western Communist Parties (Saville, 2003). Large numbers of intellectuals left the Communist Party and formed what became known as the 'New Left'. They came together around a succession of journals such as the *New Reasoner* and the *Universities and Left Review*, which merged into the *New Left Review* in 1960 under Stuart Hall's editorship (Saville, 2003: 121). Ralph Miliband's *The State in Capitalist Society* (1969) and *Parliamentary Socialism* (1973) were key pieces of Marxist writing from a political scientist who came out of the Communist Party following 1956. Miliband offered a fundamental critique of the idea of achieving socialism through social democracy. He argued for a conception of socialism that was not concerned with managing the capitalist economy better than the traditional elites; this had become the Labour Party's goal, as seen in Tony Crosland's (1956) book *The Future of Socialism*. Miliband was equally critical of the Communist Party's notion of the *British Road to Socialism* in which a socialist society would be voted in by the masses led by the Party. A rich vein of socialist writing emerged in the annual *Socialist Register*, which was edited over several decades by Miliband and Saville. Little of this writing however involved what might be termed *sociological* research that engaged the work being undertaken by the neo-Weberian sociologists, such as that discussed in the previous section, who were researching the changes taking place in the industrial and social structure of the United Kingdom.

Class was at the heart of the Marxist debate, but it was marooned within political theory or in relation to history. Many of the best historians of the post-war period were members of the Communist Party including Christopher Hill, Eric Hobsbawm and E.P. Thompson. Thompson's (1968) *Making of the English Working Class* not only rescued the Luddites from the condemnation of history, but also had a profound effect on the development of a Marxist sociology because it engaged Marxist notions of class in a robustly critical manner. In this book, Thompson pursued a resolutely humanist version of Marxism that explicitly confronted both Marxist and non-Marxist conceptions of class. In the preface, Thompson sets himself up against, on the one hand, sociologists and, on the other hand Marxists, who wanted to abstract class to a mathematical formulation that, as he saw it, had little to do with human experience:

> ... class happens when some men, as a result of common experiences (inherited or shared), feel and articulate the identity of their interests as between themselves, and as against other men whose interests are different from (and usually opposed to) theirs. The class experience is largely determined by the productive relations into which men are born – or enter involuntarily. Class-consciousness is the way

in which these experiences are handled in cultural terms: embodied in traditions, value-systems, ideas and institutional forms. If the experience appears as determined, class-consciousness does not. (Thompson, 1968: 10)

This definition of class infuriated many fellow Marxists who rooted their Marxism in the mode of production and the behaviour of the capitalist 'system'. Baran and Sweezy (1968) who wrote extensively on capitalism's monopolistic tendencies are an example of the former, whilst Althusser (1969), who focused on capitalism as a mode of production in which the exploited masses were far from visible, was an example of the latter. Thompson subsequently delivered an excoriating attack on Althusserian Marxism in *The Poverty of Theory* (1978). His 'experience is all' approach appeared to make him antagonistic to any kind of theorizing, however, and this did not necessarily endear him to those Marxists who might have been his natural allies, for example those working with Stuart Hall at the Centre for Contemporary Cultural Studies (CCCS) at the University of Birmingham who were exploring the work of the Italian Marxist Antonio Gramsci (Johnson, 1978) (see Chapter 7 for an outline of the pioneering CCCS work on youth sub-cultures). By the 1970s however, this European neo-Marxism was able to challenge the neo-Weberian orthodoxy as we see in the debates over industrial sociology and social class in Chapter 4.

Somewhat surprisingly perhaps, some of the best writing on political economy from a Marxist perspective was being undertaken in the United States notably by Baran and Sweezy (1968), both long-established Communists. In *Monopoly Capital* (1968) they focused on the monopolistic tendencies in capitalism which had originally been noted by Lenin in his work on *Imperialism* (1999 [1916]). Baran and Sweezy's work had particular application during the post-war period as the United States and its monopolistic corporations established themselves across the world whilst apparently banishing the language of class from the homeland. Baran and Sweezy also explored the nature of the relationship between race and class and argued that race was essentially a form of 'super exploitation' by capital in its monopoly phase. Their focus therefore was very much on the 'tendencies' in the mode of production of capitalist economies and, to a lesser extent, with the social relations of production.

What both Marxists and Weberians could agree about was the existence of a large manual working class employed in manufacturing industry, i.e. an industrial proletariat. The two decades that followed the ending of the Second World War marked the high point of industrial capitalism in the so-called developed world. Manufacturing dominated this era with the rise of integrated corporations based mainly in the United States but also in Europe and, towards the end of the period, in Japan. They employed large numbers of well paid and, for the most part, unionized male workers in plants that dominated their local regional economies. This period has since become known as the Fordist era in which governments, corporations and, to some extent, the representatives of their unionized workforces operated together to maintain an economy based around mass production and mass consumption (Amin, 1994a). It was this system which gave rise to the sense of affluence which so engaged many of the leading sociologists of the period as they grappled with the oxymoronic notion of working-class affluence. As we shall see in the following section, a similar paradox could be noted in the spatial organization of the economy and particularly the major urban centres of manufacturing. These finally began to fall apart in the so-called long hot summers of the mid-1960s when many North American cities experienced unprecedented social unrest by their black residents protesting against the lack of employment opportunities and entrenched racial animosity (Sugrue, 1996). This only served to increase further the abandonment of the city by the white working classes who fled to the suburbs using their new-found affluence to commute to work in the factories surrounding such cities. The kind of working-class privatism, noted by Lockwood, manifested itself in the increasing suburbanization of the city.

Urban boundaries

As we have seen, explanations of social stratification have traditionally been rooted in the 'relations' of production in general and those of employment in particular. This tendency towards 'economic determinism' has long been the source of intellectual tension amongst sociologists and their critics. In this section, we introduce the idea that space and place have an increasingly important role to play in understanding how contemporary society is stratified.

Sociologists have tended to behave as if social processes occur in a kind of 'any-place', despite the fact that many of the most famous and influential studies are often known for their geographical location. The 'Bethnal Green studies' are often used to describe the pioneering work on community by the Institute of Community Studies (Young and Willmott, 1957; Platt, 1971); the 'Luton studies' describe the work on class structure undertaken by Goldthorpe et al. (1969).

In the remainder of this chapter, we focus on the role of cities in understanding the changes that took place in the social stratification of post-war society in North America and Britain. As with the industrial working class, post-war urban resurgence and reconstruction presaged the decline of the industrial city by the late 1960s. By the time the students and others in 1968 were taking to the streets of London, Paris and Berlin, many of the cities of North America had already burned and in Britain the Labour Government was sponsoring Community Development Plans in an attempt to deal with what was now perceived as specifically *urban* deprivation and the inner-city problem (Craig et al., 1982). We start however by examining how cities became, in the context of capitalist industrialization, essentially working-class places.

The industrial city

In his classic account of the origins and development of cities, Mumford likens them to containers, initially of material culture, resources and people which then evolve:

> Not by accident ... have the old functions of the urban container been supplemented by new functions, exercized through what I shall call the functional grid:

the framework of the invisible city. Like the old container the new grid, in all its forms, industrial, cultural, urban, lends itself to both good and bad uses. But what is even more significant is the fact that the form has appeared in so many different places, as an organic response to present day needs. The new image of the city must be in part an expression of these new realities. On that score, both the old metropolis and the new conurbation lamentably fail for they have tended to efface instead of reintegrating the essential components of the city. (1961: 564–5)

Unlike the 'new world', cities in Europe were built in ongoing and contested societies and reflected their population centres and power relations. According to Burtenshaw et al. (1991), there are three traditions in European urban development. From the late nineteenth century, with the establishment of capitalism, the nation state and the subjugation of the working class, the centres of many European cities were remodelled in a neo-classical tradition. Undoubtedly, the best-known and most influential exemplar of this tradition was the remodelling of Paris in the 1870s by Baron Haussman who imposed a grid plan of long and broad avenues on the centre of the city. An important objective was to prevent a repetition of the Commune of 1871 in which the workers seized and held Paris for several months. Under the Haussman plan, even if workers did manage to throw barricades across the new boulevards, the cavalry and artillery would be able to operate with devastating effect. The centres of many European cities were remodelled in the same manner: for example, Brussels, Stockholm, Barcelona and Vienna. The tradition made a further reappearance during the Nazi era with Speer's work on Berlin; Madrid too was 'rearranged' in similar mode after the Nationalists won the Civil War in 1939.

Burtenshaw et al. (1991) argue that there was a second 'utilitarian' tradition in Britain, in which the role of the state was to provide a regulatory framework that imposed minimum standards and determined what could be built where and for what purpose. The redesign of much of central London (for instance, the building of Regent Street and Oxford Street, the Mall etc.) occurred at roughly the same time as Baron Haussman was at work in Paris. In both cities, the concern was with breaking up working-class ghettoes – known as 'ventilating the rookeries' in London. Whereas in Paris this was done under the auspices of an insecure monarch with imperialist pretensions, in London it was mainly undertaken by private capital basking in the super profits of being the world's most successful imperial power. The net effect, however, was broadly the same.

There is a third, and somewhat later, tradition in which design as a statement about values was foregrounded. This movement is associated with a number of iconic figures, most of whom actually built very little, but who nevertheless reflected the aspirations of the modern age. These figures and/or movements include Walter Gropius and the Bauhaus, Ebenezer Howard and Garden Cities movement, Frank Lloyd Wright and the extensive city and, perhaps most importantly, Le Corbusier. The latter referred to the house as being 'a machine for living'. His influence over urban design in the twentieth century was massively out of proportion to what he actually built. His basic notion was to take advantage of new technologies to build high, which would allow the elite to live near the centre with good access to administrative and cultural centres, which would be co-located there. Workers, by contrast, would live in satellites.

Approximately 85 per cent of the surface area was to be parkland. Cities were, in his view, to be designed for leisure as well as for production. When his plan for the right bank of Paris (the 'plan voisin') was turned down, he moved his allegiances from capitalism to syndicalism.

In all these accounts of the city, working-class subordination to capital is reflected in the spatial organization of the city which emphasizes the growing power of capital and the state. The working classes are moved around the inner city and their potential power over the city is increasingly circumscribed, whether undertaken by a *dirigiste* state (as in Haussman's remodelling of Paris) or the operation of the land market (as in London's West End). Le Corbusier's original 'plan voisin' for Paris was designed with this very much in mind. In the late nineteenth century, the urban hierarchy and ownership of the city was very clearly delineated; it reflected the state of relations between capital, the state and labour whether strongly established (as in Britain) or weakly (as in Bonapartist France). In the former it reflected their strength whereas in the latter it was an attempt to bolster their lack of hegemony. It was, however, in the United States, without a history of feudal cities, that the first explicit sociological analysis of urban growth emerged.

The Chicago School

In contrast to Europe, cities in the United States developed largely in locations which had not been previously urbanized in a country with cheap and extensive hinterlands. Urbanization was therefore linked much more directly to the process of industrialization and capitalist development than in Europe, parts of which had already been heavily urbanized for 500 years. In North America, the industrialization process was driven by the needs of capital accumulation, the need to absorb and settle a massive migrant labour force and to conquer a continent and remake its landscape (Hacker, 1947). Hacker refers to the 'moving frontier thesis', in which it was argued that the continual westward movement of the 'frontier' ensured a process of upward social mobility which had the effect of attracting many of the more ambitious members of the urban working class from the cities on the Eastern seaboard (Turner, 1961). These were also, potentially, the most radical and the opening up of the West contained the potential for development of political and industrial radicalism in the industrial cities on the Eastern seaboard, particularly amongst those radicals who had fled the 'old world'. The discovery of gold in California in 1849 merely hastened this huge migration westward – overland and by sea up the West Coast of the Americas. On the way, the railroads were built, the large rivers opened up to passenger and freight traffic using large flat-bottomed paddle steamers and the huge gateway cities to the mid-Western farming belt were created – St. Louis, Cincinnati but above all Chicago. Chicago was the gateway to the new farm belt of the mid-West and sat on the convergence of the Great Lakes, the Mississippi River and the new railroads being built from the East with the eventual goal of linking the Atlantic to the Pacific. The mid-West however had two more immediate uses: as sources of meat and grain. The invention of barbed wire transformed the Prairie lands enabling them to be enclosed for private ownership and farming at relatively minimal cost. Chicago became the grain elevator to the world and its stockyards the world's butchers (see Box 3.6). At the same time, it became a manufacturing centre for the farm machinery that made this level of agricultural productivity possible in a land with no traditional source of plentiful and cheap labour.

Box 3.6   **EXCERPT FROM *THE JUNGLE* BY UPTON SINCLAIR**

Promptly at seven the next morning Jurgis reported for work. He came to the door that had been pointed out to him, and he waited for nearly two hours. The boss had meant for him to enter, but had not said this, and so it was only when on his way out to hire another man that he came upon Jurgis. He gave him a good cursing, but as Jurgis did not understand a word of it, he did not object. He followed the boss, who showed him where to put his street clothes, and waited while he donned the working clothes he had bought in a second-hand shop and brought with him in a bundle; then he led him to the 'killing beds'. The work which Jurgis was to do here was very simple, and it took him but a few minutes to learn it. He was provided with a stiff besom, such as is used by street sweepers, and it was his place to follow down the line the man who drew out the smoking entrails from the carcass of the steer; this mass was to be swept into a trap, which was then closed, so that no one might slip into it. As Jurgis came in, the first cattle of the morning were just making their appearance; and so, with scarcely time to look about him, and none to speak to anyone, he fell to work. It was a sweltering day in July, and the place ran with steaming hot blood – one waded in it on the floor. The stench was almost overpowering, but to Jurgis it was nothing. His whole soul was dancing with joy – he was at work at last! He was at work and earning money! All day long he was figuring to himself. He was paid the fabulous sum of seventeen and a half cents an hour; and as it proved a rush day, and he worked until nearly seven o'clock in the evening, he went home to the family with the tidings that he had earned more than a dollar and a half in a single day!

Chicago was little more than a trading post in the 1860s yet doubled in size every decade until the depression of the late 1920s finally put an end to its period of frenetic growth. Chicago's rapid growth provided the first opportunity for the new discipline of sociology to observe how the city was able to absorb these migrants from a plethora of non-urban backgrounds and yet create some sense of order which, over time, led to a discernible spatial and social urban structure. The Chicago sociologists likened the city to an organism in which there existed a symbiosis between its people and its physical spaces. These they termed 'natural areas' which served both to socialize and be socialized by successive groups of migrants. The model developed by the founding fathers of the Chicago School and their teams of graduate students drew heavily from the ideas of Darwin about competition, succession and natural selection. The city had an ecology in which the fittest survived but did so by a continual process of outward succession – the city was like a pond into which a stone had

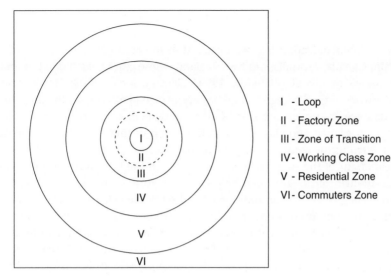

I - Loop
II - Factory Zone
III - Zone of Transition
IV- Working Class Zone
V - Residential Zone
VI- Commuters Zone

Figure 3.1   Concentric zones redrawn

been thrown and produced a series of outward ripples. This gave rise to the famous diagram, by Park's associate Edward Burgess, of the city, which he represented as a series of concentric rings (Figure 3.1).

Whilst it has been enormously influential, the Chicago School approach has also been subjected to massive criticism, mainly on the grounds that it failed to identify the dynamic for urban growth and was too specific to Chicago (Saunders, 1986; Savage et al., 2003). However, these criticisms notwithstanding, it identified the underlying outward expansion from the centre that occurred in most cities during the twentieth century. In Chicago, as elsewhere, this process came to a halt in the interwar period in response to the economic depression. The central, or downtown, areas of many US cities changed from being zones of transition for European immigrants to ghettoes for those fleeing the economic deserts which had become America's 'Deep South'. What had previously been the most dynamic areas of the city were turned into racialized no-go areas for the majority of their citizens who increasingly did not venture out of their suburbs except to go to work.

With the resumption of economic growth during and after the Second World War, the pattern of outward growth became increasingly racialized. It was not just Chicago which adopted the familiar donut shape in which the downtown area became largely deserted after working hours except for those seeking the 'pleasures' of its red light districts (Jacobs, 1962). This racialized suburbanization process became known as 'white flight' (Jackson, 1985; Avila, 2004). This was later followed by 'black flight' as the newly upwardly mobile black middle classes joined the process of urban 'leapfrog' and escaped the deindustrializing inner cities from the 1970s (Wilson, 1987), as we discuss in Chapter 5. This is epitomized in Detroit where much of what was previously the inner city is now almost literally deserted, whilst the surrounding areas (such as Dearborn) are populated by affluent middle- and working-class suburbs.

Suburbanization and the creation of social distance

The process of suburbanization has been greatest in the Anglophone countries of the world, Britain, Canada, Australia and New Zealand whose cities have tended to follow the North American model (Richards, 1990; Clapson, 1998, 2003; Harris, 2004). Although the work of the Chicago School has been challenged and largely discredited, the model describes two main patterns of urban settlement in the twentieth century: that of suburban growth and class segmentation. Both of these, we suggest, are now being restructured in the context of the post-industrial global city.

The development of the suburbs began in earnest in the inter-war period on both sides of the Atlantic, although it can be traced back to the late nineteenth century (Dyos, 1961). The growth of suburbia coincided with the expansion of the middle classes from a small group of upper middle-class professionals to a larger and more amorphous grouping which incorporated managers, technical, administrative and lower professional occupations as well as the self-employed (Lash and Urry, 1987). It is important to note here two aspects of this growth. Firstly, it was associated with the rise of new occupational groups (teachers, nurses, scientific and technical workers, administrators and 'routine' professionals), and secondly with the expansion of owner occupation in the housing market (Jackson, 1973). The emergence of this expanded middle class in the inter-war years coincided with the emergence of a 'new' working class. Both groups were associated with the development of new forms of manufacturing (mainly consumer goods based around the electrical and internal combustion engines) and the expansion of state-sponsored professions (Lash and Urry, 1987). However, it was in the decades following the end of the Second World War that these groups took off and became embedded in the social structure, particularly in owner occupied housing outside the urban core (Whyte, 1956; Gans, 1967).

Blokland and Savage (2001: 223) argue that, for much of the nineteenth and most of the twentieth century, class and space tended to overlap largely unproblematically in that social groups lived separate and exclusive lives which were largely defined by the labour market needs of the large employing organizations – factories, mines, railway yards, etc. The relative immobility of the working class, its dependence on rented accommodation and poor transportation meant that workers and their families lived near to where they worked. Cities tended to be 'quartered' along the lines of social class; there were separate areas for the upper class, the professional classes, the lower middle classes, and the working classes, albeit with some divisions amongst each group. Residential location could be explained by 'central place theory', according to which those with most resources lived nearest to the centre. However, this never worked very neatly in so far as the other group that tended to be located nearest the centre was the casually employed section of the working class whose members depended on the sweated trades for their employment. These tended to be located near to the great centres of consumption; in the case of London, this meant the City and West End (Stedman Jones, 1974).

With the development of the so-called 'railway suburbs' around London, the better off members of the working classes and the professional middle classes traded distance for quality of life (Dyos, 1961). The growing network of urban railways enabled workers who had achieved a degree of financial security to move to the outer suburbs (in the case of London, places such as Walthamstow) and commute into city employment on special 'workmen's trains' for which they paid a concessionary fare (Kellett, 1969). Labour markets tended therefore to determine the nature of the housing market in which all but the most secure professionals and the upper classes rented their homes. Working-class owner occupation was, for the most part, restricted to the industrial North of England where the activities of the mutual 'building societies' had enabled a small number of skilled 'labour aristocrats' access to capital to purchase their own homes. This began changing in the inter-war period with the development of the suburbs around London (Jackson, 1973). It was the building of these suburban developments along the new arterial roads (such as the North and South Circular roads around London) and the associated development of new centres of manufacturing around London (Dagenham, Lea Valley and Park Royal) that finally began to break down the hitherto solid elision of class and residential location (Hall, 1962; Olechnowicz, 1997).

The impact of this only fully materialized during the mass housing boom of the post-war era which saw the beginnings of a significant working-class movement out of London to the suburbs and New Towns and the development of industrial manufacturing outside the 'greenbelt' (Young and Willmott, 1957; Willmott and Young, 1960; Clapson, 1998). This suburbanization was predicated on newly affluent workers either buying their homes or renting them from local authorities; much of the housing built in the New Towns of Southeast England was publicly rented (Clapson, 1998). As Clapson details, although these suburban and New Town locations were new areas of settlement, they remained solidly working class albeit 'new working class'. Despite its findings about the privatized, home-centred nature of working-class life, Goldthorpe et al.'s (1969) study of affluent workers in Luton emphasized the continuing salience of social class and the lack of cross-class social interaction.

One important issue from our perspective was what the suburban move out of London and other cities said about status and racialized divisions *within* the working class. The Luton working class was composed largely of those with ambitions to move out of the inner city and become members of an industrial working class employed in what at the time were modern industries such as car assembly (Mackenzie, 1974; Devine, 1992a). In England, the move out from cities like London and Birmingham was connected to the desire by 'respectable' workers and their families to leave the 'rough' sections of the working class behind, a desire that included a 'white flight' element as the inner cities were becoming populated by immigrants from the New Commonwealth (Willmott and Young, 1960; Rex and Moore, 1967; Clapson, 1998; Watt, 2004).[15] The reconstruction of the post-war working class was therefore associated with a spatial reordering away from the settlements of the first and second Industrial Revolutions into new areas of working-class settlement with a privatized, as opposed to solidaristic, civic culture, a reordering that undoubtedly facilitated the exacerbation of intra-class divisions.

Conclusion

At the same time as Goldthorpe and Lockwood's findings about a new working class were appearing in print, the student revolts of 1968 marked a symbolic turning point away from much of the post-war consensus and the growth in consumerism. For the first time, a group questioned whether 'more' was necessarily 'better'. This also coincided with the beginnings of a 'back to the city movement' by renegade members of the middle classes and the counter culture, whilst white working-class flight to the suburbs began to speed up. These twin processes of middle-class gentrification and working-class suburbanization pointed to the complexity of the changes that were taking place primarily in the United States and Britain; elsewhere in Europe suburbanization was already a working-class phenomenon. These processes were indicative of changes that were occurring within and between classes as well as between generations and we will return to them in Chapters 4 and 5. Not only did they reflect the cultural and political movements of the period, but more importantly the underlying trend towards deindustrialization which had already begun by the late 1960s. If cities were the containers for industrial capitalism and its working classes, the loss of the industry that sustained both of them was to have major social and spatial consequences, which have emerged over the past three decades. In subsequent chapters, we show how this led first in the 1970s to growing social conflict and class division and ultimately in the closing two decades of the twentieth century to a neo-liberal form of restructuring whose spatial and social contours are only now becoming clear. Neither the working classes nor the cities that nurtured them in the post-war period would ever again appear as secure as they seemed to those who had lived through the depression years of the 1930s and survived the war years of the 1940s. For their children these conditions seemed the natural state of things for which they felt little obligation to be grateful as became obvious in the various youth revolts of the late 1960s and emerging industrial militancy of the 1970s.

Further reading

Marshall (1990) provides an excellent précis and appraisal of several major post-war sociological studies undertaken, including some of those referred to in this chapter. For an 'update' and critique of the affluent worker study, see Devine (1992a) and Savage (2005). The social historian Mark Clapson has written two excellent, if somewhat overly positive accounts of twentieth century suburbia: one covers working-class suburbanization in England (1998), while the other is a comparative study between England and the United States (2003). Classic sociological studies of post-war suburbia include Willmott and Young (1960) on Woodford Green on the outskirts of London, and Gans (1967) on Levittown in New Jersey.

CHAPTER FOUR

The Aftermath of Affluence

●●●●●●●●

- ■ Introduction
- ■ Dual labour markets
- ■ Marxism and the labour process
- ■ Restructuring and the collapse of work
- ■ The new space economy
- ■ Emerging spatial divisions of labour and capitalist transformation
- ■ Whatever happened to the collar line?
- ■ Conclusion

Introduction

During the 1970s and subsequent decades sociological attention shifted in several fundamental ways away from a concern with affluence and the manual working class – it is these shifts that are the subject of this chapter. Firstly, we examine the notion that the working class was internally divided, a major source of inspiration for which was Lockwood's (1966) article on 'working-class images of society' which we discussed in Chapter 3. Much of the subsequent neo-Weberian work from this perspective focused on the notion of dual labour markets which divided working-class occupations into those which were privileged, well paid and secure on the one hand, and those which were often temporary, badly paid and generally classified as unskilled or semi-skilled on the other hand (Blackburn and Mann, 1979). We discuss some of this work in the next section of this chapter.

Secondly we discuss industrial sociology and the influential Marxist work of Braverman (1974) on the 'labour process' (the nature of how commodities are produced in a capitalist labour market) and what came to be known as the deskilling thesis. According to Braverman, processes such as automation actively transferred skills from the working class to technology owned and controlled by capital. Not only did this homogenize the manual working class, but it also resulted in the downgrading or 'proletarianization' of non-manual white-collar work and workers. The subsequent proletarianization debate was, in many ways, the obverse of embourgeoisement. It focused on routine non-manual workers in clerical, secretarial and sales occupations, in other words that 'middle-class' section of the workforce that effectively represented the 'control group' in the affluent worker study (Goldthorpe et al., 1969). Marxists had long argued that, in essence, the work conditions, pay and other remuneration of these white-collar workers were little different from that of manual workers and were even worse in some cases (Westergaard and Resler, 1976). As their numbers swelled in the offices of both private firms and public agencies, and also as they were predominantly female, so their supposedly middle-class status came under increasing scrutiny.

The end of the long boom period of post-war capitalism during the early 1970s brought with it high levels of unemployment that have continued, albeit spatially unevenly, in subsequent decades. By the end of the 1970s and the early 1980s, the working class was therefore faced by a great deal more than either dual labour markets or deskilling, since many of its members were simply no longer working. In the third section we examine this 'collapse of work' (Jenkins and Sherman, 1979) associated as it is with deindustrialization and the decisive move in Britain towards a post-industrial society. However, the collapse and the attendant restructuring of socio-economic relations was by no means geographically uniform. We therefore discuss the contribution of social geographers to analyzing changing class relations and patterns of work and employment. Finally, we return to the binary blue-collar/white-collar line that we introduced at the beginning of Chapter 3 and consider its contemporary relevance for understanding class relations.

Dual labour markets

The neo-Weberian action frame of reference approach developed by Lockwood and Goldthorpe gave rise to a plethora of theoretically informed empirical studies which expanded upon Lockwood's notion that the working class was internally divided. Examples included the edited collection *Working-Class Images of Society* by Bulmer (1975), Moore's (1974) study of coal-miners, *Pitmen, Preachers and Politics*, Newby's (1977) study of agricultural workers, *The Deferential Worker*, and Blackburn and Mann's (1979) *The Working Class in the Labour Market*. Gallie (1978) argued that cultural factors were an important intervening factor in the causal relationship between the type of technology or degree of automation and the degree of social integration. Gallie criticized previous attempts to investigate this relationship, from whatever perspective, as reverting to technological determinism: the idea that technology determines workers' behaviour and attitudes. To get around this, he compared companies using the same continuous process technology, in the same multinational group, in France and Britain and argued that resulting differences were an outcome of national/cultural differences.

For the purposes of the present book with its concern for understanding social stratification, we will focus on the Blackburn and Mann (1979) study as the most interesting for the way in which it develops the 'working-class images' argument by incorporating notions of segmented labour markets. Blackburn and Mann begin by pointing out that although the labour market is a central aspect of capitalist society and has been crucial for the development of theory in sociology and economics, it has been the subject of remarkably little empirical sociological research. Blackburn and Mann argue that, in a situation where choices are limited and/or constrained by such *social* factors as skill, gender, 'race', ethnicity and religion:

> ... the labour market is increasingly divided into *primary* and *secondary* sections. Into the primary sector go the monopolies, capital-intensive, highly profitable and technologically advanced firms and industries. Into the secondary sector go small backward firms located in competitive markets – in retail trade, services and non-durable manufacturing industries such as clothing or food processing. The primary sector is high wage, highly unionized and contains internal labour markets. (1979: 21 emphasis in original).

Thus

> ...better and worse jobs tend to polarize into two sub-markets, the primary and secondary markets. As the employer has no obvious way of distinguishing the abilities of the workers, the primary sector employer employs crude 'screening devices' and discriminates against women, youth, and exploited racial and ethnic groups. Thus, the better jobs will be filled by *adult, native born, white males.* (1979: 246 emphasis in original)

They suggest that many important social, political and economic consequences flow from the nature of the labour market. Does the labour market allow the worker a significant measure of control over his [sic] economic life? Does he have opportunities to choose work he finds worthwhile or to develop genuine skills? How does his experience shape his understanding of his place in society?

> The defining characteristic of the worker within capitalism is that he sells his labour power to the employer within a free market. By selling himself, he places himself under the control of the employers and his management agents. Yet he has freely sold himself and is free at any time to choose to sell elsewhere. Whether this is a 'real' choice is an old and important question among defenders and critics of capitalism alike. (Blackburn and Mann, 1979: 1)

Blackburn and Mann's study shows that, taken as a whole, the labour market is chaotic but nevertheless it is 'workers' orientations' that provide some basis for choice about which parts of it they choose to work in. Overall, labour market position is not based on the skills required for the job because, as they show, in nearly 90 per cent of the cases, workers exercise more dexterity skills in driving to work than they do on the job!

The 'discovery' of segmented labour markets failed however to explain why a particular group's workers has more favourable working conditions and better wages than other workers. Was it because of their market position, which enabled them to extract favourable wages and conditions from employers? To what extent were differentials of skill also an outcome of labour market position rather than simply determined by the skill requirements of the job? Hardly ever, if the evidence from Blackburn and Mann's study was to be believed. Historical studies on the so-called 'labour aristocracy' of skilled workers in the nineteenth century showed that skill was an outcome of power in the labour market rather than the other way around (Gray, 1976), a coupling that was reinforced by gender inequalities (Beechey, 1987). In the textile industry, the skilled (male) workers organized unskilled (female) workers into the trade unions thereby reinforcing skill, wage and gender differences. A major role of the trade union was therefore to police the skilled/unskilled boundary. In *Brothers* (1983), Cynthia Cockburn demonstrates very clearly how gender maps on to this via the ways in which well-paid male printing workers maintained control over technology and maximized their wages through the exclusion of women. These questions, raised by Marxists, feminists and Marxist feminists were a prominent feature in the debates about deskilling and proletarianization as highlighted in Marxist work on the labour process.

Marxism and the labour process

Deskilling

As we saw in Chapter 3, the focus of academic Marxism in Britain and North America was largely confined to history or long-term trends in political economy. Baran and Sweezy's (1968) account of the development and tendencies of monopoly capitalism was a pre-eminent example of this broad brush approach. However, one of their students, Harry Braverman, focused his attention on the 'labour process' in his book *Labour and Monopoly Capital* (1974), a title which reflected the influence of his mentors.

Braverman argued that the relationship between labour and capital was complex and mediated by the nature of the work situation and the technology involved. This is not dissimilar to Lockwood's (1958) argument and also developed out of earlier work carried out by Blauner (1964), which we discussed in Chapter 3. However, contra Blauner, Braverman argued that technology did not empower workers but rather, in the longer term, represented a theft of the worker's skill which became embodied in the machine (or later the software that ran it). In other words, capitalist technology *deskilled* workers and thus increased the control of capital over the labour process; this became known as the 'deskilling thesis'.

Following Marx, Braverman argued that the capitalist expropriated from the worker the *ways* in which commodities were produced as much as the *fruits* of that production (profit/surplus). Technology was therefore not only concerned with accumulation and increasing productivity but also with removing *control* over production from the worker. This loss of control takes place through the division of labour that involves both a social (between capital and labour) and a detailed division of labour. Until the 1970s, Marxists had concentrated on accumulation, reproduction and extraction of surplus value and tended to ignore the issue of the labour process. Technology was merely seen as an adjunct to the accumulation process. Braverman showed how capitalism has widened its control over the labour process by deepening the 'detailed' division of labour. Through a process of deskilling, capital replaces labour power within the detailed division of labour by separating out the 'conception' and the 'execution' of a task – for example, the division between mental and manual labour – within the labour process. Braverman drew from Frederick Taylor's (1998) [1911] work on 'scientific management' ('Taylorism') which had been so influential for much of the twentieth century in exerting management control over how the task was done, often involving detailed ergonomic analysis. Breaking the job up into repetitive tasks and introducing technology was done as much for reasons of control as for productivity, according to Braverman.

Deskilling and the proletarianization debate

Braverman's deskilling thesis had considerable implications for the long-running proletarianization debate regarding routine white-collar workers. Marxists had long argued that, in essence, the work conditions, pay and other remuneration of these white-collar workers were little different from those of manual workers and were even worse in some cases (Westergaard and Resler, 1976). This Marxist proletarianization thesis was taken to task by Lockwood (1958) in a classic study of male office workers. He found that these office workers still had significant work and market advantages over manual workers, which dented the proletarianization thesis. This position was restated in the Oxford study of social mobility based on male heads of households and undertaken in the 1970s (Goldthorpe, 1980). Goldthorpe argued that rates of work–life mobility into service-class occupations from routine non-manual positions were far higher than those from manual working-class positions. In other words, although the present remuneration and work positions of clerks and shop assistants was not hugely dissimilar from those of manual workers, their chances of escaping such positions into unambiguous middle-class occupations (professionals and managers) was far greater. This view was reasserted in a later large-scale study of the British class structure (Marshall et al., 1988).

The Marxist response to the neo-Weberian arguments about the different life chances of the two groups relied partly upon Braverman's deskilling thesis. This suggested that the modern office was very similar to the modern factory and that both office and factory workers were subject to the same logic of capitalist deskilling that reduced both to hired machine minders exercising little discretion at work. Hence despite whatever status distinctions which might exist, clerical workers were proletarians in suits and blouses, a finding that rang directly counter to the affluent worker study which hinged around the manual/non-manual blue-collar/white-collar class divide (Goldthorpe et al., 1969). Later Marxist case studies confirmed Braverman's emphasis on deskilling, but also paid far greater attention to the gender dimension of routine clerical work. In a case study of clerical workers and computerization in banking, life insurance and local government, Crompton and Jones (1984) indicated that the vast majority exercised relatively little control or skill in their work. Furthermore, they found that although male clerks had a relatively high chance of leaving deskilled clerical work, this did not apply to their female colleagues whose work-life promotion prospects were relatively poor in comparison. Hence, arguments based upon work-life mobility rates, as found in Goldthorpe (1980), did not apply to the bulk of routine non-manual staff since the majority were female; women had been marginalized in the original Oxford Mobility Study, although they were considered in the second edition (Goldthorpe, 1987). Crompton and Jones (1984) also noted that the growth of white-collar unionism was related to the declining objective class situation of non-manual work.

The proletarianization thesis was prominent during the 1970s and 1980s; for an overview see Lane (1988). It also fed into two further, sometimes acrimonious, debates in class analysis. The first was over 'women and class' and the 'best unit' for measuring class, i.e. the household or the individual (H Roberts, 1993). The second was methodological. One of the major criticisms made by the Nuffield School of sociologists against the proletarianization thesis was that the latter's advocates, such as Crompton and Jones (1984), relied on unrepresentative case studies instead of nationally representative sample surveys (Marshall, 1997).

Worker resistance

Braverman's book put a dynamic back into Marxism that had been missing in much of the previous work on capitalism's immanent and historical tendencies as a mode of production. Rather than looking at the working class and capitalist labour process as an undifferentiated whole, it encouraged researchers to examine the variation in working relations, particularly amongst different kinds of work situations and production technologies, and more broadly it emphasized the social construction of technology itself. This helped to explain many of the struggles in the post-war period, particularly over industrial restructuring and new technology.

As well as being highly influential, Braverman's work was subject to intense criticism, notably that Taylorism was not ubiquitous within capitalism and also that he appeared to suggest that capital had all its own way since he disregarded worker resistance (Wood, 1982). Within a context of increasing labour militancy around active trade unionism and rising strike levels during the late 1960s and early 1970s, ethnographic studies in industrial sociology, such as Nichols and Beynon's (1977) account of work in a chemical factory and Beynon's (1984) *Working for Ford*, had shown how workers use a variety of formal and informal strategies to resist management control including that arising from the technology itself. For example, one issue identified by Beynon (1984) on the car assembly line at Ford was *speed-up* in which there was an increase in the actual speed at which the line passed the workers necessitating a corresponding increase in work effort. During the 1960s and 1970s, the workers at the Ford Halewood plant on Merseyside resisted speed-up via walking off the line in unofficial stoppages, necessitating a compromise on the part of management since they conceded the key that locked the assembly line to the shop stewards: 'Little Bob

Costello had the key on the A shift, and the line speeds were changed with great ceremony, watched and cheered by the workers on the line' (1984: 149). As we discuss in Chapter 7, worker resistance within the labour process is by no means limited to unionized male workers in manufacturing industry, but remains present in non-unionized post-industrial workplaces such as call centres.

Andrew Friedman's (1977) book on industrial restructuring in Coventry, *Industry and Labour*, remains a good example of a study that looks at both labour and management strategies within a broad labour process perspective. Friedman's work had its origins in the Community Development Programme set up by a worried Labour Government in the late 1960s to combat urban deprivation (Craig, et al., 1982). In the book, Friedman is concerned with two main issues. Firstly to investigate 'the persistence of areas of deprivation alongside areas of prosperity within cities or regions in spite of general prosperity in advanced capitalist countries' (1977: 3). Secondly, at the theoretical level, he attempts to construct a framework that allows the links between industrial development and the relative prosperity of small areas to be explored. He rejects neo-classical economic theory because it 'treats as exogenous technical developments, initial property endowments and many other institutional relationships which would seem to me to be important for understanding the persistence of inequality' (1977: 4). Friedman suggests that a Marxist framework is more suitable for the analysis and explanation of long-run inequality, because of its ability to

> ...deal clearly with the basic inequality between workers and capitalists and the reasons for their fundamental antagonism at the level of the capitalist mode of production as a whole. Any analysis of individual firms, of industries or of small communities, which claims to be Marxian, must begin with these macro-economic insights. (1977: 4)

However, Friedman suggests that Marx did not deal systematically with changes *within* the capitalist mode of production, which are the outcome of class struggle. Whilst for Marx the importance of worker resistance lay in its potential for the socialist transformation, for Friedman it is equally significant that worker resistance has been responsible for modifying class relations *within* the capitalist mode of production. This may not have led to the working class becoming a 'class for itself', but it may have forced an accommodation with capital and so transformed some of the manifestations of social class and hence the structuring of stratification. Not only is worker resistance itself unequally distributed, but the results of this resistance have been to shore up or even augment differentials. In particular, Friedman posits a division between 'central' and 'peripheral' workers (like the dual labour market theorists) on the basis of skill, power, and necessity:

> Central workers are, on the one hand, those who, through their skills or their contribution to the exercise of managerial authority, are considered essential by top managers to secure long run profits. On the other hand, central workers are those who, by the strength of their resistance, collectively force top managers to regard them as essential. During recessions, the employment positions of

central workers will be protected, while peripheral workers will be readily laid off. (1977: 109)

The centre-periphery distinction arises out of struggle, out of a combination of differential *worker resistance* and *managerial strategies*. It is not simply a function of attributes such as differences in race, sex, colour, nationality or skills. Whilst the distinction will often follow such divisions, it need not. The different positions of central and peripheral workers during productive activity affect several aspects of their economic and social positions: central workers will generally have more *direct control* over their work situation, be paid more and will have greater employment security. This central-peripheral division can take place within a firm, an industry or a nation. Management responds in different ways. Broadly, it deploys direct control strategies against peripheral workers whilst granting some 'responsible autonomy' towards those occupying more central positions. In other words, unlike Braverman, Friedman takes a less one-sided approach to the management of the labour process. Worker resistance is a key element to the constituting of the labour process within the capitalist mode of production. The substitution of technology for labour by capital is a crucial part of this process and Friedman gives a good account of this historically through an examination of how Coventry lost its industrial and manufacturing base during the 1970s. It is this process of deindustrialization that we turn to examine next.

Restructuring and the collapse of work

Until the 1970s, the successful legacy of the Keynes-Beveridge settlement had meant that full employment (roughly three per cent unemployment) could more or less be taken for granted and the main issue was who got what jobs. However, from the late 1960s this assumption began to look increasingly unsteady. Unemployment rose, as did inflation, giving rise to 'stagflation', not seen since the 1930s, in which output stagnated yet prices rose. By the mid-1970s, prices were rising by up to 25 per cent a year and unemployment in Britain was pushing through the one million mark – some way off the three million it would hit during the 1980s, but nevertheless worrying in a society that had been nurtured on so-called 'full employment'. The reasons for the reappearance of the terrible twins of the depression years were multifaceted and complex. To some extent, they were the outcome of the successful policies that had driven the Western industrial economies through 30 years of sustained growth. Taxes had risen and, so it was argued, the entrepreneurial spirit and labour productivity had suffered, as had the level of corporate profits. Managers, allegedly, spent more time on the golf course working out how to mitigate their tax bills than raising productivity and innovating. The recourse by the state to running the printing presses (therefore expanding the money supply) to keep unemployment at bay had blunted the efficient but brutal discipline of unemployment while trade unions had become adept at maintaining both levels of employment and real wage rises.

The resurgence of the devastated economies of Western Europe and Japan, following the Second World War, together with those of the more recent industrializing economies of South East Asia had all showed how far behind the British economy had fallen. By the mid to late 1970s, the economic and industrial problems became seen as '*The* crisis' and it was increasingly clear that many industries would not survive. The Labour Government under James Callaghan had to accept the humiliation in 1978 of being put on the International Monetary Fund's (IMF) critical list and being forced to cut 'the social wage' (public expenditure). This process accelerated after the election in 1979 of a Conservative Government under Margaret Thatcher, which embraced the 'supply side' economic policies of Professor Milton Friedman with all the enthusiasm of the neophyte.[16] Ironically, it was the votes of the skilled workers in the manufacturing industry in the West Midlands who deserted Labour in favour of the Conservatives in 1979, partly in order to retain their skill differentials in the face of limits on pay, which arguably won the election for Mrs Thatcher. Subsequently, many of them saw 'their' industries and jobs disappear for ever.

In this context, neo-Weberian theories about 'action frames of reference' and dual labour markets found themselves being faced down by the logic of an 'old fashioned' crisis of capitalism in which companies went out of business, wages were cut and workers lost their jobs, as predicted by classical Marxism (Armstrong et al., 1984). Friedman's (1977) work can help to explain how unemployment occurred since the most valued 'central' as well as peripheral workers were dispensed with as technology was used to displace their skills. The new ideology of monetarism and the hands-off state meant that government made a virtue of doing nothing. The picture was similar across North America and Europe, despite a short-lived attempt by the French government under François Mitterrand to buy its way out of recession (Armstrong et al., 1984). For the first time since the 1930s, there were millions of people whose livelihoods depended not on wages but on state benefits. Income differentials, which had been narrowing steadily in the post-war period, began to increase in the late 1970s and accelerated during the 1980s, a process that was particularly prominent in the UK (Pond, 1989; Hills, 1995). Inequality also took a pronounced geographical form with a revival of talk about a 'North–South divide' in Britain (Massey and Allen, 1988).

For some, the disappearance of work was seen as a 'good thing' in the sense that it would rid society of drudgery and allow people to concentrate on more fulfilling activities (Gorz, 1985). By contrast, Jenkins and Sherman (1979) highlighted the potentially negative social consequences of high levels of enforced unemployment, or the 'collapse of work'. They saw the main issue as being the so-called third industrial revolution based around micro electronics – the previous ones having been based on steam and the electric motor. This would create what they termed technological unemployment. There were two options in their view – either we could sit back and wait for the consequences (largely the breakdown of social cohesion) or we could change our attitudes and regard this as 'the ascent to leisure'. However, in order to achieve this, the government would need to invest (using North Sea oil revenues) and ensure that the UK was at the leading edge of the new technology. The consequences, they argued, of doing nothing would be cataclysmic because now, unlike the 1930s, people had more things to lose and would not accept high unemployment.

Mass unemployment proved to be a crude but effective indicator of the large-scale restructuring of not only the British economy but also of its social structure and spatial configuration. If anything, Jenkins and Sherman underestimated its negative impact given the structural nature of the economic downturn, hitting jobs in traditional male industries such as coal-mining, steel, ship-building, engineering and vehicle manufacturing particularly hard (Alcock et al., 2003). With a rise to over three million unemployed in Britain by the mid-1980s, there was a sociological shift of attention away from the 'working' class towards the 'no-longer working' class (Westergaard et al., 1989; Morris, 1995). Gallie (1994a: 134) has summarized the damaging economic, psychological and social effects of unemployment:

> Unemployment continues to lead to a major fall in household income and to a sharp reduction in consumption standards. It leads to substantially higher levels of psychological distress, and this affects not only the unemployed person but also their partner. It produces severe tension within families, markedly lower levels of satisfaction with family life and higher rates of marital break-up. Finally, it is associated with lower levels of sociability and with weaker social support systems, reinforcing the exclusion of the unemployed from the labour market.

The effects of mass unemployment were not evenly spread geographically, but instead were particularly hard-felt in the ex-coalfields regions, the Northern cities and towns, the West Midlands and inner London. These areas have witnessed some of the most dramatic social changes associated with deindustrialization and resultant joblessness, prompting some commentators to suggest that an unemployed 'underclass' is in the process of formation (Lash and Urry, 1994). Leaving this issue aside for now (see Chapter 6), we will sketch out the nature of what has been lost in such areas by quoting Beynon's (1997: 20-1) perceptive ruminations on the town in South Wales (where he was brought up in the post-war period) in which the social ordering of available jobs, by gender, age and education, was clearly understood by all:

> There were 'jobs' in the steel works and in the coal mines. Boys who left school at fifteen or sixteen went into either of these work-places and became coal miners or steel workers. Those with academic qualifications became apprentices and were prepared for jobs as skilled maintenance workers in these industries. All of them understood their job to involve a powerful occupational identity and to be a 'job for life'. ... There were comparatively few manual jobs for women. The girls who left school at fifteen worked as machinists in the one garment factory in the town; alternative employment was offered in local shops and, for those with some academic qualifications, in the local 'council offices'. The strong expectation was that young women would marry and not return to employment'.

This old social order has been swept away, as Beynon indicates, alongside the closure of the steel works, coal mines and other industries. In such ex-industrial areas, there have been several significant changes which reflect the ways that economic restructuring and attendant unemployment have been associated with the reframing of existing gender/age inequalities and differences (see inter alia Coffield et al., 1986; Westergaard et al., 1989; Morris, 1995; Bradley, 1999; Buck and Gordon, 2000; Alcock et al., 2003; Watt, 2003; MacDonald and Marsh, 2005).

- The decline of the 'male breadwinner' household model that dominated many traditional working-class areas. This is partly brought about by male unemployment, but also by the feminization of employment as the wives and daughters of redundant manual workers became the economically active members of the household.
- Labour market detachment on the part of adult males, particularly those over 50, as they have failed to gain jobs in depressed labour markets (Alcock et al., 2003). This initially manifested itself in high rates of long-term unemployment, but these have gradually morphed into higher levels of economic inactivity in the form of early retirement, long-term sickness and disability as a consequence of the interaction of labour markets with the benefits system. As Alcock and colleagues argue, there is in effect extensive 'hidden unemployment'. There is also a profound sense of loss of identity among some middle-aged and older men. (Beynon, 1997; Watt, 2003)
- Fragmentary school-to-work transitions among working-class youth. As Beynon indicates above, such transitions were relatively straightforward during post-war Fordism as young men moved directly from school to factory, coal mine or building site, and young women went from school to office, shop or factory.[17] During the last 25 years, and especially in deindustrialized areas, although young men's and women's transitions remain gendered, they are also characterized by frequent periods of unemployment and generally more hazardous career routes (see Chapter 7).

These changes have prompted debates around the notion that a new group of poor people has been created, one surplus to labour market needs (Bauman, 1998). We will discuss this further in Chapters 5 and 6 when we consider the underclass, poverty and social exclusion.

The new space economy

The economic downturn that had its origins in the 1960s rapidly gathered pace in the 1970s. It was, like previous crises in capitalist economies, a process of 'creative destruction' (Schumpeter, 1943). Many industries were being destroyed whilst, simultaneously, new ones were also being created – in different locations and with new forms of labour process (Martin, 1988; Massey, 1988). These included service sector industries, but particularly the so-called 'knowledge economies' of finance and business services which were disproportionately concentrated in London and the South East (Sassen, 1991).

During the decade in which global antagonisms between the United States and the USSR flared up, what started as a severe economic downturn soon became '*the* crisis' with global connections (Cooke, 1989). With hindsight, it can be seen that these were all symptoms of a classic crisis of profitability within the capitalist nations; taken together they constituted a 'crossroads' for the capitalist economy worldwide (Harris, 1988).

With the declining rate of profit, two things happened. Firstly, many firms were forced to reorganize in order to make a profit again. Secondly, as these firms have groped towards a new regime of capital accumulation, so a new system of regulation, based upon new national and international institutions, has shown signs of coming into being; out of the old order comes the new. To summarize, that fundamental something underlying the economic crisis has been capitalism 'putting its books in order'. Whereas the world-economic crisis was brought on by essentially national phenomena (albeit triggered by an international event), the solution adopted by many corporations and banks was essentially international. At the heart of the new world-economic order, then, is a very simple process – the internationalization of capital. (Thrift, 1988: 9)

This restructuring of social, economic and spatial relations affected almost every part of the global economy. It also led to changes in territorial *identity*, which to some extent have replaced – or at least nuanced – dominant and national class identities.

> Territorial identity is at the root of the worldwide surge of local and regional governments as significant actors in both representation and intervention, better suited to adapt to the endless variation of global flows. The reinvention of the city-state is a salient characteristic of this new age of globalization, as it was related to the rise of a trading, international economy at the origin of the Modern Age (Castells, 1996a: 357).

Part of what has been happening in Europe, as it grapples with the forces of economic globalization, can be rather inelegantly described as a process of 're-territorialization' (Brenner, 1998). Some of the nation state's powers have been devolved upwards to the European level and the others 'downward' to that of the city and the region. This is not to argue that the nation state is necessarily 'withering away' but rather to suggest that, in the long term, the nation may not be the appropriate mode of political, social and cultural representation in an economically globalized society. Whereas the local was previously 'taken for granted', it is now self-consciously seen as 'local' in the context of a globalized culture – as, for example, in the well-worn phrase 'think global, act local'. If the forces of economic globalization are pushing towards a homogenization of cities and urban life, then the cultural and historical experience of cities is still straining towards some degree of uniqueness. According to Brenner (1998: 16), it is both an outcome of the crisis of restructuring and a focus for state-led re-industrialization. In sum, what seems to have happened over the last 25 years is that the economy has become de-territorialized whilst politics has become re-territorialized (Sassen, 2001; Blokland, 2003). In particular, cities and city regions now compete with each other nationally, regionally and globally.

Whereas in industrial capitalism, cities hosted factories and their working classes produced manufactured commodities, in the emerging 'informational capitalism' the focus has shifted to the networked global cities and their knowledge workers. Some cities, notably London and New York, have achieved a makeover becoming both centres of economic activity (mainly in finance and business services) and of consumption and culture; others have continued to decline. The consequences of this process of urban renaissance and decline have been complex: the worst effects have been concentrated in many of what used to be Northern Europe's industrial urban and port centres and North America's 'rustbelt' cities. Several generations of working-class people in these cities lost employment and, in many cases, their children have never experienced formal paid employment.[18] On the other hand, many of the cities on Europe's southern periphery have bloomed. This has been, in part, a consequence of EU strategies of supporting peripheral regions, as well as a consequence of their attractions as tourist, convention and governance centres; their relative lack of congestion, their benign climate and their accumulation of many centuries' worth of material culture have also helped.

According to Brenner (1998: 16), cities are the 'nodes' of economic power and the 'co-ordinates' of territorial power. During the period of Fordism/Keynesianism these two aspects of urbanization were 'spatially co-extensive' within the container of the nation state. This is no longer the case although there are major differences in the relationship across Europe between cities and their respective nation states. This can, for example, be illustrated by the difference between London and Frankfurt – the former works as a centralizing urban space whilst the latter is a regionalizing space. The Randstad in the Netherlands is half way between these two poles.[19] What these contrasting experiences show is that the response to restructuring has been diverse both spatially and socially.

Although, with hindsight, we should not be particularly surprised that cities are witnessing a renaissance and once more becoming centres of economic, cultural and intellectual innovation; what has been surprising is the speed with which a downturn in urban fortunes became an upturn for *some* resurgent cities. During the 1970s New York City was seen to be in terminal decline with jokes about 'the last person to leave please put the lights out' as corporate capital fled to the sunny South West from the rustbelt North East (O'Connor, 1973). Now, as the events of September 11th demonstrated so tragically, New York is the unchallenged capital of global capital.

------- **Emerging spatial divisions of labour and capitalist transformation** -------

Doreen Massey's path-breaking *Spatial Divisions of Labour* (1984) indicated that the geography of economic restructuring was a crucial element in explaining how work was changing. She brought both a Marxist and geographical perspective to the ways in which space was used by capital to restructure its operations. In particular, she argued that new spatial divisions of labour emerged as space was actively used to restructure the labour process and labour relations. 'Command and control' functions were centralized around London and Southeast England, whereas manufacturing was taking place in the periphery of the UK and increasingly the globe. Research and development became separated from manufacturing and was relocated into such 'sunrise' areas of the United Kingdom as the M4 corridor west of London or M11 area around Cambridge ('Silicon Fen'). Much the same was happening elsewhere in the United States (the research triangle of North Carolina, Route 128 around Boston or the research parks of Northern California) and Europe (Baden Württemberg and around Grenoble). Advances in technology meant that manufacturing became an increasingly less central part of the process of production and could almost be located anywhere with cheap and compliant labour. Workers became less powerful and increasingly what had been a male preserve became a female reserve.

Massey (1984) showed how areas such as South Wales became 'screw driver' assembly plants, using standardized components to build consumer goods. In almost all cases, they employed 'green' labour, which had had little or no previous experience of paid work. The plants were often not unionized or the product of 'sweetheart' single union agreements signed with compliant national officials. The fact that many of the workers came from families with traditions of union militancy was doubly ironic. These households were, however, ones in which the men had done the paid work and the women supported them domestically and so had limited employment traditions of their own. The collapse of the coal and steel industries in South Wales meant that many households now became dependent on the female wage earner. Massey shows that similar processes were happening in Cornwall where the traditional industries of farming, fishing and tourism again created the 'right' conditions for a compliant workforce. In other words, she argued that not only was capital deepening the technical division of labour but was achieving this by using space, thus creating the new spatial divisions of labour in which there are radically new patterns of work.

We will discuss this new work further in Chapter 7 as we come to examine the 'McJobs' in which people flip burgers in globally branded restaurants or travel across the globe to care for other people's children. Employment is increasingly feminized and Massey demonstrated ways in which gender helped to structure these new divisions of labour. Massey's work presaged a change in focus away from the factory, and from national class aggregates based around employment, to those of identity and inequality which are globally produced but locally conditioned.

These changes are often associated with the transition from Fordism to post-Fordism, 'flexible specialization', outsourcing and the re-engineering of production hierarchies. A starting point for any analysis of what is meant by Fordism and post-Fordism is the collapse of the so-called 'Keynes-Beveridge Settlement' in which the state played a crucial mediating role between the two essentially conflictual goals of economic competitiveness and social justice. According to Amin, 'Fordism is summarized as the age of "intensive accumulation" with "monopolistic regulation" of the economy' (1994a: 9). 'Fordism' became shorthand for an economy based around mass production and mass consumption in which broadly similar products were produced by large numbers of workers using the techniques of mass production (long runs, assembly line technology, etc.) (Phillimore, 1989). It also relied on a high level of co-operation between management and workers which, in Europe, tended to be mediated by the state (Piore and Sabel, 1984; Amin, 1994b; Aglietta, 2000). Relatively high levels of taxation enabled the state to provide 'collective consumption' via public services in fields such as education, transport, health and housing, for example the National Health Service and local authority rental housing in Britain

(Rustin, 1989). By the late 1970s, as we have seen, this economic system was struggling as profitability fell, inflation rose and the demand for taxation-funded welfare services seemed unending.

> These appear to be times of bewildering transformation and change in the structure and organization of modern Western economy and society. It seems that capitalism is at a crossroads in its historical development signalling the emergence of forces – technological, market, social and institutional – that will be very different from those which dominated the economy after the Second World War. Though not uncontroversial, there is an emerging consensus in the social sciences that the period since the mid-1970s represents a transition from one distinct phase of capitalist development to a new phase. Thus, there is a sense that these are times of epoch-making transformation in the very forces which drive, stabilize and reproduce the capitalist world. Terms such as 'structural crisis', 'transformation' and 'transition' have become common descriptors of the present, while new epithets such as 'post-Fordist', 'post-industrial' 'postmodern', 'fifth Kondratiev' and 'post-collective' have been coined by the academic prophets of our times to describe the emerging new age of capitalism. (Amin, 1994a: 1)

Whatever happened to the collar line?

We have seen how post-war sociological class analysis in both its Marxist and Weberian forms was dominated by debates over the status of the blue-collar/white-collar line, both in relation to embourgeoisement and proletarianization. Considering the voluminous literature devoted to each debate, it is noteworthy that neither occupies the pivotal role in class analysis that they once did. This arguably reflects the more recent iteration of capitalism in which issues around 'flexibility' have become prominent both for non-manual and manual employees. What can we say about the contemporary status of the collar line? Several sociologists of stratification continue to use the manual/non-manual distinction as a significant boundary marker in class divisions (Devine, 1997; Roberts, 2001; Kerbo, 2003). Alternatively, others consider the collar line to be less significant than it once was and they locate the majority of routine non-manual employees alongside manual workers within a reshaped working class juxtaposed to a professional-managerial middle class (Crompton, 1998; Savage, 2000; Zweig, 2000), a view that we largely support.

In terms of income, Table 4.1 shows full-time earnings across different occupational groups in Britain. The figures show clear gender divisions in pay across each occupational group. As Savage (2000: 52) notes, the main difference within the genders is not between manual and non-manual, but between the managerial and professional occupations (the 'top three' groups) and the rest. Among men, both craft workers and machine operatives have higher weekly incomes than clerical staff. The position is reversed among women, but the gap between clerical workers on the one hand and managers and professionals on the other is far more marked. What is also

Table 4.1   Mean weekly incomes by occupational group, 1998 (£)

Occupational group	Men, full-time	Women, full-time
Managers and administrators	625.6	435.3
Professionals	568.4	458.4
Associate professionals	515.9	375.8
Clerical and secretarial	291.9	257.6
Personal and protective services	339.5	220.1
Sales occupations	339.6	231.0
Craft workers	360.4	217.7
Plant and machine operatives	332.9	228.6
Others	280.4	193.3
Average	427.1	309.6

Source: New Earnings Survey in Savage (2000: 52, Table 3.3)

striking about this table is the way that it is only among the associate professionals and above that the gender earnings gap is substantially surmounted, since female professionals and managers have higher earnings than *all* male groups below associate professional level.

On other criteria, such as job security and on the nature of the relationship with management, there seems to be some convergence between lower non-manual and manual employees, as Gallie (1996) admits, even though he ultimately rejects the proletarianization thesis overall. Although sales staff in shops were traditionally regarded as 'white collar' and middle class, there is now widespread recognition, including from the Nuffield School, that the majority of shop assistants and supermarket cashiers are undertaking jobs equivalent to manual employment in terms of control and promotion prospects (Goldthorpe, 1987; Marshall, 1988). In her ethnographic study of female shop assistants in a department store, Webb (1990) found the women had little control over their work-time and expressed a rich variety of anti-management views. Among those using the Nuffield class scheme, there is now a routine separation of class 3B (sales assistants and personal service workers) from class 3A (clerical workers), with the former included alongside semi and unskilled manual workers (Gallie, 1996; Marshall et al., 1996; Gallie et al., 1998) and the latter put in an 'intermediate' class position.

The downgrading of non-manual employment seems to have occurred in previously relatively stable white-collar organizations, such as banking, which has experienced considerable restructuring including the increased use of part-time workers lying outside traditional career structures (Halford et al., 1997). Restructuring and the downgrading of white-collar staff is also a prominent feature of the public sector, as seen, for example, in the expansion of temporary workers (Conley, 2002). In *Gender and Power in the Workplace*, Harriet Bradley (1999) uses case study research to examine class and gender relations at five organizations in the North East of England including a group of hospitals, a regional branch of the civil service, a bank, a supermarket chain and a chemical factory. Job insecurity and fear of redundancy were least marked among the shop and factory workers, but were greater among the bank staff and most prominent among the non-manual public sector workers: 'this suggests that it is white-collar workers who formerly felt secure and who, indeed, often chose their careers especially because they appeared to offer "a job for life" who articulate the clearest subjective experience of insecurity' (1999: 123). Bradley concludes that, although some distinctions remain between white-collar and manual workers in terms of promotion prospects and job content, heightened insecurity, diminished autonomy and in many cases lower pay have all contributed towards considerable convergence across the collar divide with claims about a 'white collar proletariat' having some merit. Furthermore, as Crompton and Jones (1984) rightly pointed out, Bradley (1999) also emphasizes the intertwining of gender with class whereby the fact that many white-collar jobs are feminized contributes towards their lower status. The term 'pink collar' has been used to denote the gendered inadequacies of the blue/white-collar divide – it refers to those occupational enclaves comprised almost exclusively of women, as, for example, in the case of flight attendants:

> Service work (such as flight attending) ... never fell neatly into the blue-collar/white-collar distinction between manual and non-manual work. Instead it straddles the two, being charactersitc of neither archetype. ... Partly because of their gender, flight attendants have not had access to a career structure and their income at various points in their history has been at proletarian levels. Their work control has always been limited. Despite middle class trappings, in analytic terms flight attendants were proletarianised by gender. (Williams, 1988: 3)

Among emergent office-based industry sectors such as call centres, involving nominally white-collar workers, the balance of evidence would suggest that such employees are not anything other than 'working class' in terms of remuneration and working conditions (see Chapter 7). Annual turnover rates of 30 per cent and above have been reported among call centre staff in Britain (Taylor and Bain, 1999; Richardson et al., 2000; Taylor et al., 2003), rates that are very similar to those found among that most alienated section of the manual Fordist workforce, car assembly workers, during the 1960s (Beynon, 1984: 102).

The collar line was most relevant in industrial society when the workforce was pre-dominantly male and large numbers were employed in factories. Case studies high-lighted the social distinctions made by blue-collar 'workers' between themselves ('us') and the office 'staff' who were nominally attached to the factory ('them') (Goldthorpe et al., 1969; Beynon, 1984). This worker/staff divide was expressed via status distinc-tions, as, for example, in the existence of separate canteens. As industrial factory employment has shrunk dramatically since the 1970s, particularly in the United States and Britain, and as the workforce has become increasingly feminized, so the binary blue/white-collar line has far less sociological relevance.

Conclusion

During the three decades following the ending of the Second World War, the working classes (or in North American parlance the middle class) achieved unprecedented levels of affluence and influence, becoming the major focus of interest not just for sociologists and politicians but also for society as a whole. It is therefore perhaps not surprising that there was so much interest in social class and that this revolved around the elision of the concept with a particular class. In Britain at least, class became an obsession – whose disappearance as a marker of social conflict and whose persistence as an indicator of cultural identity were celebrated in equal and disconcerting measure (Cannadine, 1998). Many key sociological texts became best sellers on both sides of the Atlantic – a situation that academics and their publishers would kill for today.

At the same time as this love–hate relationship with social class was working its way through the changing cultural landscape, particularly in Britain, the economic structure was undergoing far-reaching changes. It was only in the late 1970s that the word 'restructuring' entered the lexicons of professionals, journalists and the population as a whole. Its origins lay in the process of *perestroika* under Gorbachev in the former Soviet Union, whose economy and politics collapsed at about the same time as the industries that had formed the backbone of the British space economy since the late eighteenth century. Until this restructuring began, and began to be talked about as such, much of the work on social class in Britain was undertaken by sociologists working in a Weberian tradition. Marxist industrial sociology only came to the game relatively late and it remains the case today that the most single-minded sociological attempt to characterize Britain as being in the iron grip of a class structure has been that of John Goldthorpe and his Oxford colleagues. Many other class analysts have long conceded the need to refocus both methodologically and conceptually. As we shall see in Chapter 5, sociology's long ties, not just to social class but also to history, have been weakened and forced to grant an increasingly important place (literally) to geography and concepts of space. This has partly been an issue of ontology (Soja, 1989) but mainly as a consequence of the emergence of processes of 'time-space compression' (Harvey, 1989; see Box 2.1 on page 13). Sociologists have embraced not only concepts of space, but also given due weight to those of 'race', ethnicity, gender, identity and difference. Work and occupation have steadily lost their purchase as the source for understanding social behaviour, while class consciousness has morphed into identity (See Chapter 8).

The 'sociology wars' that emerged in these last two chapters are largely a thing of the past as sociology, human geography and cultural studies struggle to come to terms with the huge changes that have taken place since the late 1970s. Sociologists today are willing to borrow extensively from different fields, disciplines and traditions if it will aid understanding. In recent years, the increased emphasis by sociologists and others on qualitative methods such as ethnography, in-depth interviews and even discourse analysis has enabled it to reveal the deep, or thick, meanings (Geertz,

1993) underlying the apparently contradictory actions of consumers, voters and others. The sociology wars between class theorists therefore reflected not only the dying gasps of monopoly capitalism or high modernity, but also perhaps of a sociology based in a less complex set of behaviours and structures. The transition to post-Fordism, post-industrialism or 'informational capitalism' requires a more nuanced approach by social science to the subjects and objects of study. Sociologists simply cannot afford to base their enquiries on how some white, male manual workers earn their living in a society where this group is now not only in a numerical minority, but also is increasingly on the political and cultural margins. We will explore aspects of this 'new world' in subsequent chapters which look at the emerging space-economies of nation states and urban centres, as well as identifying new processes of class formation (for example, gentrification), new forms of social exclusion (for example, youth unemployment), and new forms of labour process (for example, call centres).

Further reading

Bulmer (1975) brings together a collection of key works on the working-class images literature. Massey and Allen (1988) and Allen and Massey (1988), which were written for the Open University course *Restructuring Modern Britain* D314, remain an excellent collection of chapters on the remaking of the British space economy following the collapse of Fordism in the early 1980s. The companion volumes, Hamnett et al. (1989) and McDowell et al. (1989), chart the associated changes in society, social divisions and social policy. The collection edited by Amin (1994b) remains one of the best sources of writing about the rise of post-Fordism. Lash and Urry (1987, 1994) chart the downfall of 'organized capitalism', as they term it, and its replacement with a post-Fordist post-industrial service economy.

CHAPTER FIVE

New Spatial and Social Divisions of Labour

- Introduction
- World cities
- Los Angeles and the 'LA School'
- Social polarization
- Gentrification and the urban-seeking middle classes
- The ghetto and the urban underclass
- Methodology and urban social polarization
- Conclusion

Introduction

We have seen how explanations of social stratification have traditionally been rooted in employment relations. In Chapters 3 and 4, however, we introduced the idea that space and place play an increasingly important role in understanding how contemporary society is stratified and this idea is developed further in this chapter. Sociologists have only relatively recently begun to heed the assertions of human geographers that 'space matters', as hinted in the discussion on restructuring at the end of Chapter 4 (Massey, 1984; Soja, 1989). In recent years, these ideas have been taken up in the context of urban change (Blokland, 2003). Cities are effectively the prism through which the economic restructuring of the last quarter of the twentieth century is refracted. They have now become the focus for social and economic change across the globe and for discussions about changing cultural landscapes (Graham and Marvin, 2001; Amin and Thrift, 2002; Abrahamson, 2004). Some sociologists have even begun to suggest that the attachment to place may have begun to usurp occupation as the means by which identity becomes articulated (Savage et al., 2005a). Cities have become the habitat of both the new social groups that have emerged out of recent international restructuring and those disposed by it. It is in this increasingly urbanized landscape that a new articulation of social and spatial relations is beginning to occur (Blokland, 2003). As we shall see later in the chapter, a number of writers have claimed that it is this interaction of the social and spatial that 'all comes together' in polycentric Los Angeles' post-industrial landscape. Leaving to one side the veracity of these claims, what is certain is that social scientists are currently engaged in re-engineering the relationship between the social and the spatial.

In this chapter, we focus on the role of cities in understanding social stratification in contemporary advanced societies. This involves a discussion of the decline of the industrial city in the second half of the twentieth century and the recent 'resurgence' of 'world cities' as staging posts in the new globalized economy.[20] This has had direct implications for their populations and how we think about them (Amin and Thrift, 2002; Parker, 2004).

World cities

Since the 1960s world cities have been routinely ranked in various ways with reference to their location within the world system (Beaverstock et al., 1999). This notion was expanded upon by Friedmann who argued that the emergence of world cities as control centres of capital in the global economy was associated with a number of developing trends (Friedmann and Woolff, 1982; Friedmann, 1986). He put these forward as a series of linked hypotheses that became the subject of much academic debate (see Box 5.1).

Box 5.1   THE WORLD CITY HYPOTHESES

- Are world cities 'global centres?
- What spatial forms are world city regions taking?
- Are all parts of the world integrated within the world-city-focused global accumulation structure?
- What are the implications of the migration of unskilled workers to world cities?
- How will Tokyo, Hong Kong and Singapore survive as world cities with their stringent immigration controls?
- What is the nature of class struggle in world cities?
- What is the role of world cities in world politics?
- What types of architecture are world cities bequeathing to the world?
- Are world cities a new phenomenon or merely continuations of long trends that began in the eleventh century?

Source: Johnston (1994: 150–2)

There has been considerable work over the last decade on the emergence of world or global cities, much of it in response to the Friedmann hypotheses. Much of this work has concentrated on London and New York, but also to a lesser extent Tokyo, Paris, Frankfurt and Los Angeles, and has focused on how these cities became keystones of the new global financial system and the international division of labour (Thrift, 1988; Sassen, 1991; Fainstein et al., 1992; Sassen, 1994; Leyshon and Thrift, 1997; Beaverstock et al., 1999). There is a continuing debate about the ranking of the lesser world cities and where they should be located in this international urban network:

> There is then a second rank of urban centres (European examples of which include Paris, Frankfurt and Zurich; global examples Singapore, Los Angeles, Hong Kong) which are important links in the international system with financial responsibilities for their zones. Finally, there are regional centres – Milan, Madrid, Edinburgh, Amsterdam and Brussels in Europe, and globally Sydney, Chicago, Dallas, Miami, Toronto, São Paulo and San Francisco – which 'host many corporate offices and foreign financial outlets [but] they are not essential links in the international financial system'. (Thrift, 1988: 40)

Different cities could be added and/or subtracted from the list; see Beaverstock et al. (1999) and Abrahamson (2004) for two alternatives based upon differing sets of world city criteria. The crucial point, however, is that since 1990, economic growth has centred around such cities. More recently, it has been suggested that there are really only two dominant global cities (London and New York) with Tokyo and Hong Kong fighting to represent the Asia Pacific time zone. It is also clear that over the last decade there has begun to be a discernible concentration on a global scale of manu-facturing to China and of services to India, resulting in predictions that Shanghai and Mumbai will join the list of global cities along with London and New York (Macrae, 2004). These changes have clearly had major implications for the inhabi-tants in cities that have been both 'winners' and 'losers', as the new era describes them, and those that live in them. We will now turn to examine one such world city, Los Angeles.

Los Angeles and the 'LA School'

Los Angeles – the original polycentric 'non city' for much of the twentieth century has become emblematic of the changed nature of the city, just as Chicago was for the industrial city.

> A city seventy miles square but rarely seventy miles deep apart from a small downtown not yet two centuries old and a few other pockets of ancienty, Los Angeles is instant architecture in an instant townscape. Most of its buildings are the first and only structures on their particular parcels of land; they are couched in a dozen different styles, most them imported, exploited, and ruined within living memory. Yet the city has a comprehensible, even consistent, quality to its built form, unified enough to rank as a fit subject for an historical monograph. (Banham, 1971: 21)

Despite its built environment, Los Angeles has an exaggeratedly conventional economy and that is perhaps what makes it such an interesting case study for the post-industrial city. This can be epitomized by, on the one hand, Tinsel Town in which flickering images underpinned a whole entertainment economy and, on the other, by the 'high tech' parts of the military industrial complex – particularly aerospace. Both sectors had their origins in the years leading up to the Second World War and were consolidated during the war and subsequent Cold War. The power of the United States, during this period, was represented through, on the one hand, the good guy of the Hollywood image machine and, on the other hand, the destructive might of the intercontinental ballistic missile – both of which were 'made in Los Angeles'. The Reagan presidency drawing on his links both with Hollywood and the major defence industries represented this 'fantasy-fact' nature of the United States to the rest of the world.

In the last two decades of the last century, the argument on Los Angeles began to shift – as symbolic of the dystopic urban future. The film *Blade Runner* with its portrayal of the city of 'have nots' and 'have lots' to the background of an utterly commercialized culture, was believably based on what Los Angeles was rapidly becoming. This notion of Los Angeles ('LaLaLand') became a focus for debate amongst some of the city's leading 'celebrity' academic commentators who saw in it an expression of the changes that, they perceived, were taking place more generally in North American culture and society. This became encapsulated in the so-called 'LA School' whose members, whilst sharing some 'common turf', were almost gang-like in their behaviour over and towards it and each other.[21] They tended to agree that 'it all comes together in Los Angeles' (Soja, 1989) and shared an assumption that in some sense Los Angeles was the 'capital of the twentieth century' (Dear, 2002: 10). This did not simply refer to the economy of the high tech or digital image but to its social and cultural accompaniments and its rapidly changing ethnoscape; whites are a minority in what is predominantly now a Hispanic city.

The LA School brings together a number of scholars working at two major Universities in Los Angeles – University of California, Los Angeles (UCLA) and the University of Southern California (USC) – across a number of schools and centres. They come at this work from very different backgrounds and perspectives. Michael Dear (2000), one of the leading protagonists for the construction of a postmodern urban theory based around the study of Los Angeles, has this to say:

> ... until recently, Los Angeles was not taken seriously by most urbanists. The least-studied major city in the United States, LA has consistently been portrayed as an exception to the rules governing US urban dynamics, a *sui generis* invention on an isolated continental margin ... What is Southern California trying to tell us?
>
> Los Angeles is a polycentric, polycultural, polyglot metropolis regarded by many as the prototype of contemporary urbanization. It is a burgeoning capital of the Pacific Rim, undergoing a simultaneous deindustrialization and reindustrialization. It is an ungovernable city of intense socio-economic polarization, where (it is said) a glittering 'First World' sits atop an impoverished 'Third World' substructure. Los Angeles is a collection of theme parks where

privatized, partitioned spaces exist for all tastes – communities of industry, leisure, sexual preference, and so on. The residents of such packaged dream-scapes evince some of the most fantastic consumption patterns in the world. But equally importantly, they have produced a multi-cultural mosaic in which the existing social contract is under stress. Acute socio-economic polarization, crises in political representation, racism, and community fragmentation pro-duced in 1992 the worse civil unrest experienced in twentieth century urban America. It is a city that cannibalistically devoured its greatest asset – its natural environment. (Dear, 2000: 3)

This description of Los Angeles is probably common ground amongst the various writers but what follows from that isn't. Some see this as the future and a brave new world, despite the polarization, while others find in Los Angeles the continued rapa-cious growth of American corporate capitalism. In all the accounts however, it is the *growth* of Los Angeles that is at the heart of what it does. It consumes people and places in a headlong expansion that regularly trips over itself in the greatest of nat-ural or man made disasters. Mike Davis (1990, 1998) likens the Los Angeles leviathan to an addict with no option other than to live on the edge. In his writing, the nat-ural beauty of much of Los Angeles, its ecological fragility and its vulnerability to fire, flood and earthquake, merely adds to the frisson of capitalist development. The imperative to flee the city by the affluent Anglos not only requires that they live in dangerously flammable semi-wilderness areas but that the resources of the whole city region are disproportionately deployed to enable them to do so. They benefit from subsidized property insurance, despite the well-known risks of huge fires in the chaparral every few years. They cost disproportionately more to connect up to utili-ties and the costs are borne by those living in the cramped and crowded conditions of South Central and Hollywood where the fire dangers are man made rather than a function of natural conditions. The relationship between people and their environ-ment mirrors that of the ways in which the economy operates. It is crisis ridden: the Los Angeles River is concreted over and channelled, wildlife is culled, the chaparral is preserved and the geological fault lines built over. In each case, the 'big one' (flood, fire, a child being savaged by a wild lynx or catastrophic earthquake) is an inevitabil-ity and the question only remains 'when?'. What is always clear, however, is that the state will be mobilized to rebuild along the existing lines of social and economic priv-ilege.[22] Disaster relief will be a direct transfer from those most in need to those whose needs are fanned by the fear of those from whom they flee. In his two main books, *City of Quartz* (1990) and *The Ecology of Fear* (1998), Davis points to this underlying dynamic that is Los Angeles. It has been thus for the last 100 years or so, since it was discovered as the promised land that had none of the hardships of the East Coast and the Midwest.

The apocalyptic images of the movie *Blade Runner* often seem anything but fictitious in Los Angeles. Air quality in the region is the worst in the country, despite increasingly draconian regulations. The physical expansion of the urban-ized areas has generated other acute, human-induced environmental crises, especially those connected urban services such as water supply, toxic waste disposal, and sewage. These problems, together with the region's especially hazardous natural environment (earthquakes, floods, landslides, and fires), are proving increasingly intractable as the region struggles to maintain the economic impetus. (Dear et al., 1996: 11)

In essence, Los Angeles manages to bring together the most rapacious forms of capitalist development in an environment – physical and human – from which there is continual pressure to escape its immediate consequences. This however simply stokes up more problems for the future – be it lack of water, congestion on the free-ways with four-hour commutes, fire risk, or pollution. As Dear indicated above, this is echoed by the worst riots in North American urban history that took place in 1992 when police officers were acquitted of beating up a black motorist – Rodney King – despite video evidence showing him being attacked beside his car on the freeway by members of the LAPD. The spatial and the social reinforce these tensions in Los Angeles but, in both cases, come up against the finite limits of the mountains that ring the bay as well as the absolute level of deprivation in the city. Unsurprisingly, Mike Davis has made himself very unpopular with many people in Los Angeles and has found his work subject to massive and minute examination and criticism. In addition, the economic cycle in Los Angeles is more exaggerated than elsewhere; it went into the recession of the early 1990s deeper and longer than elsewhere in the United States. Conversely, it benefited disproportionately when the economic upturn finally came in the mid-1990s. Dear and colleagues sum up the consequences in terms with which the more radical members of the School could not but agree:

> In social terms, Los Angeles is now characterized as a 'First World' city flourishing atop a 'Third World' city. The latter term refers to the burgeoning population either engaged in the informal economy or paid poverty-level wages. They tend to be only marginally housed by conventional standards, or even homeless. The postmodern metropolis is increasingly polarized along class, income, racial, and ethnic lines … The disadvantaged classes are overwhelmingly people of color. Their family lives are disrupted by the demands of a flexible, disorganized work-place (e.g. the pressure on both parents to work and the need for families to crowd together to be able to afford housing). These trends have been aggravated by a strong ideology of privatism, as well as the practical effects of privatization at all levels of government during the last two decades. (1996: 11)

Allen Scott, another leading member of the LA School, has based his work on a study of the changing economy of Los Angeles and, in particular, the way in which a cul-tural economy works. He has undertaken comparative work between Paris and Los Angeles to look at how the exploitative social and labour relations in Los Angeles influence the nature of its cultural economy (Scott, 2000a, 2000b). He has taken Los Angeles as an indicator of the kind of changes that are likely to occur in the US economy and has shown how it is perfectly feasible to run a first and third world economy side by side, or more likely on top of one another, and how this impacts on the ecology of the city. Like Davis, Scott sees parallels between contemporary Los Angeles and Chicago in the 1920s – both were major growth poles in the national economies of their time. In the case of Los Angeles today this is in the context of a global economy, particularly given Los Angeles' role as the eastern gateway to the Pacific Rim economy and to its Latin American hinterland (Scott, 1988).

Ed Soja (1995) has developed this into an argument that space becomes the major form of social contestation. In this context, Los Angeles is not simply a case study but rather an exemplar of the way in which space has been used as a tool for capitalist development over the last 150 years. Space has also become the means with which to ensure social stratification between Los Angeles' various populations working through differences of social class and ethnicity, as illustrated in the 2004 film *Crash,* directed by Paul Haggis. The fact that, as an urban and ecological system, it is highly unstable adds, rather than detracts, from its dynamism. Although Los Angeles (like Chicago before it) is an extreme case, it does provide a means of understanding some of the socio-spatial interactions that now infest 'advanced' and rapidly post-industrializing societies – these, it can be claimed, are predominantly urban. Whereas in the Chicago School approach the city was ordered from the centre outwards, as Dear (2002: 16) puts it, for Los Angeles 'the hinterlands organize what remains of the center'.

Social polarization

As mentioned above, one of the major conceptual prisms through which global cities are said to be re-stratifying is that of 'social polarization'. This term is particularly associated with the work of Saskia Sassen in her influential book *The Global City* (1991) which offers a penetrating analysis of the three first league global cities, New York, London and Tokyo. According to Sassen, such cities function as concentrated command points in the global economy and as key locations for financial and producer services firms in accountancy, banking, insurance, legal services, etc. This spatial concentration of financial activity alongside deindustrialization has reshaped and effectively polarized the occupational structure in global cities. There has been an expansion of both highly paid professional jobs, such as accountants, lawyers and merchant bankers, as well as low paid service jobs such as cleaners, security guards and waiting staff. The latter service the former's needs and wants either in the offices of the expanding downtown financial districts or in gentrified residential settings. Income polarization matches occupational polarization with a prominent decline in those middle-income, often unionized jobs, which were prominent in the cities' manufacturing districts up until the 1980s. Many of the low-wage service jobs are filled by new migrants to the city who tend to come from a wide range of less developed countries, as we saw in Chapter 2. Migrants in global cities often find themselves working in low-paid entry level jobs, either formal or informal, at the bottom of the labour market. Illegal immigrants can find themselves working in what Kwong

(1997: 113) describes as 'indentured slave-like conditions', as in the case of Fuzhounese illegals working in the Chinese ethnic enclave in New York.

Chris Hamnett (1994, 1996, 1998, 2003) has offered a sustained critique of Sassen's polarization thesis. On the basis of official statistical data for London and the Randstad in the Netherlands (see note 19), he argues that whilst there has been growing income inequality, there is no evidence of polarization. Rather than low-skilled and high-skilled service jobs *both* expanding in an hourglass shaped pattern, as Sassen argues, only the latter professional and managerial occupations have grown, resulting in an overall upgrading (professionalization) of the workforce. While Sassen's theory seems appropriate for New York or Los Angeles, Hamnett suggests that it is less applicable to European cities including London. Not only have these not witnessed an equivalent expansion of low-skilled service sector jobs as North American cities, but they have also not experienced the same immigration levels of people to fill such positions. Hamnett (1996, 2003) concedes that there may well be polarization in European cities, but that it takes a different form to the occupational version advocated by Sassen. This form is not that of a polarizing workforce, but instead between a group of employed 'insiders' and the long-term unemployed, early retirees and discouraged workers who are effectively 'outside' the labour force: 'the problem in London and key European cities may not be that there are too many low-skilled jobs but that there are not enough to provide work for those with few educational qualifications' (Hamnett, 2003: 61).

Even though he argues against occupational social polarization *à la* Sassen, Hamnett accepts that London has witnessed widening income inequality which has taken the housing-based shape of 'socio-tenurial polarisation' (2003: 147) with a growing division between home-owners and council housing tenants. This housing tenure divide manifests itself spatially via the demarcation between upmarket gentrified houses and council estates containing the growing ranks of the unemployed, poor and socially excluded.

Hamnett's contribution to the debate on social polarization is significant not least because of the implication that cities such as New York and Los Angeles 'are special cases and not representative of urban developments in general' (Burgers, 1996: 100). Importantly, Hamnett highlights the potential role played by different national welfare states or 'welfare regimes' (Esping-Andersen, 1990, 1993), a topic we discuss further in Chapter 6. Following Esping-Andersen, Hamnett (1998) argues that the poor in the United States are more likely to take up the expanding number of low-paid jobs due to the paucity of welfare benefits, whereas in Europe the relatively generous welfare states encourage the development of an 'outsider surplus population' external to the labour force.

In relation to London, there is certainly support for Hamnett's professionalization thesis with respect to the occupied workforce (Buck et al., 2002). Furthermore, as Hamnett suggests, divisions between housing tenures are indeed a significant marker of social and economic inequalities as predominantly white and affluent home-owning gentrifiers are awkwardly juxtaposed to ethnically mixed and often deprived council tenants in inner London (Butler with Robson, 2003; Watt, 2003, 2006). However, four main criticisms can also be made of Hamnett's position. Firstly, that he has paid insufficient attention to both the gendered and racialized operation of welfare regimes and urban labour markets (Bruegel, 1996; Burgers, 1996; Cox and Watt, 2002). As Burgers notes in relation to Dutch cities, the division between those in employment and those depending on welfare 'strongly correlates with ethnicity' (1996: 102), with much higher rates of unemployment among minority groups. Secondly, by relying upon official statistics derived from the Census, Hamnett may well have underestimated the extent of low-wage service employment in London because some of it takes place informally, 'off the cards', for example in the case of paid domestic workers (Cox and Watt, 2002) (see Chapter 7 for discussions of both informal employment and paid domestic workers). Thirdly, aspects of Hamnett's (1998) application of welfare regime theory are debatable, especially in the case of London. The bracketing of London with continental European cities can be challenged from the standpoint of regime theory given the way that, according to Esping-Andersen (1990, 1996), the British welfare state is closer in many ways to the liberal regime, as found in the United States, than the continental European social democratic or corporatist regimes (see Chapter 6). Finally and relatedly, Hamnett's positing of a hermetic break between groups of supposedly privileged labour market 'insiders' and disadvantaged 'outsiders' ignores the limited role played by low-paid and often insecure work in alleviating poverty and social exclusion in London and Britain more generally (see Chapters 6 and 7).

Although Sassen and Hamnett disagree upon the exact form that social polarization takes, their respective analyses concur in the sense that global cities in the United States and Europe are subject to profound processes of widening income and wealth inequalities. Such polarization takes different forms in different cities and is therefore at least partly dependent upon the continued efficacy of national welfare states as Hamnett argues, for example as in the cases of Amsterdam (Amersfoort and Cortie, 1996; Burgers, 1996) or Paris characterized as a 'soft' global city by Body-Gendrot (1996). The argument that global cities have become socially polarized is one of the more disturbing images that has been put forward and balances the glitzier one of 'urban renaissance' and 'cappuccino culture' regularly projected onto our screens (Atkinson, 2003b; Lees, 2003a). Moreover, such polarization is not restricted to global cities *per se* even if it is most keenly expressed there. Instead social polarization is manifest in a wide range of 'globalizing cities' (Marcuse and Van Kempen, 2000a) that, despite not being necessarily locatable in a league table of world cities, are nevertheless 'touched by the process of globalization' (Marcuse and Van Kempen, 2000b: 263). These include deindustrialized now ostensibly 'regenerated' cities, for example Manchester in the North of England (Peck and Ward, 2002) and Lille in Northern France (Moulaert et al., 2001).

One of the main effects of global restructuring has been to accentuate and reshape, rather than ameliorate, existing patterns of inequality based around class, ethnic and gender divisions via social polarization (Perrons, 2004). This reshaping has taken a spatial form in cities, not only in relation to the relevance of space for access to resources such as jobs or housing, but also in terms of people's conceptions of place, as we discuss below. Although a dualistic division between the zones of the 'have lots' and the 'have nots' is overly simplistic (Fainstein et al., 1992; Marcuse and Van Kempen, 2000a), social polarization is nevertheless enmeshed with the spatial recon-figuration of cities:

> Cities have always shown functional, cultural and status divisions, but the differentiation between areas has grown and lines between the areas have hard-ened, sometimes literally in the form of walls that function to protect the rich from the poor. (Marcuse and Van Kempen, 2000b: 250)

One of the most obvious physical expressions of this hardening of spatial divisions is the concentration of dereliction and poverty in the stigmatized ghettos of the United States, as well as inner cities and peripheral housing estates in Britain and continental Europe (Wacquant, 1996; Power, 1997; Byrne, 1999; Marcuse and Van Kempen, 2000a). Although in one sense such 'no-go areas' are effectively rendered invisible to the majority of people, as Littlewood and Herkommer (1999: 16) suggest, in another they are all too visible via media-fuelled representations of concentrated deviance (Hargreaves, 1996; Wacquant, 1997). Wacquant has referred to this con-centrated socio-spatial disadvantage as a 'new regime of urban marginality' (1999), and we will discuss its most extreme manifestation in the form of the ghetto under-class in North American cities below. The rise of gated communities (Low, 2004) represents another stark manifestation of the hardening of socio-spatial divisions, 'in which the new rich locked themselves in and "the other" out' (Butler with Robson, 2003: 64), as, for example, seen in the Docklands area of east London. This is only the most overt form of a new wider socio-spatial formation in polarized world cities, i.e. gentrification.

Gentrification and the urban-seeking middle classes

Space, place and the service class

Over the last decade, but especially in the Anglophone nations of Europe, North America and Australasia, social and economic restructuring has resulted in the remarkable growth of consumer services and a swollen 'service class' recruited from an expanded higher education system. That service class has itself, however, become increasingly polarized between a high earning group of largely private sector and/or self-employed professionals and another group mainly working in the public and voluntary sectors (McDowell, 1997; Crompton, 1999, 2000; Devine, 2004a). The latter group includes university lecturers, public service lawyers and many health professionals, who have increasingly become reliant on two professional incomes in order to maintain an adequate and secure household income.

> Social classes, which are conventionally taken as focused around place, national spaces and organized hierarchies, are one of the victims of such disorganization.

They are simultaneously localized and globalized, transformed by the flows of people, images and information. Classes in the sense of hierarchically organized national entities are rapidly dissolving, at the very time that social and spatial inequalities rapidly increase. (Lash and Urry, 1994: 323)

Whilst this was a perceptive claim to have been making in the early 1990s, the consequences have been rather more complex than Lash and Urry suggest. The globalization process has not led in any simple way to hypermobility of people except at the extreme ends of the social and economic spectrums (see Chapter 2). Whilst it is true that a small proportion of the top echelon of business elite move from one global location to another, this is not true of the group as a whole who often demonstrate considerable loyalty to particular cities and devote significant resources to putting down 'roots'. For most of the service class, a sense of place appears to be one of the remaining sheet anchors in their lives. For example, in a recent study of middle-class people in the North of England, Savage et al. (2005a) only came across two respondents for whom where they lived made relatively little difference to their lives; for the rest it was of critical importance to their sense of identity and well-being.

Richard Sennett (1998) has argued that the re-engineering process, undertaken by many of today's professionals in their work, has had profoundly disturbing effects in their personal lives (see Box 5.2). They have, in effect, taken the long term out of the value chain with flat hierarchies, just-in-time supply chains and flexible manufacturing methods. This may have been good for their business but it means that they increasingly find themselves unable to rely on the 'hinterland' of traditional values when bringing up their children. Living in a world where they are only as good as their last consultancy, and their children having become mall rats fixated on the latest consumption fads, has meant that many are now seeking out forms of meaning in places where they choose to live. As Butler with Robson (2003) argue, it is this search for belonging and a sense of place that drives London's contemporary gentrification, as we discuss below. What matters is 'putting down roots'; these are increasingly signified, it is suggested, by a sense of place. Thus, whilst the economy may have become more globalized and amorphous, there is an increasing sense of the local in day-to-day life, as, for example, in concerns over education (Butler and Hamnett, forthcoming). Whilst work may have become all consuming, social status is realized in consumption in which the consumption of place (the home and where it is located, for example) is an increasingly important factor. As we will see later in the chapter, similar arguments have been made about the importance of a sense of space for the 'ghetto underclass'.

Box 5.2   THE COSTS OF SUCCESS

In *The Corrosion of Character: the personal consequences of work in the new capitalism*, Sennett (1998) encapsulates the lives of these post-war 'baby boomers'. The subtitle tells it all. His respondents are, for the most part, the winners in what is euphemistically called the 'new economy' but, as the story unfolds, it becomes apparent that they are not 'taking all'. Some, if not all, of the people Sennett interviewed expressed open contempt for their parents' generation and the certainties that governed their lives. Take Rico, for example. Rico was brought up in a 'middle'[23] American family as one of the baby boomer generation. His father was a janitor, his mother ran the home (we might now say she worked in the domestic economy as a homemaker). The family knew exactly for how much longer the father would have to work, at the end of which there would be a pension. Things were done properly, corners were not cut and Rico's father handed wisdom down to him about how he should approach a task in the form of practically based homilies which derived either from his work or his hobbies. Rico worked hard at school and could not wait to leave this stultifying environment. He made it, his wife made it: they moved around and they moved up. He now has his own consultancy; she is something in financial engineering. He fears their kids have become 'mall rats'. They (the kids), of course, do not appreciate the achievement that Rico's upward journey represents – their lives are as they are. Whilst intensely proud of how far he has come, Rico worries intensely that he is only as good as his last report, and that the 'twenty somethings' who he struggles to hire and then retain already know more than he does and that he is in imminent danger of becoming technologically redundant. What he has done, in the grand scheme of things, is to take the long term out of capitalism and successfully re-engineer its supply chains so that all that matters is 'now'. This may work in terms of driving forward a new logistics strategy but it has infected his home life as well; it means, in effect, that he has no moral authority to preach the same deferred gratification and pride in the task to his kids as his parents did to him. The personal consequences of the new capitalism can therefore be profoundly unsettling to those regularly settling into business class seats on their transcontinental missions to add yet more to the bottom line by taking out further costs.

Gentrification

Ruth Glass (1964) first coined the term 'gentrification' in the 1960s, although it was not until the large scale deindustrialization of Britain 20 years later that the re-urbanization of sections of the middle classes became widespread:

> One by one, many of the working-class quarters of London have been invaded by the middle-class – upper and lower – shabby modest mews and cottages … they have been taken over when their leases expired, and have become elegant, expensive residences. Larger Victorian houses, downgraded in an earlier or recent period – which were used as lodging houses or were otherwise in multiple occupation – have been upgraded once again … Once this process of 'gentrification' starts in a district it goes on rapidly until all or most of the working-class occupiers are displaced and the whole social character of the district is changed. (Glass, 1964: xviii)

A 'post-1968' generation was starting to repopulate inner areas of some major cities of the UK and to a lesser extent Europe (where they had less often left them) replacing the working class which begun leaving in large numbers. The expansion of student numbers in the late 1960s contributed and has continued to contribute to this process (Bondi, 1999). At about the same time, the quadrupling of oil prices by the Organization of Petrol Exporting Countries (OPEC) in 1973 in the wake of the Arab–Israeli war led to concerns about sustainability. Sections of the middle classes began to question the rationality of long distance commuting with all its associated costs (Hamnett, 1984). The evidence shows that this wasn't a return to the city by those living in the suburbs but rather a tendency to remain in the city by at least some of the highly educated young professionals who might have been expected to migrate to their natural habitat of the suburbs when they formed households (Butler and Hamnett, 1994; Butler, 1997). This did not mark a massive restructuring of social and spatial relations away from single class suburbs to more mixed residential patterns but it did indicate, as we have seen, the start of a process of social and spatial diversification *within* a changing middle class (Butler and Savage, 1995). Mixing was, however, not simply a function of class but also of gender, ethnicity and cultural politics (Ley, 1994, 2003). Whilst middle-class households, including those with young children, began to repopulate inner-city districts, particularly in London, white working-class households with sufficient economic resources began to flee the cities for the white outlands of Essex and Kent (Hamnett and Randolph, 1988; Robson, 2000; Watt, 2004). Patterns of sociospatial settlement have become increasingly complex and it is really only over lengthy periods of time that the long-term trends are discernable (Hamnett and Randolph, 1988; Ford and Champion, 2000). Nevertheless, labour and housing market trends do begin to suggest that inner London has become divided between an affluent and predominantly white home-owning middle class and a deprived and economically insecure multi-ethnic group reliant on social housing (Buck et al., 2002; Hamnett, 2003). In other British metropolitan centres, the middle classes have largely continued to leave the centre for the suburbs, abandoning the inner city to those living in social housing (Champion and Ford, 1998). There has been a small and recent trend towards the gentrification of the inner core of many such cities by a young 24/7 group who have been attracted by rehabilitated industrial housing (Lambert and Boddy, 2002; Bridge, 2003; Dutton, 2003).

Gentrification has become a metaphor for social change and demonstrates many of the themes expounded in this book, notably the tension that exists between consumption and production and between structure and action in explaining social processes. The interdisciplinary and political cross cuts that are represented by gentrification and its explanation have been well described by Atkinson:

> The conceptual language with which gentrification has been explained has predominantly drawn on the central ideas of Neil Smith's rent gap theory of neighbourhood change (Smith, 1979, 1996) and David Ley's views of the necessary role of consumer preference linked to the emerging fractions of the middle class (Ley, 1986, 1996). Implicit in the rent gap theory was a materialistic interpretation of neighbourhood change driven by wider cycles of disinvestment and uneven development thus creating new opportunities for

speculation. While this body of theory has been modified, it continues to act as a counterpoint to Ley's ideas about the rise of a new middle class whose tastes and housing preferences led them to demand stock in the inner city. The implied economic and cultural imperatives central to each theory have often been interpreted as a sign of mutual exclusivity, although this is perhaps something of an 'overdistinction'. Nevertheless, there has been general acknowledgment that both writers generally failed to accept either the complementarity or necessity of each other's ideas in a more integrated theory (Hamnett, 1991; Clark, 1992; Lees, 1994).

Outside the debates of what gentrification is (definitional), why it occurs (theoretical), who it affects and what should be done about it (political), the process has provided a significant theme in the field of urban studies that overstepped what some saw as a generally insignificant phenomenon (Berry, 1985; Bourne, 1993a and b). For many, the attraction of the gentrification debates has been the interdisciplinary and ideological intersections that it provided. Geographers found themselves with similar concerns to those of political scientists while the theoretical perspectives of sociologists became enmeshed with the analytical standpoints of economists at the epistemological crossroads that gentrification represented. (Atkinson, 2003b: 2344)

The concept of gentrification has more recently become a forum for debate amongst those who might wish to dispense with the language of class (Lees, 1994; Redfern, 2003) but has also been a useful vehicle for those wishing to understand the urban and non-urban (Phillips, 2004; Hoggart and Hiscock, 2005) consequences of globalization (Lees, 2000; Butler with Robson, 2003). Lees (2000, 2003b) argues that there has been a process that she terms super gentrification in Brooklyn and arguably parts of London which represents more than a simple upscaling of existing gentrification processes in such areas as Islington (Butler and Lees, forthcoming). This process represents the housing market activities of the 'masters of the universe' working in global financial markets and their close subsidiaries. More traditional gentrifiers are typified by 'Lucy' whose story is told in Box 5.3.

Box 5.3   THE MIDDLE CLASSES COME TO HACKNEY

Lucy: Originally we came here in the late 1970s because we knew we wanted to buy somewhere to live and we had been looking at flats in West London and we began to realize that we might be able to buy houses with tenants on the ground floor; we somehow got the idea that we might be able to buy a house not a flat. A friend who was living in Islington mentioned that there were nice houses in this area and we came here by chance. We walked over one day after we had been at a Rock Against Racism thing at Victoria Park which was about the first time that I had been to the East End; I can't claim any relationship with this area at all, it was like the back of beyond to me and I had never been anywhere near it and we saw this house in Nayland Road and it was three floors and there was nothing wrong with it. We had actually spent about a year looking at houses in Fulham and Wandsworth and they were always terrible – you would always go into a street and the one with stone-cladding was the one that you had the details of, there was always something really terrible about it and this house, though it was dilapidated, was a fine house, lots of space and it was incredibly cheap. Then it was £13,000 – in 1978. So we moved there originally and I think there was always the sense that it was not the greatest area in the world in terms of the upkeep of the buildings, and the streets were really dirty and nobody ever cleaned them but it was quite lively and it never seemed threatening or worrying and it was always nice to be near the park and then Fraser got the job at the River and then it was useful to be in the area and we got more involved in the area and knew more people here.

We had no idea of staying here for long, it was not the idea of 'here I am going to settle and spend my life in'; we were quite young and without much cash and it was the idea that here we could have a nice house and we were just thinking the other day that we could not believe we had been here this long – we have been here ten years. I cannot envisage moving in the next five or six years or ten years.

TB: Were you working at the time?
Lucy: No I was doing my graduate research, so I was on a grant and it was conve-nient. The main advantage was cheap economy but at the same time in an urban set-ting. We had been living in a rented flat in Fulham and part of me thought that living in the inner city was quite interesting but part of me was quite embarrassed about hav-ing to explain where it was as nobody knew it. I used to kick myself for hearing myself almost apologising for living here; I would go into a long explanation about 'that was where I lived and it was really very interesting and full of local colour' whereas if you said something like Primrose Hill you wouldn't have to say anything with it. There was the sense that when you were talking to people from the same class or background that you were being somewhat rebellious or strange to be living in Stoke Newington, not just that you were poor.

TB: Might the suburbs have been an alternative?
Lucy: No, never looked, no never thought of it.

Interview with a gentrifier in Stoke Newington in 1988 (Butler, 1992)

Many of these people (the 'baby boomers') were the sons and, significantly, daugh-ters of the post-war suburban middle classes. Their experience of university was such as to attract them to life in inner London's gentrified belt and to repel them from the suburbs for life – even when children arrived (Butler and Hamnett, 1994). Whilst they subsequently fretted about the children's education and their quality of life, they could not for the most part face the trek in from the suburbs and the isolation from metropolitan culture (Butler, 1997).

Recent work on the gentrification of inner London points to an increasing *diversity* amongst the middle class who now make up an increasing percentage of its inhabi-tants, especially in inner London. Butler with Robson (2003) argue that there is now a distinctive geography of gentrification in inner London by which internal divi-sions within the middle classes are reflected in their residential locations. These reflect distinctions of lifestyle across several key fields within the middle-class *metropolitan habitus*. This serves firstly to distinguish the urban-seeking professional middle classes from the urban-fleeing ones (Lockwood, 1995), but also mark key differences amongst this essentially cosmopolitan group. The presence of artists and even middle-class council tenants amongst this group are good indicators of its diversity (McRobbie, 2004; Watt, 2005). These differences cannot be reduced to occupational or wealth and income differences but represent broader differences in terms of culture, politics and notions of self-identity. Just as the differences between the ownership of a BMW, Mercedes or Saab mark out different forms of middle-class self-identity, so does where you choose to live within gentrified inner London – assuming you can still afford the cost of entry.

The ghetto and the urban underclass

Traditionally ghettos have been regarded as enclaves of cities dominated by a single ethnic or religious group, as, for example, in the case of the Jewish ghettos in inter-war European cities (Wacquant, 1997). More recently the term 'ghetto' has been associated with processes of widening urban inequality as constituting a zone of intense poverty and deprivation, ethnic concentration and heightened social pathology. Marcuse and Van Kempen refer more explicitly to an 'excluded ghetto' defined as 'a ghetto in which race or ethnicity is combined with class in a spatially concentrated area where residents are excluded from the economic life of the surrounding society, which does not profit from its existence' (2000c: 19). For some writers the contemporary ghetto represents the spatial location of a developing urban underclass (Wilson, 1987; Massey and Denton, 1993).

This begs the question, 'what is meant by an underclass'? The existence of poverty is not by itself sufficient to declare that an underclass either exists or is in the process of formation. Instead, the underclass refers to 'poverty plus', that is, a group which not only lacks material resources but is also socially, culturally and politically distinctive. This distinctiveness has a decidedly moral set of connotations whereby the putative underclass is said to go against mainstream norms, values and behaviour (Levitas, 1998). Furthermore the underclass is regarded as in some sense 'dangerous', notably via its mooted association with various forms of criminality (Morris, 1994). Roberts (1997) has provided one of the clearest definitions of the underclass based around having four features.[24]

1. Economic disadvantage – the underclass stratum is economically disadvantaged compared to 'the lowest class in the gainfully employed population' (1997: 42). Chronic joblessness is considered a central aspect of underclass membership by many commentators (Wilson, 1987; Murray, 1984, 1990; Buckingham, 1999).
2. Social immobility – the members of the underclass have to be in this disadvantaged position 'for the duration of their entire lives and, indeed, across the generations' (Roberts, 1997: 42).

3. Socio-cultural distinction – 'the underclass should be a socio-cultural formation as well as an economic aggregate' (Roberts, 1997: 42). In other words, the underclass has different values, lifestyles and lives in separate areas compared to the rest of the population. In the United States, this socio-cultural distinctiveness is both racialized (via a concentration of black and Hispanics) and spatialized (via the inner city ghetto).

4. Cultural sustainability – the distinctive culture of the underclass is maintained even if the material circumstances which have sustained it have changed: such a culture will distinguish an underclass, if one exists, from a 'reserve army of labour' who are excluded from employment purely by lack of opportunity and take jobs when their labour is in demand. (see chapter 6 for a discussion of the Marxist reserve army of labour theory)

The debates over the existence of an underclass are multifarious and are also complicated by the way that the concept is inserted into existing traditions of social scientific thought which tend to emphasize different aspects of social stratification, with a North American emphasis on race and a British emphasis on class (Silver, 1996). In the United States, the underclass debate has tended to focus upon the black African-American poor, and to a lesser extent Latina poor, living in inner-city ghettos. Ghetto areas such as Harlem, South Central Los Angeles and South Side Chicago have assumed a postmodern Baudrillardian hyper-real status in the eyes of Americans as well as globally via Hollywood movies and TV cop shows (Jackson, 2001). As Baudrillard (1988: 56) says, 'the American city seems to have stepped right out of the movies. To grasp its secret, you should not, then, begin with the city and move inwards to the screen; you should begin with the screen and move outwards to the city'. 'Harlem' is thus a media construct as well as a 'real' place (Jackson, 2001). Underclass perspectives on such ghetto areas highlight both socio-economic circumstances, notably chronic joblessness and poverty, and socio-cultural factors, or indicators of 'social dislocation', such as high levels of teenage pregnancy, female-headed households, criminality, drug and alcohol dependency (Wilson, 1987). Accounts of the black underclass in ghetto areas have focused on the relative interplay of race, class and space in producing what appears to be a unique set of social conditions.

There have been five main explanatory approaches to the urban underclass (adapted from Massey and Denton, 1993).

1. Culture of poverty – according to this explanation, ghetto residents display distinctive cultural traits and abide by an alternative set of values and norms to those that are found in the rest of American society. In effect a 'culture of poverty' (Lewis, 1966) is said to exist in which the short-time and hedonistic values of ghetto residents mean that they are trapped in a vicious circle of grinding material poverty plus poverty of expectations.

2. Institutional racism – ghetto problems are the result of the disadvantages black African-Americans face across a range of key institutions including education, employment and housing. Blacks are effectively disadvantaged in the ghetto areas because there are societal-wide processes of racial disadvantage which put them at the base of the institutional order when good schools, jobs and housing are being allocated. Whereas recent migrants to the United States have been able to take up low-skilled

positions in urban labour markets, established African-Americans have found themselves increasingly destined to exclusion from such positions (Wilson, 1996; Fainstein,
1998). As we discuss in Chapter 7, the latter are effectively at the end of the 'hiring
queue' of sought-after workers (Talwar, 2001; Waldinger and Lichter, 2003).

3. Liberal welfare policies – right-wing commentators, notably Charles Murray (1984),
   argued that far from solving the problems of the ghetto underclass, the 1960s' liberal
   welfare policies, for example the 'War on Poverty', brought about further deterioration in the lives of ghetto residents.[25] Murray emphasized the deleterious effect of
   welfare policies on the work ethic in the ghetto; generous welfare payments meant
   work did not pay and black mothers therefore opted for a life on welfare. Joblessness
   therefore results from ghetto residents' rational choice to live on welfare rather than
   employment.

4. Deindustrialization and black flight – in his influential book *The Truly Disadvantaged*
   (1987), William Julius Wilson argued that the overt vicious racism of the early and
   mid-twentieth century is of dwindling significance, largely as a consequence of the
   liberal anti-discrimination and positive action programmes of the 1960s. By expanding educational, job and housing opportunities for African-Americans, these programmes facilitated the rapid expansion of the black middle class. If this was the case,
   then why were so many blacks trapped in the ghettos? Wilson's answer is two-fold.
   First of all, there was the massive impact of deindustrialization and economic restructuring on black employment patterns and prospects, particularly those of males in
   blue-collar jobs. As the auto plants, steel mills and factories of the major cities of the
   North East and Midwest shut down or relocated during the 1970s and 1980s, many
   black men were thrown onto the unemployment scrapheap. This is crucial in relation
   to Wilson's approach to the underclass because his point is that the 'underclass
   behaviours', such as out-of-wedlock births and separation, all followed from the
   decline in jobs. In other words, materialist causes brought about the cultural
   responses and not vice versa, as in both the culture of poverty and liberal welfare
   explanations. For Wilson, the decline of the black family in ghetto areas was directly
   attributable to the destruction of the material infrastructure provided by well-paid
   manual jobs which supported the nuclear family. Ghetto joblessness was therefore
   not the result of a rational choice to live on benefits, as Murray suggested, but
   followed on from economic restructuring and deindustrialization (Wilson, 1996).

Deindustrialization, however, was by itself insufficient. The second explanatory factor
was socio-spatial and related to the expansion of the black middle classes. According
to Wilson, as the latter expanded, they joined the exodus to the suburbs in exactly
the same way as whites had done in the immediate post-war period. In other words,
'black flight' followed 'white flight' away from the inner-city areas to the suburbs (see
Chapter 3). The result was there were no black teachers, social workers or business
people for young ghetto residents to aspire to; in other words an absence of role
models. In conditions of full employment this may not in itself have been that significant.
However under conditions of joblessness, its effects were devastating. No jobs or role
models led to the creation of the 'truly disadvantaged' black ghetto underclass.
Although Wilson (1991) later came to reject the term 'underclass' and instead opted
for the less condemnatory 'ghetto poor', the essence of his approach as being class-
based has remained. In a subsequent book, Wilson (1996) focused on the impact of
joblessness on the ghetto poor in Chicago.

5. Racial segregation – according to Massey and Denton, the above approaches are inadequate because they do not deal adequately with racial segregation:

> Our fundamental argument is that racial segregation – and its characteristic institutional form, the black ghetto – are the key structural factors responsible for the perpetuation of black poverty in the United States. Residential segregation is the principal organizational feature of American society that is responsible for the creation of the urban underclass. (1993: 9)

Massey and Denton focus on the operations of the housing market and its chief players in the form of realtors, financial institutions and governments. Between them, these institutions have allowed and helped to perpetuate a system in which white prejudice and discrimination produces the spatial segregation of black African-Americans. Although the 1968 Fair Housing Act was supposed to end discrimination in the housing market, all it did was effectively remove the most visible signs of discrimination, typified by the 'no Negroes' signs in realtors windows and replace it with 'discrimination with a smile' (1993: 96). Processes of subtle and not immediately detectable 'racial steering' and urban disinvestment by governments and financial institutions have remained.

Massey and Denton accept that each of the first four approaches above has something to contribute to explaining the underclass, but only after what they regard as the over-riding explanation – racial segregation – is placed centre-stage. Thus they suggest that instead of a 'culture of poverty', there exists a 'culture of segregation' which has developed only because black Americans are spatially isolated in ghetto areas. Racism impacts upon black people across all aspects of their lives, but its main impact is in the housing market and their racial segregation. Deindustrialization undoubtedly worsened black life chances, as Wilson argues, but the impact of this economic restructuring was so devastating on black communities because they were spatially isolated. Similarly, as Murray suggests, federal welfare policies also played a part in the rise of the underclass, but only because higher levels of welfare receipt were spatially concentrated in ghetto areas. One effect of racial segregation has been that although a black middle class has been created, as Wilson argues, it does not live in the same suburbs as the white middle class. Instead, the suburbanization of black Americans has uniquely been to black-dominated suburbs:

> Although the problem is most acute for the poor, segregation confines all blacks to segregated neighbourhoods regardless of social class, so working- and middle-class blacks also have a very difficult time insulating their children from the competing values and attitudes of the street. Compared with children of middle-class whites, children of middle-class blacks are much more likely to be exposed to poverty, drugs, teenage pregnancy, family disruption, and violence in the neighbourhoods where they live. (Massey and Denton, 1993: 178)

This latter point is supported by Pattillo-McCoy (1999) in her study of a black middle-class suburb on Chicago's South Side ('Groveland'). Like Massey and Denton, she argues that racial segregation has meant that the black middle class has remained close to the inner city within predominantly black suburbs set apart from white suburbs.

The debate over the North American ghetto underclass is complicated and beset by terminological and methodological disputes. The concept of the underclass is said to have an in-built 'blaming the victim' connotation since its alleged 'members', who are often among the poorest members of society, are either implicitly or explicitly at fault for their lifestyles and as such should be morally condemned, a perspective which suits neo-liberal welfare and economic policies (Levitas, 1998). The focus of attention on the moral behaviour of the poor detracts attention from the rich: 'one never hears of the Wall Street underclass demoralized by their junk bond dependency culture' (Bagguley and Mann, 1992: 123). Many social scientists of a structural persuasion are therefore reluctant to use the underclass term for fear that it would be giving it some kind of academic legitimacy, a position that Wilson (1991, 1996) him-self later came to adopt via his preference for the term 'ghetto poor'.

If the 'underclass' is a problematic term, Wacquant (1997) has also questioned whether the contemporary use of the term 'ghetto', to mean an aggregation of poor people, 'dilutes' the ghetto's institutional form as an ethnic or racial socio-spatial formation. Perhaps a more telling criticism made by Wacquant about the ghetto underclass debate is methodological in that the reliance on survey data and official statistics can result in an outsider perspective that simply replays supposedly 'common-sense' fears about dangerous people and places. Wacquant has suggested that urban studies which use official statistics have effectively 'exoticized the ghetto' whereby the dangerous and deviant aspects of ghetto life, such as violent crime, drug consumption and teenage pregnancy, are all highlighted at the expense of consider-ation of more mundane social activities which do not fit the stereotype of 'life in the hood'. Social dislocation is read off from quantitative indicators, such as welfare recipient and crime levels, but these fail to capture the range of socio-economic activ-ities and the complexity of socio-cultural practices found in ghetto areas and there-fore result in a simplistic one-sided picture. In opposition to this quantitative approach, Wacquant (1997: 346) advocates the greater use of 'close-up, first-hand observation' of an ethnographic kind. The results from this kind of research (see *inter alia* Danziger and Lin, 2000; Venkatesh, 2000; Jackson, 2001) highlight the simplifi-cations and even distortions redolent in ghetto underclass accounts, as we now discuss in relation to welfare and work.

Surviving in the inner-city ghetto

One of the distinguishing features of the ghetto underclass is its marginalization from the world of work, meaning paid employment. From the standpoint of main-stream American culture, the absence of people regularly going out to work is a major deviant aspect of the ghetto (Massey and Denton, 1993). Neo-liberals assume that it is precisely *because* the urban poor are on welfare that their work ethic has been eroded and hence they do not take up whatever employment opportunities are avail-able (Murray, 1984, 1990). On the other hand, structural explanations emphasize the way that joblessness results from insufficient numbers of jobs to go around (Wilson,

1996). Either way, the urban underclass or ghetto poor are passively dependent upon benefit payments and permanently excluded from paid work. Joblessness is certainly a feature of ghetto areas of the United States, albeit a feature that varies to an extent with the machinations of the business cycle (Newman and Lennon, 2004). However, insider qualitative research on the so-called ghetto underclass, as advocated by Wacquant (1997), reveals a more nuanced relationship to paid work than the notion of blanket welfare dependency indicates.

> The black people I met in Harlem (as much as people anywhere else in the United States) have lives that shoot through overly rigid, static, either/or designations of class. They have juggled college education with welfare, homelessness with unionized jobs, drug dealing with steady-service sector employment. (Jackson, 2001: 86)

Two studies of black Americans living in ghetto areas, one focusing on mothers (Puntenney, 2000) and one upon males (Venkatesh, 1994), found that although only a minority of their samples were working formally at the time of the interview, the vast majority had at least one period of formal paid employment during their lives. Moreover, movement between welfare and paid work was common, while many men and women worked informally on a cash-in-hand basis to supplement their incomes, an aspect of inner-city life we examine in detail below.[26] The women did in-home babysitting and cooking and also provided services such as hair and nail care (Puntenney, 2000), while the men did plumbing and household maintenance, as well as selling drugs in the illegal economy (Venkatesh, 1994). However, as Venkatesh argues, most of the men he interviewed 'explicitly frame their participation in part-time, irregular, or informal work as a temporary survival strategy until they can find steady full-time employment' (1994: 177). In other words, it is not necessarily the *lack* of jobs that is the main problem for ghetto residents, but rather the *kind* of jobs that are on offer. This view is endorsed in another qualitative study of low-income young black men living in a poor area of Chicago. None of the 26 men Young (2000) interviewed were working at the time of the interview and their work experience was limited to short-term jobs lasting a few months. Nevertheless, all demonstrated a commitment to working but in secure and stable jobs, in other words a 'good job' that allowed them to use manual skills and demonstrate physical dexterity. The problem is that such jobs no longer existed in that part of Chicago:

> They fixed their interests on unionized factory work and, to a lesser extent, on the moderately skilled municipal service sector such as the postal service. Conspicuously absent in their remarks was a desire for inclusion in the employment sector that continues to be the fastest growing in Chicago – the white-collar service sector. (Young, 2000: 162)

This hints at a far more subtle, as well as gendered, set of processes based around what Philippe Bourgois (1995: 114) has called the 'cultural dislocations of the new service economy'. In his ethnography of Puerto Rican crack dealers in East Harlem in

New York City, *In Search of Respect: Selling Crack in El Barrio,* Bourgois (1995) has dramatically highlighted the links between masculinity, respect and work (Box 5.4).

Box 5.4 **WORK AND RESPECT AMONG CRACK DEALERS IN EAST HARLEM**

Bourgois (1995) was surprised that the dealers had not completely withdrawn from the legal economy. They engaged in a series of just-above minimum wage jobs, such as security guard, before being fired and going back to crack dealing. In their early youth, 'they had been energetically pursuing the immigrant's working-class dream of finding a tough macho factory job and working hard for steady wages' (1995: 137). This dream evaporated along with the factory jobs in New York and the Puerto Ricans rotated between one low-wage job after another in a 'horizontal mobility' fashion (see Box 7.2 on page 141). Although some of the dealers found employment in the expanding service sector, they found working in offices humiliating since it provided no space for their overtly macho 'street culture' to be respected:

> Street culture is in direct contradiction to the humble, obedient modes of subservient social interaction that are essential for upward mobility in high-rise office jobs. ... When these office managers are not intimidated by street culture, they ridicule it. Workers like Caesar and Primo appear inarticulate to their professional supervisors when they try to imitate the language of power in the workplace, and instead stumble pathetically over the enunciation of unfamiliar words. They cannot decipher the hastily scribbled instructions – rife with mysterious abbreviations – that are left for them by harried office managers on diminutive Post-its. ... Their interpersonal skills are even more inadequate than their limited professional capacities. They do not know how to look at their fellow service workers – let alone their supervisors – without intimidating them. They cannot walk down the hallway to the water fountain without unconsciously swaying their shoulders aggressively as if patrolling their home turf. Gender barriers are an even more culturally charged realm. They are repeatedly reprimanded for offending co-workers with sexually aggressive behavior. (1995: 142–3)

Those males who display strongly macho forms of bodily comportment are unlikely to thrive in the offices, shops and restaurants of the late twentieth century global city. The alternative is not to passively accept their structural victimhood, but instead to embrace the street culture via drug dealing since it offers a sense of 'respect' that post-industrial workplaces do not.

As well as the ghetto poor not being as estranged from the world of employment as blanket 'underclass' accounts suggest, there is also evidence that African-Americans in particular are systematically disadvantaged when it comes to the hiring of new workers for post-industrial jobs, as we examine further in Chapter 7.

────────────────── **Methodology and urban social polarization** ──────────────────

One important question facing urban social scientists is how should one try to capture the shifting patterns of social polarization that characterize city life, especially as found in global cities with their extremes of wealth and poverty? Official statistics are often used and these involve complex operationalization and measurement issues (Hamnett, 2003). Mapping spatial patterns of segregation (shapes on the ground) and relating those patterns to social inequalities (shapes in society) are also fraught with well-known difficulties (Cannadine, 1982). Furthermore, as highlighted above, there are also problems with over-relying on official statistics given the way that emergent social groups, for example, informal or illegal workers, are likely to fall under the radar of state-sponsored data gathering techniques (Bourgois, 1995; Cox and Watt, 2002).

While qualitative ethnographic accounts of deprived urban neighbourhoods capture something of the internal dynamics of such areas, it is not always made clear how the residents of such areas interact with the broader city. What is therefore harder to grasp is an overall sense of the urban dynamic. The same criticism can be leveled at those studies which examine the opposite end of the polarization spectrum, in other words the new middle class. Despite the rapidly growing literature on gentrification and gentrifiers (Ley, 1996; Butler, 1997; Lees, 2000; Butler with Robson, 2003; Ley, 2003), one problem with this literature is that it generally fails to examine the social interactions in these new urban quarters from the perspective of *all* the social groups concerned (Slater et al., 2004). What therefore seems to be missing is the approach adopted by the practitioners of community studies who attempted to understand communities as 'local social systems' (Bell and Newby, 1971). This methodological difficulty undoubtedly reflects the increasingly complex patterns of social inequalities found in globalizing cities and the bewildering array of urban lifestyles found within them. Furthermore, such lifestyles are not restricted by any spatial container since they spill out beyond the putative boundaries of individual residential neighbourhoods (Blokland, 2003) and well beyond the city itself via global interconnections (Durrschimdt, 2000).

Butler and Robson (2001) have introduced the term 'tectonic' to describe the social interactions in some of the areas of gentrified inner London that they studied. This refers to the ways in which different social groups move past each other in separate worlds and have almost no interaction on any systematic basis – the social relations between the different groups are parallel and not integrative. These findings point to the need to undertake work which examines these different universes in such a way as to plot the interactions in order to understand how they are generative of particular sets of social relations at different geographic scales – the city, the district and the neighbourhood, for example. Nevertheless, the notion of 'social tectonics' is useful in thinking about how social groups work in the city. In particular, it points to how social relations have changed with the slow demise of cities as constructed around social classes.

Conclusion

In this chapter, we have used the discussion of cities to examine the ways in which a sense of place has come to inform people's identity. We have argued that this now underlies and, in some respects, has replaced class identities. Whilst Soja (1989) is undoubtedly correct in his critique of sociology for privileging time to the exclusion of space, it is also clear that processes of time-space compression that have happened with developing ICT and economic globalization have meant that space rather than time has now become foregrounded into people's sense of identity. We have suggested, in this chapter, that cities have become the places where these identities have been fought out – whether in global cities which are the nodes of economic power or the declining cities whose sense of identity are reinforced by their marginalization by and from the forces of global power. Given that these cities are now engaged in ruthless competition with each other for a share of economic investment, these contested views of place assume not just a cultural and social importance but also an economic one.

Further reading

There have been a number of recent texts on the city which are worth following up for those wishing to delve further into the issues raised in this chapter, notably Amin and Thrift (2002), Savage et al. (2003) and Parker (2004). See Abrahamson (2004) for a readable overview of global cities. Although somewhat dated now, Davis (1990) remains an exhilarating account of Los Angeles. Two very worthwhile recent accounts of social and economic change in London are Buck et al. (2002) and Hamnett (2003), each of which challenges various aspects of the global cities approach. Musterd and Ostendorf (1998) is a very good edited book on urban inequality, segregation and welfare states, while the collection from Marcuse and Van Kempen (2000a) takes a more explicitly spatial approach. A seminal text on gentrification from a Marxist perspective is Smith (1996). In contrast, a lesser known, but worthwhile book on gentrification in Toronto from a more cultural perspective is Caulfield (1994). Atkinson and Bridge (2005) provide a useful collection of chapters on gentrification in a global context. Two excellent ethnographies which in different ways challenge the ghetto underclass thesis are a study of the infamous Robert Taylor Homes public housing project in Chicago by Venkatesh (2000) and a study of Harlem by Jackson (2001).s

For global cities, see the Globalization and World Cities website at Loughborough University: www.lboro.ac.uk/gawc. The ESRC Centre for Neighbourhood Research website provides a large number of downloadable papers based both upon British and cross-national research – http://www.neighbourhoodcentre.org.uk/.

Poverty, Social Exclusion and the Welfare State

CHAPTER SIX
●●●●●●●●

- ■ Introduction
- ■ Welfare state regimes
- ■ Poverty and social exclusion
- ■ Poverty in the United States
- ■ Poverty and social exclusion in Britain
- ■ Poverty and social exclusion in Europe
- ■ Conclusion: towards a liberal welfare convergence?

Introduction

In Chapter 3, we saw how a major theme in post-war British sociology was the impact of affluence on the working class. During the 1960s, poverty was 'rediscovered' by Abel-Smith and Townsend (1965) and this concern with poverty has grown during the last 30 years alongside deindustrialization and global economic restructuring. One of the main challenges facing European and North American societies has been high and sustained levels of poverty since the end of the long boom in the early 1970s. The 'underclass' has been the dominant concept in grasping the expansion and deepening of poverty in North America, as seen in the debate over the ghetto urban underclass discussed in Chapter 5. Whilst the underclass debate has had some resonance in Western Europe, especially in Britain (Silver, 1994, 1996; Levitas, 1998; Herkommer and Koch, 1999), the more influential concept has been that of 'social exclusion', a term that is virtually absent from policy debate in the United States (Steinert, 2003: 47). In this chapter, we offer a guide to debates about contemporary poverty and social exclusion by drawing on material from both Europe and the United States.

• 100 •

Traditionally in Britain the academic analysis of poverty and the welfare state was the provenance of social policy and administration rather than sociology, while the latter dealt with social class. Sociological class analysts have tended to focus on employment and property relations and in so doing have often downplayed the potential role of welfare and poverty in understanding stratification; neither makes much of an appearance in Savage (2000) for example. However, it could be argued that as poverty has both expanded and deepened during the last 30 years, so the relevance of traditional social policy concerns for understanding stratification has grown, as emphasized by Zuberi (2006) in his comparative account of the working poor in the United States and Canada. Post-war poverty research was concerned with not only calibrating the size of and composition of 'the poor', but also with estimating the impact of government welfare policy on poverty and refining that policy in order to reduce or eliminate poverty altogether (Rowntree and Lavers, 1951; Abel-Smith and Townsend, 1965; Townsend, 1979). This reforming aspect can also be identified in the more recent academic agenda on exclusion as social scientists undertake research commissioned by government and voluntary agencies under the auspices of 'tackling social exclusion'. Although we make reference to policy reforms, our primary focus in this chapter is the sociological aspect of the poverty and social exclusion literature in relation to understanding and explaining patterns of disadvantage and inequality.

We saw in Chapter 5 how the notion of differential welfare regimes can help to illuminate comparative patterns of social polarization in global cities. In the first section of this chapter, we expand upon this theme by focusing on the contribution of Gosta Esping-Andersen to welfare regime theory. In the second section, we present a 'conceptual guide' to the definition and operationalization of poverty and social exclusion, as well as a discussion of the various theoretical approaches and explanations which have been used in relation to these phenomena. Thirdly, we discuss poverty in the United States, the paradigmatic liberal welfare regime nation. In particular, we emphasize how poverty in the USA is not just associated with a lack of paid employment, but is also linked with low pay via poor work and the 'working poor'. In the fifth section, we examine poverty and social exclusion in Britain, a nation which has increasingly moved in a liberal welfare regime direction. In the sixth section we discuss poverty and social exclusion in Europe more generally, and in particular we examine three 'at risk' groups – the unemployed, young unemployed and migrants. In the conclusion, we consider whether or not the differential nature of welfare state regimes is breaking down and if there is therefore a move towards a 'liberal convergence'.

Welfare state regimes

Three types of welfare state regime

One of the most significant ways of analyzing differences in capitalist societies from the standpoint of stratification is predicated on welfare regime theory and the construction of welfare state regime typologies. There are several different, and to an extent, competing typologies in existence (Bonoli, 1997; Hammer, 2003a). In this section, we focus on probably the most influential typology, that developed by Gosta Esping-Andersen (1990) in *The Three Worlds of Welfare Capitalism*. In this, Esping-Andersen puts forward the view that welfare states are not merely mechanisms that intervene in the structure of social inequality, but that instead they actively operate as systems of stratification since they confer differential rights to benefits. Such rights are predicated on the balance of forces between state, market and family, a balance that varies from society to society. According to Esping-Andersen, such variations cluster in distinct welfare state regimes which have arisen as a consequence of differential political mobilization on the part of national working classes, often in concert with other social classes. He constructs a regime typology in which different welfare states are clustered around their ability to promote 'decommodification' in relation to three social welfare programmes: pensions, sickness and unemployment cash benefits: 'decommodification occurs when a service is rendered as a matter of right, and when a person can maintain a livelihood without reliance on the market' (Esping-Andersen, 1990: 21–22). In other words, decommodification refers to the extent to which people can uphold a reasonable standard of living even if they are not working in paid employment, for example when they retire, are sick or unemployed. The more generous the benefits the state pays under such circumstances and the easier the eligibility rules the state sets, the greater the degree of decommodification. As well as decommodification, the welfare regimes are distinguished by the nature of their engagement with the labour market in relation to conditions of entry (as in the welfare state's own role as an employer) and exit (retirement and paid absence from work).[27]

In a later self-critique, Esping-Andersen (1999: 47) admits to not paying a great deal of attention to the family in *The Three Worlds of Welfare Capitalism*. In other words, he focused on the state/market relation at the expense of adequately understanding the state/family relation. As feminist critics have argued, 'decommodification' assumes a male breadwinner model of work and welfare which does not take into account the gendered nature of benefit payments and care work – much of it unpaid (O'Connor, 1993; Sainsbury, 1994). Hence, as Esping-Andersen admits, for many women dependence upon the family is effectively the equivalent of market dependency for men. In order to address this issue, he introduces the concept of 'familialism' which refers to whether families are meant to be the main focus of welfare provision. 'De-familialization' is thus equivalent to decommodification and refers to, 'policies that lessen individuals' reliance on the family; that maximize individuals' command of economic resources independently of familial or conjugal reciprocities' (Esping-Andersen, 1999: 45).

A summary of the main characteristics of the three welfare state regimes is provided in Table 6.1. It is worth emphasizing that Esping-Andersen (1999: 73) is not concerned with either welfare states *per se* or with individual welfare policies, but rather with 'regimes': 'the ways in which welfare production is allocated between state, market, and households'. The three-fold regime typology represents an ideal type, the main features of which are discussed below.

Table 6.1   Welfare regime characteristics

	Liberal	Social democratic	Conservative
Role of:			
Market	Central	Marginal	Marginal
State	Marginal	Central	Subsidiary
Family	Marginal	Marginal	Central
Welfare state:			
Dominant locus of solidarity	Market	State	Family
Degree of decommodification	Minimal	Maximum	High (for breadwinner)
Examples	USA	Sweden	Germany

Source: adapted version of Table 5.4 from *Social Foundations of Postindustrial Economies* (Esping-Andersen, 1999). By permission of Oxford University Press.

Liberal regime – the welfare state has a residual role since non-work benefits are modest and cater mainly to low-income groups. The state encourages the market, either passively, in the shape of only providing stigmatized means-tested public benefits, or actively by subsidizing private welfare schemes. As a consequence, decommodification is minimal. There is a class-political dualism between welfare dependent minorities and market dependent majorities. Taxation levels, on both companies and households, are generally low. Although both total and female labour force participation rates are high, this is not due to state involvement but instead occurs as a result of market pressures. The regime is not familialist. The prototypical liberal welfare state is the United States with other prominent examples including Anglo-Saxon countries such as the UK, Canada, Australia and Ireland.[28]

Social democratic regime – the welfare state plays a major role in providing high non-work benefits that keep their recipients out of poverty. Consequently decommodification is advanced and there is an emphasis on providing universal welfare benefits: 'all benefit; all are dependent; and all will presumably feel obliged to pay' (Esping-Andersen, 1990: 28). Taxation levels, on both companies and households, are generally high. Gender equality is valued and publicly recognized via state-provided childcare systems. There is an emphasis on maximising labour market supply for both women and men and the welfare state itself is a major female employer. Typical social democratic welfare states included Scandinavian nations such as Sweden and Denmark.

Conservative (or corporatist) regime – unlike the liberal regime, conservative welfare states do not emphasize market efficiency. Instead, there is a predominant concern with the preservation of status segmentation and familialism. Status differentials are important, notably in relation to gender divisions in which social insurance excludes non-working wives while benefits encourage motherhood. Familialism based upon traditional gender role is strongest within the conservative regime since women act as welfare providers for families. The conservative regimes offer a high level of non-work benefits, but only to a group of labour market 'insiders' rather than universally. The historical role of the Church is strong in the conservative regime countries. The conservative regime discourages labour market supply by providing easy exit routes and also disincentives to female participation. Nations which have a conservative regime include continental European nations such as Germany, Austria, France and Italy.

Welfare states and post-industrial class structures

Having set out a comparative model of welfare states in advanced capitalist societies, Esping-Andersen then proceeds to demonstrate how, 'the welfare state is a midwife of post-industrial employment evolution. Different welfare-state/labour-market interactions produce different post-industrial trajectories' (1990: 192). This approach is developed further in later work on post-industrial class structures (Esping-Andersen, 1993, 1999). Although he recognizes some broad commonalities, for example the expansion in professional employment and the decline of manual jobs, Esping-Andersen also highlights several differences. Service job growth in post-industrial society is strongest in the liberal and social democratic welfare states, such as the United States and Sweden respectively, but far weaker in conservative nations such as Germany. Using these three nations as prototypical examples, Esping-Andersen (1999: 107–11) provides a three-way comparison of the regimes in relation to employment and welfare.

Liberal regime (United States) – the market provides the main source of new service jobs. These are prominent both in business-related management and professional occupations and in low-skilled jobs, for example cleaners, waiters, bar workers employed in the leisure industry. The residual welfare state in the United States means that the poor are effectively forced into taking low-paid service jobs. Hence the 'outsider population', that percentage of the working-age population not in employment, is relatively small, a factor aided by the increase in the total number of jobs.

Social democratic regime (Sweden) – service job growth is also high but this occurs as a result of state rather than market activity. The service jobs created here are a combination of professional jobs within the welfare state itself, such as teachers and nurses, and low-skilled service jobs. The outsider population is relatively small as redundant ex-industrial workers are recycled into alternative jobs via retraining schemes and women are absorbed into the low-skilled public service jobs.

Conservative regime (Germany) – remains heavily reliant on traditional industry even if such manufacturing jobs are in long-term decline. The conservative regime is least likely to produce job growth in services at all, either public or private sector. The result is a highly gendered job distribution, heavily weighted towards traditional male workers. The relatively generous welfare benefits, coupled with a wide range of exit routes from the labour force, for example via unemployment and early retirement among older workers (Knuth and Kalina, 2002), means that there is a large benefit dependent outsider population composed of the long-term unemployed, early retirees and female dependents.

Criticisms of the 'three worlds' welfare regime typology

Esping-Andersen's work has proved hugely influential, notably in relation to the cross-national analysis of poverty, social exclusion and urban deprivation. It has also been subject to several criticisms, including by Esping-Andersen himself (1999: 73–94).

1. Feminist critics have questioned whether his version of welfare regime theory does justice to the gendered nature of welfare provision, labour market participation and caring reponsibilities which locate women in a different and in many ways more disadvantaged position in the state/market/family nexus (O'Connor, 1993; Sainsbury, 1994).

2. Access to employment, entitlement to benefits and welfare provision generally are highly dependent upon racialized conceptions of citizenship that differentiate national populations on the basis of both migrant and ethnic statuses (Ginsburg, 1992; Morissens and Sainsbury, 2005), as highlighted by the case of asylum seekers in the UK (Geddes, 2000). The relationship between ethnicity, welfare and labour markets is often uneven and more complex than regime theory would seem to suggest.

3. Relatedly, by operating at the national level, welfare regime theory provides only a partial guide as to how different social groups are inserted into contemporary processes of socio-spatial polarization in particular cities (Musterd and Ostendorf, 1998). As we saw in Chapter 5, regime theory was used by Hamnett (1998) in relation to explaining variations in social polarization between global cities. However, while the relative size of the outsider surplus population is generally lower in North American as opposed to continental European cities, this does not mean to say that joblessness is not an issue in the United States, as we saw in relation to the debate over the ghetto underclass. Furthermore, as Beck (2000: 117) highlights, the so-called US 'jobs miracle' obscures the unparalleled rate of incarceration' of 1.6 million Americans – mainly young, black and male.

4. By focusing on benefit entitlements, it has been suggested that Esping-Andersen has neglected the wider nature of the welfare states within which such benefit programmes are embedded. In particular, there is little discussion of housing, health or education, all of which can potentially have significant decommodifying effects.[29] In other words, the focus should be on the way that the state provides 'collective consumption' in a broad sense, rather than simply benefits.

5. As an ideal type, the 'three worlds' typology has difficulties in accommodating certain 'ambiguous countries'. Esping-Andersen has himself recognized that existing nations contain welfare elements drawn from other regime types and therefore that 'no regime, let alone country, is pure' (1999: 88). Prominent examples include the Netherlands (Kloosterman, 1996), Canada (Murdie, 1998; Zuberi, 2006) and Britain (see Box 6.1).

6. Over and above the criticism that there are ambiguous countries, a more serious charge levelled against Esping-Andersen's typology is that it is not exhaustive and that there is in effect a 'fourth world' comprising a qualitatively distinct welfare regime (Esping-Andersen, 1999: 88). Several candidates have been put forward for this fourth regime including Southern Europe, East Asia (Japan, Korea and Taiwan), and the Antipodes (Australia and New Zealand). Here we will limit our discussion to Southern Europe.[30] Social assistance, in the form of out-of-work benefits, takes a minimal, highly residual form in Southern European countries such as Greece, Italy, Spain

and Portugal. In such countries, there are powerful expectations that the family will provide social aid and assistance and these are characterized by strong familialism in Esping-Andersen's terms. Esping-Andersen (1999: 90, 92–4 and 138) doubts whether this is sufficient to sub-divide the conservative regime into 'Southern' and 'Continental' European branches. Other comparative poverty and social exclusion analysts disagree and therefore advocate a four-fold welfare regime typology incorporating the 'three worlds' model plus a fourth 'residual' or 'sub-protective' Southern European regime cluster (see *inter alia* Gallie and Paugam, 2000; Hammer, 2003b; Layte and Whelan, 2003; Berthoud, 2004); we return to this typology below in our discussion of poverty and social exclusion in Europe.

Box 6.1 THE BRITISH WELFARE STATE REGIME: LIBERAL, SOCIAL DEMOCRATIC OR HYBRID?

Esping-Andersen (1990, 1993, 1999) places Britain in the liberal welfare regime cluster, as do many comparative welfare analysts. This is justified in relation to social security benefits, given, for example, its incomplete coverage of the unemployed population and its low level of benefit payments to the unemployed (Gallie and Paugam, 2000). However, the early post-war welfare state also contained universalistic elements of state provision, notably in health, via the National Health Service, as well as primary and secondary education, plus significant if not universal elements of public local authority rental housing (Murie, 1998, 2005). Such extensive state services are in stark contrast to the United States with its highly residual public health and housing schemes (Harloe, 1995; Murie, 1998). The British welfare state has therefore been considered by some as representing a 'hybrid' welfare regime combining liberal and social democratic elements (Cochrane, 1993: 239). However the direction of change has been firmly away from the latter as a result of the neo-liberal welfare and economic policies pursued by the Conservative and Labour Governments during the 1980s and 1990s (Alcock and Craig, 2001; Clarke et al., 2001). This liberal shift has 'recommodified' elements of welfare provision, notably in the field of housing as nearly one in three council homes were sold to sitting tenants between 1979 and 1994 and therefore transferred from public to private ownership: 'in the period since 1979, welfare state restructuring has been significant and more radical than elsewhere in Europe. If the post-war redistributive, integrative welfare state had already been eroded, the changes of the 1980s went further in the direction of creating a liberal welfare state.' (Murie, 1998: 124)

Poverty and social exclusion

Poverty

Social scientists usually distinguish between three definitions of poverty: absolute, relative and subjective.

1. *Absolute poverty* – this is defined by the United Nations as 'a condition characterized by severe deprivation of basic human needs, including food, safe drinking water, sanitation facilities, health, shelter, education and information. It depends not only on income but also on access to services' (cited in Gordon et al., 2000: 9). Such absolute definitions are meant to be cross-cultural and trans-historical, but problems of making comparisons over time have led most contemporary poverty researchers to use a relative definition.
2. *Relative poverty* – this refers to poverty which is relative to the standards of living that exist in a society at a particular point in time. To quote Townsend (1979: 31):

> Individuals, families and groups in the population can be said to be in poverty when they lack the resources to obtain the types of diets, participate in the activities and have the living conditions and amenities which are customary, or at least widely encouraged or approved, in the societies to which they belong. Their resources are so seriously below those commanded by the average individual or family that they are, in effect, excluded from ordinary living patterns, customs and activities.

3. *Subjective poverty* – this refers to whether or not people feel themselves to be in financial hardship.

Estimating the number of people living in poverty at any one time is based upon how the concept is both defined and 'operationalized', i.e. how it is measured. As a general rule, measures based on an absolute definition will tend to produce lower rates of poverty than measures based on a relative definition. Gordon et al. (2000: 72–75) have identified four main approaches to measuring poverty.

1. *Budget standards* – this approach is based upon pricing a basket of goods essential for minimum subsistence and then calculating how many people's incomes fall below the level of the valuation. This was adopted by Seebohm Rowntree in his three studies of poverty in York, the last of which was undertaken in 1950 (Rowntree and Lavers, 1951). Budget standards also underpinned the National Assistance scales devized by Beveridge in 1942.
2. *Income threshold* – this approach defines poverty in terms of low income measured by an income line; people are poor if their income falls below that line. This is the commonest way of measuring poverty, for example the European Community's uses of an income threshold of 60 per cent of median household income after housing costs, a measure also used by the British Government in their *Households Below Average Income* (HBAI) data (Flaherty et al., 2004).
3. *Social indicators/consensual approach* – this approach is based on constructing an index of deprivation based on an assessment of which items are 'necessary' within a society, as Townsend (1979) did in which he personally decided which items were to be included. A later variation is the consensual approach, as used by Gordon et al. (2000), which uses a deprivation index based upon public perceptions of necessary items instead of relying upon expert opinion.
4. *Subjective measures* – these are based on estimations by people as to which minimum income level they could live on 'decently'.

Poverty can be explained in a number of ways. A 'common-sense' explanation, often seen in the mass media, is that the individual moral or intellectual characteristics of the poor cause poverty. In other words, the poor are themselves to blame for their poverty since they are morally deficient (they are lazy) and/or intellectually defective (they have low intelligence). This individualistic approach is one that few social scientists would accept; instead structural and to a lesser extent cultural explanations are preferred (Spicker, 1993: 74–86; Kerbo, 2003: 268–82; Lister, 2004). Structural explanations shift attention away from the poor themselves towards the wider social, economic and political structures that generate poverty. These structures include capitalism itself, socio-economic inequality in the form of social class, as well as inequalities arising from gender, 'race' and disability (Lister, 2004).

According to Marxism, capitalism is an economic system which by its very nature generates both extreme wealth, for the capitalist class, and inevitable poverty among sections of the working class. Marx (1974: 589) invoked the theory of an 'industrial reserve army' or, more commonly, the 'reserve army of labour' to explain how capitalists draw previously marginal groups into the workforce during times of economic boom, but then eject such groups again during slump periods. The reserve army therefore varies in size according to the machinations of the business cycle, but its general function is to depress wage levels while its members suffer from various degrees of poverty as a result of either irregular or absent employment – see the section on social exclusion below. For Marxists, the welfare state under capitalism merely shifts resources around in the middle range of the class structure while not fundamentally challenging the basic source of poverty that is capitalism itself (Westergaard and Resler, 1976).

Weberian sociologists and social democratic policy analysts have tended to emphasize skill differentials in allocating particular occupational groups to poverty. If the occupational reward structure is based upon differential access to well-paid jobs on the basis of skills, those with the least skills will be clustered in the lowest paid jobs and will also be the most likely to find themselves unemployed. The fact that many people located in low-skilled jobs are in poverty reflects the structurally related rewards accruing to different jobs rather than anything about the individuals who occupy such positions. Townsend (1979) found that around half of unskilled manual workers and their families were in poverty resulting not only from the low pay typical of such jobs, but also from the absence of sick pay and paid holidays, as well as the inherent insecurity of unskilled manual labour.

Feminists have argued that traditional Marxist and non-Marxist approaches to poverty ignore gender inequalities in relation to households, labour markets and welfare states resulting in a 'feminization of poverty' (Pascall, 1997; Jonsson, 1999). Such inequalities mean that 'women are at far greater risk of poverty than men; at any given stage in their lives, women are far more likely than men to be poor and their experience of poverty is also likely to be far more acute' (Millar and Glendinning, 1989: 363). Certain groups of women, such as lone parents, are especially prone to poverty. Racism in the operation of labour markets and welfare states increases the likelihood of poverty among minority ethnic groups. Social disadvantages facing disabled people and the elderly mean that they are also more prone to poverty (Lister, 2004).

If the above structural factors tend to dominate social scientific explanations for poverty, cultural factors have also been considered significant. Thus Lewis (1966) argued that poverty results from a 'culture of poverty' in the sense that the poor are said to have distinctive cultural traits and abide by an alternative set of values and norms from the rest of society, a poverty that is passed down from one generation to another.

Social exclusion

If poverty has a long-established pedigree, the term 'social exclusion' is a more recent arrival to the social science lexicon (Littlewood and Herkommer, 1999). The current usage of the term is rooted in French social policy in the 1980s from where it received wider recognition at the European Union level (Berghman, 1995). During the 1990s, social exclusion effectively replaced poverty in the EU vocabulary and 'it was then re-exported to all the European countries' (Murard, 2002: 41). Subsequently, it has come to dominate political, media and social scientific discourses about poverty and disadvantage in Europe, so much so that 'the key term in the language of European policy is *social exclusion*' (Chamberlayne, 2002: 271; original emphasis).

What, then, is social exclusion? Two different ways of answering this question can be identified. The first approach highlights the concept's ambiguities and theoretical differences: 'the expression is so evocative, ambiguous, multidimensional and elastic that it can be defined in many different ways' (Silver, 1994: 541). Silver painstakingly analyzes three distinct social exclusion 'paradigms' rooted in differing and even opposed theories and national political discourses. Similarly, Ruth Levitas (1998) has identified three separate 'discourses of social exclusion' within British political and social policy debates which inform New Labour thinking and practices (see Box 6.2). 'Discourse' means that 'sets of interrelated concepts act together as a matrix through which we understand the social world. As this matrix structures our understanding, so it in turn governs the paths of action which appear to be open to us' (Levitas, 1998: 3).

Box 6.2   THREE DISCOURSES OF SOCIAL EXCLUSION

Levitas (1998) shows how New Labour, with its 'broad tent' political appeal, has drawn upon three different discourses of social exclusion:

RED – a redistributionist discourse that emphasizes poverty and the lack of full citizenship rights.

MUD – a moral underclass discourse whose main concern is with the morality and behaviour of the excluded themselves.

SID – a social integrationist discourse that emphasizes the significance of paid work for social inclusion.

While Levitas is not suggesting that language is the essence of social reality in an idealist sense, her discursive approach resonates with the poststructural emphasis on language as creatively constitutive of social reality. This discursive approach has resulted in empirical studies that have not so much focused on describing and explaining social exclusion 'out there' in society, but instead on excavating the various meanings of social exclusion as embedded within official policy documents (Stenson and Watt, 1999; Watt and Jacobs, 2000).

The second approach to defining social exclusion is less concerned with tracing its philosophical origins and discursive ambiguities and more with trying to focus on areas of consensus. This approach is particularly important among those social scientists attempting to outline and explain patterns of exclusion with reference to empirical research on contemporary social conditions. There is a Durkheimian influence underpinning much of this research given Durkheim's concern with the moral order of society and the emphasis in social exclusion on whether people are able to participate in collective social life (Levitas, 1998). As Andersen (1999: 129) notes, this could be seen to represent a shift away from a vertical model of stratification along Marxist-Weberian lines with an emphasis on class, towards a horizontal perspective focused around an insider-outsider distinction. Several common themes can be identified within this second approach to social exclusion (adapted from Littlewood and Herkommer, 1999: 11–18):

1. *Novelty* – social exclusion refers to 'new' phenomena in two main ways. Firstly, that mass poverty and widening inequalities are something that have re-entered Western capitalist societies after their muted existence in the immediate post-war period. Secondly, that many aspects of social exclusion are irreducible to class since they depend upon 'other' stratification axes, notably ethnicity, migrant status, gender or age.

2. *Economic restructuring* – deindustrialization, globalization and neo-liberalism are said to be the underlying causes of social exclusion. This restructuring has been given different theoretical emphases, however, with Bauman (1998) suggesting that social exclusion refers to a surplus population that is no longer necessary for capital accumulation, whereas Byrne (1999) invokes the Marxist notion of a reserve army of labour under post-Fordist conditions (see Kennedy (2005) for a commentary).

3. *Multi-dimensionality* – whereas poverty is focused upon distribution issues and the lack of individual or household resources, 'notions such as social exclusion focus primarily on relational issues, in other words, inadequate social participation, lack of social integration and lack of power' (Room, 1995: 5). Exclusion is therefore multidimensional. Berghman (1995) points to considerable overlap between exclusion and the concept of 'relative deprivation', devised by Townsend (1979), which refers to being unable to participate in those social activities which are customary in a particular society, a non-participation which could result from poverty. Berghman suggests that social exclusion could be regarded as the process of which deprivation is the outcome.

4. *Non-participation* – exclusion refers to non-participation in the economic, social and political life and institutions of national societies. As Room (1995) points out, exclusion is therefore closely related to T.H. Marshall's concept of citizenship since exclusion is effectively the obverse of integration and the full participation of the societal member as a citizen. Poverty could well be the reason for this non-participation but, as seen in point 3 above, exclusion can be caused by factors other than lack of material resources. For example, disabled wheelchair users may not be living below the

poverty line in strict monetary terms, but they may be excluded from participation in leisure activities because public transport or buildings do not accommodate their mobility needs.

5. *Dynamic and processual* – social exclusion is not only concerned with a 'state of being' and outcomes, but is also about a 'state of becoming' in which persons or groups can lose their links to others and society as a whole over time.

6. *Cumulative* – the processual and multidimensional nature of social exclusion means that there are cumulative effects over time.

7. *Spatial dimension* – as we saw when discussing the ghetto underclass debate, social exclusionary processes reinforce and are reinforced in turn by the spatial concentration of deprived people living in certain locales, what Wacquant (1999) has referred to as a 'new regime of urban marginality'.

Despite the current widespread usage of 'social exclusion' by politicians and social scientists alike, the latter have also offered several criticisms. First of all, there are those who emphasize the politicized and analytically confused nature of the concept (Silver, 1994; Levitas, 1998). According to Murard (2002), social exclusion is an 'empty box' given by the French state to the social scientific community via the auspices of the EU, which social scientists, as well as others, have subsequently 'filled' with a huge number of studies and publications. This filling is rooted in an analytical imprecision which means that social exclusion encompasses a large number of quite distinct phenomena ranging from poverty, unemployment and racism to crime and 'anti-social behaviour' (Levitas, 1998; Watt and Jacobs, 2000). Secondly, the multidimensional nature of social exclusion means that it detracts attention away from poverty, and this is especially the case if the behavioural 'underclass' dimensions of social exclusion are emphasized (Levitas, 1998). Thirdly, social exclusion, like poverty, focuses on a narrow social group and therefore it downplays class inequalities (Savage, 2003). In so doing, the broader impact of changes associated with globalization and welfare restructuring are downplayed, for example in attempts by the French state to depoliticize issues of welfare retrenchment: 'exclusion is a word to denote a small number of excluded people, when the issues raised by the word are in fact a source of anxiety for a very large part of society, especially in the working class and lower middle class' (Murard, 2002: 42).

In conclusion, provided social exclusion is not used in a manner that either denies or obscures material inequalities and poverty, it can offer a potentially useful framework for describing and analyzing the multiple ways that the various axes of inequality impact negatively upon the increasingly complex web of groups who find themselves economically marginalized, socially disadvantaged and politically powerless in contemporary society. As contemporary societies have become more complex as a consequence of globalization, for example via increased migratory flows, so traditional hierarchical models of inequality and poverty increasingly struggle to capture the multilayered nature of disadvantage. Social exclusion, therefore, captures the dynamic and multi-faceted nature of contemporary patterns of disadvantage and inequality in a way that poverty alone does not. In capturing the multi-dimensionality of contemporary disadvantage, social exclusion is also superior to an 'underclass' perspective since it does not

operate with a simplistic bi-polar notion of inequality in which a singular deviant 'outgroup' is compared to the rest of society.

Poverty in the United States

US poverty in comparative perspective

We saw in Chapter 1 how inequality was particularly extreme in the United States. Official US poverty data show that 34.6 million people were below the official poverty line, or 12.1 per cent of the population, up from 11.7 per cent in 2001 (Proctor and Dalaker, 2003: 1). The official figures are based on a budget standards approach, that is an estimation of what it costs for a family to buy food, housing and other necessities. Poverty income thresholds are then calculated for different family types. If a family's total income (before tax and not including non-cash benefits such as food stamps) is below the threshold, then the family and all its members are considered to be in poverty. The poverty income thresholds in 2002 were calculated as follows (Proctor and Dalaker, 2003: 4):

- Single adult aged under 65 years – $9,359
- Two adults under 65 years – $12,047
- Three people (one adult and two children under 18 years) – $14,494
- Four people (two adults and two children under 18 years) – $18,244.

Critics have claimed that the official measure underestimates the extent of poverty since the poverty line is gauged too low (Ehrenreich, 2002; Kerbo, 2003: 254); it certainly results in a lower level than when using a relative measure, as we see below.

Cross-national poverty data, including figures for the United States, can be found in Kerbo (2003: 256–7) and Smeeding et al. (2000). In terms of absolute measures, Smeeding and colleagues compared the household poverty rate in the United States to rates found in other nations using the USA poverty line, about 42 per cent of median household income. The results, shown in Table 6.2, indicate that the country with the highest aggregate income per capita is tiny Luxembourg followed by the USA. All other countries have considerably lower averages than the latter with the UK appearing at the bottom around 33 per cent below that of the United States level. As Smeeding and colleagues note, it is not surprising that Australia and the UK have higher absolute poverty rates than the United States given that their per capita aggregate incomes are below that of the United States. However, the USA has a higher rate of absolute poverty despite having a greater per capita aggregate income than most of the countries listed:

> ... it seems clear that among these rich nations, the distribution of income is as important as average absolute income in determining the level of poverty. Poor countries can have lower poverty rates than rich ones if their income distributions are compressed; rich countries can have higher poverty rates than poor ones if their incomes are very unequally distributed. (Smeeding et al., 2000: 169–70)

Table 6.2   Absolute poverty rates for OECD nations using the US poverty line, 1994 and 1995

Nation	Year	Poverty rate %	GDP per capita 1995 US$	GDP per capita 1995 (USA = 100)
Australia	1994	17.6	21,459	77
UK	1995	15.7	18,743	67
USA	1994	13.6	27,895	100
France	1994	9.9	20,192	72
Canada	1994	7.4	22,951	82
Germany	1994	7.3	21,357	77
Netherlands	1994	7.1	21,222	76
Sweden	1995	6.3	19,949	72
Finland	1995	4.8	18,861	68
Norway	1995	4.3	23,316	84
Luxembourg	1994	0.3	36,570	131
Overall average		8.6	22,956	82.4

Source: Smeeding et al. (2000: 169, Table 5.1)

This finding is all the more remarkable given that the USA in particular, and to a lesser extent Australia and the UK, have recently experienced faster economic growth and lower joblessness rates than many other OECD countries. Smeeding and colleagues go on to examine two measures of relative poverty, 40 and 50 per cent of national median personal income based on 19 affluent countries, mainly in North America and Europe. Using the 50 per cent measure, the average poverty rate in the early to middle 1990s was 8.6 per cent (Smeeding et al., 2000: 186). The lowest rate was 3.9 per cent in Luxembourg and the highest was 17.8 per cent in the United States. Countries with high overall levels of poverty had higher rates of inequality, for example the USA and Italy, or minimal welfare systems, for example Spain. The lowest poverty rates were found in countries with high-spending welfare states in Europe such as Finland, Belgium and Norway.

According to Smeeding and colleagues, the higher levels of inequality and poverty found in the United States can be explained by the existence of low wages and limited public benefits. In fact they suggest that a considerable amount of the variance in cross-national poverty rates is accounted for by the cross-national variation in the incidence of low pay. Minimum wage levels in the USA are considerably lower than those in the European Union with the exception of the United Kingdom, as seen in Table 6.3.

Poor work and the working poor

Joblessness is undoubtedly a significant factor leading to poverty in the United States, as we saw in our discussion of the ghetto underclass in Chapter 5. Official figures on poverty for 2002 indicate that the chances of being in poverty in the United States were far higher for those out of work (21.0 per cent) compared to those in work

Table 6.3   Ratio of minimum wage to average
wage in the United States and Europe, 1991–94

France	0.50
Germany	0.55
Sweden	0.52
United Kingdom	0.40
European Union	0.53
United States	0.39

Source: OECD in Alesina and Glaeser (2004: 39 Table 2.9)

(5.9 per cent) (Proctor and Dalaker, 2003: 8). At the same time, official data show that low pay has become an increasingly significant factor leading to poverty: 45 per cent of those in poverty lived in a family with at least one full-time worker in 1993 but this increased to 54 per cent in 2000 (adapted from Kerbo, 2003: 259, Table 9-4). There has been increased scholarly and journalistic attention given to the plight of the working poor in the United States (see *inter alia* Newman, 1999; Ehrenreich 2002; Appelbaum et al., 2003; Shulman, 2003; Newman and Lennon, 2004; Talwar, 2004). In 2001, it was estimated that 27.5 million Americans, or nearly one quarter of the labour force, earned less than $8.70 an hour, while in the late 1990s 29 per cent of working families with children under 12 had lower incomes than the basic family budget for their communities (Appelbaum et al., 2003). Low-wage workers are found across a range of industries and are employed in a wide variety of occupations in both service and manufacturing industries.

In the United States, work is regarded as the *only* way out of poverty by governments, as seen in the development of 'workfare' policies to compel the unemployed off welfare and into work by time-limiting welfare payments (Gray, 2004: 164–7). Smeeding et al. (2000) conclude, on the other hand, that this emphasis on the US job creation engine to alleviate poverty is misplaced given the linkage between low wages and poverty. In 1996, the national means-tested welfare programme, Aid to Families with Dependent Children (AFDC) was replaced with Temporary Assistance to Needy Families (TANF), a state-operated programme that required most recipients to work for their benefits and also restricted life-time payments to five years. According to Newman and Lennon (2004), the impact of TANF has been to reduce the numbers on welfare, but to simultaneously swell the ranks of the working poor as many people found themselves in the low-wage labour force.

In the best-selling *Nickel and Dimed: Undercover in Low-Wage USA*, Barbara Ehrenreich (2002) details what it is like to work in a variety of low-wage jobs. Her before tax earnings at Wal-Mart in Minneapolis from her $7 an hour sales job amounted to $1,120 a month which would result in an annual income of $13,440, while in Key West, Florida she earned the minimum wage of $5.15 an hour, including tips, working as a waitress. Her highest earnings were in Portland, Maine at $300 per week after tax. However, this involved working seven days a week at two jobs, domestic cleaning and residential care. At each location, Ehrenreich earned *above* the poverty level threshold for a single person of $9,935.[31] But what Ehrenreich details with such lack of sentimentality is the sheer day-in-day-out difficulty of getting by on the wages she earned, not least because of the exorbitant rental costs she faced:

> Something is wrong, very wrong, when a single person in good health, a person who in addition possesses a working car, can barely support herself by the sweat of her brow. You don't need a degree in economics to see that wages are too low and rents too high. (2002: 199)

Her wage levels meant that she was forced to live in sub-standard accommodation, for example in motels, because she could not afford rents never mind mortgage payments. Given the difficulties Ehrenreich, a single healthy woman, faced surviving on such wages, it would seem that the official poverty threshold is indeed set at too low a level.[32] It could be objected that one cannot read too much into a short-term 'experiment' of the kind Ehrenreich undertook. But if anything, the limited timespan she spent in poor work underlines the notion that the wages she earned were inadequate since real life low-wage earners have to exist for years on their incomes and so incur the kinds of costs, for example health care, that Ehrenreich's sojourn in the land of the working poor avoided. Her experiences also indicate that the absence of European-style social wages, in the form of public health care or subsidized housing, exacerbate the problems of living on low wages in the USA. Box 6.3 offers an exercise for students to estimate what a living wage would be for a single person in their area. We return to the working poor in Chapter 7.

BOX 6.3   WHAT IS A LIVING WAGE FOR A SINGLE PERSON IN THE AREA YOU LIVE?

1. Estimate how much you would need to live in your area independently (not in the parental home) by adding up the following costs per week – if possible, try to find out what the actual cost for each item is in your area:

   - Housing (rent for a one-bed flat)
   - Lighting, heating and water (electricity, gas, water)
   - Food (three meals a day)
   - Clothes
   - Public transport to get to work for five days from approx. 3 miles away (bus or train)
   - Communication (phone, internet)
   - At-home entertainment (TV, radio, computer)
   - Out-of-home entertainment (one evening out after work for a drink or meal and one weekend visit to the cinema)
   - Modest savings (for treats, holidays, etc.)

2. Calculate how much you would need to earn (per hour for a 40 hour-week) in order to match the above total costs.

3. Find out what the wage rates are in your area for jobs such as waiter, bar or pub worker, sales assistant, cleaner, care assistant, security guard, hairdresser, etc.
4. Find out what state benefits, if any, you would be entitled to.
5. Compare the wages in point 3 with point 2. Discuss whether the low-wage workers are paid a living wage in your locality, taking into account any state benefits to which they might be entitled.
6. Discuss whether people could live on these wages for, firstly, a month and secondly, for a year.

- Compare your answers with the accounts of working in low-paid jobs by Abrams (2002) and Toynbee (2003) in Britain, and Ehrenreich (2002) in the United States.
- Have they exaggerated or downplayed the difficulties faced by low-paid workers?

Poverty and social exclusion in Britain

The British debate about poverty and stratification has tended to straddle the two discourses of the underclass and social exclusion prominent in the United States and Europe respectively (Silver 1994, 1996; Levitas, 1998). This analytical ambiguity may well reflect a wider ambivalence regarding the nature of the British welfare state (see Box 6.1 earlier in this chapter).

Poverty

In the early post-war period, it was widely thought that poverty was a thing of the past as a result of full employment and the establishment of the Beveridge welfare state. Based upon a budget standards methodology, Rowntree and Lavers found a 'remarkable decrease in poverty between 1936 and 1950' (1951: 32) in York, down from 18 per cent to less than two per cent of the city's population. However, poverty was 'rediscovered' during the 1960s largely due to the pioneering work of Abel-Smith and Townsend (1965) employing an income threshold approach based upon national data on those below an income of less than 140 per cent of the then National Assistance scale; this was therefore a more relative approach than that of Rowntree and Lavers.

It is widely accepted that both poverty and inequality have increased dramatically in Britain since the late 1970s and at rates faster than most other European countries (Pond, 1989; Hills, 1995; Flaherty et al., 2004). In a recent study, *Poverty and Social Exclusion in Britain* (PSE), Gordon et al. (2000) used a consensual approach to measuring poverty in which the public were asked to say which items from a list of household goods and activities they thought were necessities. The researchers then calculated a poverty threshold on the basis that people were classified as 'poor' if there were at least two socially defined necessities that they were unable to afford. On this basis, it was calculated that 25.6 per cent of the population of Britain, or 14.5 million people, were poor. Some groups, however, had far higher percentages in poverty than this:

- Non-retired people who were not working because of unemployment (77 per cent) or sickness/disability (61 per cent)
- People on income support (70 per cent)
- Lone parents (62 per cent)
- Local authority tenants (61 per cent) and housing association tenants (57 per cent)
- Divorced or separated people (46 per cent)
- Households with 3+ children (46 per cent)
- Younger people – 16–24 year olds (34 per cent).

Women (29 per cent) were more likely to be poor than men (22 per cent), while minority ethnic groups, particularly Bangladeshi and Black groups, also had higher poverty rates. The findings confirm those from other studies about which groups are most vulnerable to poverty (Glendinning and Millar, 1992; Hills, 1995; Flaherty et al., 2004).

The PSE data allow Gordon and colleagues to makes comparisons with earlier surveys that used a similar consensus methodology. In 1983, 14 per cent of households were living in poverty, while by 1990 this figure had increased by nearly half, standing at 21 per cent. The poverty rate for households continued to increase during the 1990s, albeit at a lower rate. Gordon et al. (2000: 52) conclude, 'this dramatic rise in poverty, in terms of the enforced lack of necessities, occurred while the majority of the British population became richer'. A combination of economic restructuring allied to the neo-liberal welfare and economic policies pursued by the Conservative Governments from 1979–97 have been largely responsible for the increase in poverty and inequality with the following representing the most commonly identified factors (Pond, 1989; Hills, 1995; Walker and Walker, 1997; Flaherty et al., 2004; Hills and Stewart, 2005).

- An increase in the proportion of workless households, i.e. with no earner – this was initially brought about by the rapid increase in unemployment, which peaked at over three million in 1986 and again in 1993 with just under three million, although it has fallen since then to below one million in July 2003.[33] The numbers on incapacity benefits have tripled in the period from 1979 to 2002 to stand at 2.7 million, suggesting considerable 'hidden unemployment' (Flaherty et al., 2004); see Chapter 4.
- A dramatic widening in the dispersion of earnings between low-skilled and high-skilled workers. At the bottom end of the distribution, this has been affected by a reduction in the numbers covered by trade unions (see Chapter 7), plus the decline and then abolishment of Wages Councils in 1993 which set minimum wages in various industries. The Labour Government introduced a National Minimum Wage in 1999.
- Changes in taxation have favoured the better off, for example significant reductions in income tax, whilst increases in indirect taxes bear down more heavily on low income households.

- Changes in welfare benefits have reduced their relative value over time, for example by uprating them in line with prices rather than earnings.
- Demographic changes have led to an increase in groups with low incomes, notably lone parent families, pensioners and single adult households below pension age without children.

The PSE results indicate that lack of employment as a result of unemployment, sickness or disability dramatically increases the risk of being poor. However, it is also the case that 28 per cent of households containing one worker were poor while slightly over half of all households in poverty contained someone in work (Gordon et al., 2000: 20). This suggests that although joblessness is a major cause of household poverty in Britain, low pay is also a significant contributory factor (Stewart, 1999; Nickell, 2004). The North American policy emphasis on 'welfare to work' has become increasingly influential on British and European approaches to unemployment and is also the cornerstone of New Labour thinking (Levitas, 1998; Gray, 2004). We will explore this question in greater detail since it illustrates not only the dynamic nature of poverty, but also the nature of the new types of work (see Chapter 7).

Poverty, unemployment and low pay are not necessarily lifetime phenomena for the working-age population; people can and do escape from each of these disadvantageous states (Stewart, 1999, 2004; Burgess and Propper, 2002). Nevertheless, poverty is often self-perpetuating since people who experience poverty once are more likely than not to be in poverty in the future, a feature which is particularly prominent in the USA and UK with liberal welfare regimes (Burgess and Propper, 2002). As with poverty, so with unemployment and low pay. Stewart (2004) has argued that people earning low pay in one period are more likely to be low-paid in subsequent periods while the experience of unemployment makes future unemployment more likely. Moreover unemployment and low pay are themselves interlinked via the 'low pay – no pay cycle' in which 'the low-paid are more likely to be out of work in the future; those out of work are more likely to be low-paid on re-entry; and are even more likely to be so if they had been low-paid prior to being out of work' (Stewart, 1999: 239). According to Stewart, 'low-wage jobs act as the main conduit for repeat unemployment' (2004: 28). The numbers and proportions of low-paid jobs increased over the last 25 years, while the relative earnings of low-paid workers have fallen (McKnight, 2002). McKnight summarizes the consequences of these trends for achieving 'ladders out of poverty': 'while worklessness virtually guarantees poverty, work is now less likely to lift a household out of poverty than in the past' (2002: 117). Given that a low-paid job does not necessarily lead onto improved future prospects, McKnight suggests that there are limitations to a policy emphasis on paid work as being the main route out of poverty.

During the 1979–97 period, poverty was effectively 'off' the Conservative Government's political agenda, as seen in the cool official response to the reports on widening health inequalities in the 1980s (Townsend et al., 1988). Under 'New' Labour, poverty is back on the political agenda, alongside social exclusion (Levitas, 1998). This can be seen in the Labour Government's ambitious commitment to ending child poverty by 2020, as well as its far greater willingness to measure the extent of poverty (Flaherty et al.,

2004; Hills and Stewart, 2005). In a review of poverty and inequality under New Labour, Sefton and Sutherland (2005) found little change in income inequality, but that Gordon Brown's tax-benefit changes have produced some reduction in poverty among children and pensioners – those groups that the Government is most concerned about. However, 'it is probably too early to judge whether the small progress made under New Labour is "scratching the surface" of the problem or whether it does indeed represent the beginning of a new trend towards greater equality' (2005: 249).

Social exclusion

As well as a greater concern with poverty, New Labour has committed itself to 'tackling social exclusion', as seen in the establishment of the Social Exclusion Unit (Levitas, 1998). As discussed above, although poverty is a major aspect of social exclusion, the latter has multidimensional features that are more than simply lack of material resources. This has prompted researchers to devise measures to capture this multi-dimensionality. In one report assessing the Labour Government's inheritance following 18 years of Conservative rule, Howarth et al. (1998) utilized no fewer than 46 indicators of social exclusion including children living in workless households, suicides among young people and anxiety in older people. Whilst such an approach is certainly multidimensional, it lacks analytical focus.

In comparison, one of the clearest attempts to operationalize social exclusion in survey research is that from the Centre for Analysis of Social Exclusion (CASE) at the London School of Economics who developed a multidimensional measure of exclusion in relation to data from the longitudinal British Household Panel Survey (Burchardt et al., 1999, 2002). They considered an individual to be 'socially excluded if he or she does not participate in key activities of the society in which he or she lives' (Burchardt et al., 2002: 30). Four dimensions of exclusion were identified, consumption, production, political engagement and social interaction, each of which was operationalized via a series of indicators. The indicators and results for the 1997 wave are shown in Table 6.4. One fifth were politically excluded compared to only one tenth who were lacking in social interaction. While around 30 per cent of the sample were excluded on one dimension, only 0.1 per cent were simultaneously excluded on all four dimensions. Taking the period 1991–98, Burchardt et al. found that the majority of the population, 63 per cent, were excluded on at least one dimension. Social exclusionary processes are therefore widespread, but the data do not point to an 'underclass' of the multiple and permanently excluded: 'inclusion and exclusion are found to be on a continuum, both across dimensions of exclusion and by duration' (2002: 41). This issue, of the existence of an underclass in Britain, has been one that has generated a great deal of attention and we return to it below.

The lack of paid employment is often considered to be a major factor leading to social exclusion, as the CASE study highlights via its 'production' dimension and as also emphasized in New Labour's pursuit of welfare-to-work policies as constituting the major factor promoting social inclusion (Levitas, 1998). Again, as with the discussion

Table 6.4   Indicators of social exclusion and percentage of working-age
population excluded on each dimension in Britain, 1997

Dimension	Indicator and threshold	%
Consumption	Equivalized household net income is under half mean income	16
Production	Not employed or self-employed, in education or training, or looking after family	12
Political engagement	Did not vote in general election and not a member of a campaigning organization	21
Social interaction	In any one of five respects lacks someone who will offer support (listen, comfort, help in crisis, relax with, really appreciates you)	9

Source: adapted from Burchardt et al., 2002: 34–5, Tables 3.1 and 3.2

above on poverty and low pay, critics have emphasized structural shifts *within* paid employment including greater insecurity as well as the lower wages increasingly on offer in the formal labour market (Smith, 2005); as Byrne (1999: 69) pithily comments, 'poor work is the big story'.

Poor neighbourhoods

There has been a concern with the spatial nature of poverty ever since Engels' (1987) *The Condition of the Working Class in England* was published in 1845 in which he described the appalling living and housing conditions faced by the first industrial proletariat in the Northern towns, notably Manchester. The notion that poverty is concentrated in certain largely urban areas has been a prominent one throughout the nineteenth and twentieth centuries, even if the names have changed from 'slums', to the 'inner cities' and more recently 'peripheral estates'. If anything, the geography of poverty and social exclusion has proved even more significant during the last 25 years, as we saw in Chapter 4 at the regional level between the North–South divide, and also in our discussion of social polarization in globalizing cities in Chapter 5:

> Even at local authority level, the gap between the poorest areas and the rest is widening. Moreover, the 1980s saw a particular increase in intra-urban polarization, with increasing contrasts between poorer and more affluent electoral wards *within* cities. ... It appears that poverty is becoming more concentrated in certain neighbourhoods. (Lupton and Power, 2002: 118; original emphasis)

A report by the Social Exclusion Unit (1998) identified up to 4,000 'poor neighbourhoods', which are said to suffer from various aspects of social exclusion including high levels of unemployment, deprivation, crime and anti-social behaviour.[34] These poor neighbourhoods are particularly prevalent in those areas of Britain that have suffered the most from economic restructuring and deindustrialization, for example in old ex-industrial regions in Northern England or those parts of London which have remained relatively untouched by gentrification and any post-industrial 'urban renaissance'. Pockets of deprivation can even be found in otherwise affluent areas of the country, such as Southeast England (Stenson and Watt, 1999).

Poor neighbourhoods can comprise of various types of housing, including areas of run-down owner occupation and private renting in some cities, but they often include stigmatized council housing estates typically characterized by high and persistent levels of poverty and joblessness (Lee and Murie, 1997; Brennan et al., 2000; Lupton and Power, 2002). In terms of ethnicity, poor neighbourhoods are not necessarily associated with any one ethnic group, although there is a notable concentration of the poorest minority ethnic groups, Pakistanis and Bangladeshis, in certain deindustrialized Northern English towns and cities (Byrne, 1998; Webster, 2003).

Poor places are constituted not only by a spatial concentration of poor people ('people poverty'), but also by the impact of the residential area itself on people's life chances, i.e. 'place poverty' (Powell et al., 2001). Typical characteristics of poor neighbourhoods include (Lupton and Power, 2002: 134):

- Poor physical environment (e.g. dumped cars)
- Inadequate private and public services (e.g. few shops, failing schools)
- Lack of sense of control and inclusion (e.g. sense of stigma because of area)
- Social disorganization (e.g. mistrust of neighbours)
- Social disorder (e.g. high crime).

An issue of continuing debate, in Britain, Europe and North America, is the extent to which there are additional effects from living in poor neighbourhoods which add to the disadvantages already experienced by their poor inhabitants (Friedrichs et al., 2005).

A British urban underclass?

A legitimate question is whether or not a parallel process of underclass formation, as arguably found in the ghettos of US cities, is underway in equivalent zones of urban marginality in Britain. Several potential candidates have been put forward for potential underclass status in Britain notably the unemployed, but also disadvantaged youth, as well as black and Asian minority ethnic groups (see *inter alia* Smith, 1992; Gallie, 1994b; Payne and Payne, 1994; Morris, 1995; Marshall et al., 1996; MacDonald, 1997; Buckingham, 1999; Pilkington, 2003; MacDonald and Marsh, 2005). With some exceptions (Buckingham, 1999; Roberts, 2001), there is widespread doubt regarding the evidence for underclass formation at the national level. The unemployed are not very different from employed low-skilled manual workers (Gallie, 1994b; Marshall et al., 1996). Black and Asian minority ethnic groups are far too heterogeneous, both economically and culturally, to constitute a singular 'underclass' (Pilkington, 2003).

At the same time, it has also been suggested that more credence *could* be given to the development of an underclass within specific localities and especially in the poorest neighbourhoods which suffer from multiple and overlapping processes of social exclusion (Payne and Payne, 1994; Blackman, 1997; Leonard, 1998a). Some writers have explicitly taken Wilson's ghetto underclass formulation and tried to directly apply it to social housing estates in British and European cities (Power, 1997; Page, 2000). Lash and Urry (1994), for example, suggest that black and white council tenants in Britain, as well as immigrants in Germany, occupy a parallel socio-structural position to African-Americans in the US ghetto. Saunders (1990) has also argued that council tenants in Britain constitute a self-reproducing underclass along housing tenure lines since their children are unlikely to be able to afford home ownership.

Despite this, the applicability of the North American ghetto underclass model to British cities remains questionable. Several in-depth analyses have been undertaken in various deprived urban areas including council housing estates, for example in Hartlepool (Morris, 1995) and Teeside (MacDonald and Marsh, 2000, 2005) in deindustrialized North East England, Belfast (Leonard, 1998a), as well as inner London (Watt, 1996, 2001, 2003) and outer London (Smith, 2005). These studies have found considerable poverty and various forms of social exclusion, including housing deprivation and homelessness, largely centering on combinations of joblessness and low-paid insecure work (see Chapter 7). They have not, however, revealed any qualitatively distinct underclass stratum: 'unemployment, job insecurity and underemployment have become common working-class experiences rather than the preserve of an underclass separated from and beneath them' (MacDonald and Marsh, 2000: 132). Moreover, Saunders' (1990) notion, that council tenants form a self-reproducing hereditary underclass, is challenged by evidence of significant rates of mobility out of council renting into owner occupation both within and across the generations (Savage et al., 1990; Watt, 1996). In comparing the situation in London as a whole with Wilson's (1996) findings in Chicago, Buck et al.

> ... did not find a major growth of the 'truly excluded' in London ... as found by Wilson in Chicago. He found that in large areas of the city there were very high concentrations of exclusion with all that that implied socially and economically. We did not find this, either from our statistical analyses of segregation or from our interviews. To be sure, the 'truly excluded' do exist in London – but on nothing like the scale that some imagine. (2002: 257)

Buck and colleagues emphasize how labour markets and housing markets in London are not as divided as they are in Chicago, primarily by race, while the welfare state, family and community relations are not as eroded as in Chicago.

Poverty and social exclusion in Europe

Since 1975 and the launch of the First Community Programme to Combat Poverty, there has been systematic research and policy concern with poverty at the European Union level. By the 1990s, the EU emphasis had shifted away from poverty towards the broader concept of social exclusion. This EU emphasis has contributed either directly or indirectly towards a large number of pieces of research which have attempted to assess the extent and causes of poverty and social exclusion within a European cross-national perspective (see *inter alia* Gallie and Paugam, 2000; Barnes et al., 2002; Chamberlayne et al., 2002; Eurostat, 2004; Apospori and Millar, 2003; Hammer, 2003b; Layte and Whelan, 2003; Steinart and Pilgrim, 2003; Berthoud, 2004; Fouarge and Layte, 2005). It is impossible here to do justice to this rich vein of comparative research and there are certainly different analytical emphases in all of these studies. However, the following propositions represent what can be regarded as a distillation of the main thrust of the findings, and they will provide the focus for the subsequent discussion in this section.

- Poverty and social exclusion (or at least exclusionary processes) are widespread across European societies.
- Poverty and exclusion vary by country at least partly according to the welfare state regime in place.
- Certain social groups are more at risk of poverty and exclusion than others.
- The degree of risk of poverty and exclusion among at-risk groups varies at least partly according to the welfare state regime in place.
- Poverty and exclusion have a spatial dimension based upon the concentration of at-risk groups in certain areas.

Poverty, social exclusion, welfare state regimes and at-risk groups in Europe

On the basis of European Community Household Panel survey data for 1999, Berthoud (2004) calculates that the average poverty rate across the EU is 16 per cent, using a measure of poverty at less than 60 per cent of national median income. However, this measure is taken at a single point in time so therefore does not take into account the dynamic nature of poverty. With reference to the latter, Fouarge and Layte (2005) found that one third of the EU population experienced poverty at least once during the 1994–98 period while 12 per cent were persistently poor across three consecutive years.

We saw in Table 6.2 on page 113 how the poverty rate varies between European countries, with a particularly high rate in the UK, the lowest rates among the Scandinavian countries and with France and Germany in-between. Table 6.5 provides data on poverty rates for 15 EU countries based on 60 per cent of national median income; it also shows the average poverty rate for the four welfare regime types (see above). As would be expected from Esping-Andersen's theory, the regime averages do indeed reflect the extent of decommodification with the lowest average poverty rate found among the Scandinavian social democratic countries of Sweden, Finland and Denmark, and the highest average among the liberal regime countries of the UK and Ireland. Welfare regimes influence both the extent and duration of poverty since, 'countries in the social democratic tradition do a better job of preventing both short- and long-term poverty. Countries in the liberal tradition and Southern European countries display much higher rates of poverty and longer durations of poverty spells, while countries in the corporatist tradition take an intermediate position' (Fouarge and Layte, 2005: 423).

Table 6.5   Poverty rates for EU countries using the 60% of
median threshold, 1999 (%)

Country	Poverty rate (%)
Denmark	13.3
Finland	16.0
Sweden	10.8
Average for social democratic regime type	12.7
Ireland	22.7
UK	19.4
Average for liberal regime type	19.5
Austria	15.4
Belgium	14.1
France	16.1
Germany	13.4
Luxembourg	12.2
Netherlands	10.9
Average for corporatist regime type	14.2
Greece	21.1
Italy	17.7
Portugal	22.8
Spain	17.8
Average for residual regime type	18.5

Source: adapted from Berthoud (2004: 14 Table 4.1)

Having noted the impact of welfare regimes, there are at least two caveats to make. Firstly, Berthoud (2004) suggests that the differences in poverty rates may also be accounted for by variations in national median incomes. Secondly, while the averages do indeed follow regime types as expected, there are also intra-regime variations. In particular, the Netherlands has a poverty rate of 10.9 per cent, which is considerably below the social democratic average and is close to the Swedish figure of 10.8 per cent. This possibly indicates the ambivalent position of the Netherlands within the corporatist regime, as mentioned above.

Across the EU, certain groups are at greater risk of poverty and social exclusion than others (Eurostat, 2002: 47–52), including:

■ Lone parents
■ The unemployed, especially the long-term unemployed
■ Ethnic minorities, especially migrants
■ Young adults, especially unemployed and/or unqualified youth
■ Retired people.

As noted above, the degree of risk of poverty and exclusion among at-risk groups is not constant across the EU, but instead varies at least partly according to the welfare state regime in place. In the following sections, we illustrate aspects of poverty and exclusion with reference to three at-risk groups: the unemployed, the young unemployed and migrants.

Unemployment and poverty

A transition from employment to unemployment leads to over three times the risk of becoming poor, while a move in the other direction, from unemployment to employment, improves the odds of leaving poverty by 1.5 times (Eurostat, 2002). However, at the same time there are also sharp cross-country differentials in the risk of poverty if an individual is unemployed (Gallie and Paugam, 2000; Eurostat, 2004; Gallie, 2004). Data from Eurostat (2004: 66) show that the average poverty rate in 1999 for the unemployed across all 15 EU countries was 39 per cent. However, this rate varied considerably from around half of the unemployed population in Ireland, Italy and the UK, compared to only around one in five in Austria, Sweden and the Netherlands, while a mere seven per cent of the Danish unemployed were poor. To what extent are these kinds of differentials in the unemployment poverty rate explained by welfare regimes? Hauser and Nolan (2000) considered this question with reference to eight European countries. From the mid-1980s to the mid-1990s, poverty among the unemployed increased between four to seven percentage points with the exception of Denmark where it remained at roughly the same low level. Hauser and Nolan found that universalistic Sweden, but more especially Denmark, managed to keep poverty among the unemployed at a low to medium level despite the difficult economic circumstances from the mid-1980s to mid-1990s. Among the three corporatist countries, France, Germany and the Netherlands, the latter had unemployment poverty rates similar to the countries with a universalistic welfare regime, while Germany protected a much smaller proportion of its unemployed against poverty. There was also considerable divergence among the two liberal welfare regime countries, Ireland and the UK, since the former managed to improve its unemployment poverty rate over the period in question while the UK experienced the worst deterioration in its relative position of all eight countries. Hauser and Nolan (2000: 45) conclude that:

> Neither the extent of poverty among the unemployed nor the changes of the poverty rates over time can be explained purely in terms of the social policies of the different countries, though these did clearly play a major role. Countries belonging to the same type of unemployment welfare regime were not homogenous.

Unemployment in Europe is a major contributory factor to poverty in both objective and subjective terms (Gallie and Paugam, 2004). Unemployment policies therefore play a major role in mediating this impact even if this mediation does not necessarily follow neatly along welfare regime types.

The young unemployed and social exclusion

Young people are particularly at risk from becoming socially excluded not least since their unemployment rate (16 per cent) within the European Union is over twice as high as for adults (7 per cent; figures for 2000). Researchers undertook a comparative study based on a standardized survey of nearly 17,000 young unemployed people aged 18–24 years old in 10 countries; the Youth Unemployment and Social Exclusion

Table 6.6 Unemployment rate and labour force participation for 15–24 year-olds in EU countries (%)

Country – year in brackets	Unemployment rate	Labour force participation
Denmark (1997)	8.1	74.2
Finland (1997)	25.3	44.6
France (2000)	20.7	29.5
Germany (2000)	7.7	52.5
Iceland (1997)	7.7	60.3
Italy (2000)	31.5	38.1
Norway (1997)	10.6	61.6
Spain (2000)	25.5	48.2
Sweden (1997)	21.0	50.2
UK (1998)*	12.3	69.5
European Union (2000)	15.6	48.3

Note: *this figure is for the UK as a whole, although the YUSE survey was undertaken in Scotland alone.
Source: OECD (in Hammer, 2003a: Table 1.1)

in Europe (YUSE) project (Hammer, 2003b). Eligible respondents had been unemployed for a period of at least three months during the previous six months. By the time interviews took place, some young people had either gone on to study or work while others remained unemployed. The choice of countries allows comparison of welfare state regimes. The unemployment and labour force participation rates among 15–24 year olds for each country are shown in Table 6.6.

Theoretically, the cross-national team were interested in unraveling both the objective and subjective dimensions of social exclusion; in other words not only young people's experiences of poverty or unemployment, but also what these experiences meant to them in terms of their values, attitudes and views about the future. One way of thinking about the various elements of exclusion is to contrast them to what 'social integration' might mean in an ideal type format (Box 6.4). Given the processual and multidimensional nature of social exclusion, the YUSE team also utilized an intermediate concept of 'marginalization'. This refers to the notion that some people may be excluded on some dimensions of social exclusion, but not all, which therefore means they are in an intermediate position between full integration and social exclusion. 'Marginalization' is particularly useful when discussing young people 'because the situation of young people can often be characterized as an intermediate position in which we know little about the final outcome' (Hammer, 2003a: 3).

Box 6.4   INTEGRATION VERSUS EXCLUSION: IDEAL TYPES

Social integration	**Social exclusion**
Employment/sporadic unemployment	Long-term unemployment
High employment commitment	Low employment commitment
Financial security	Financial insecurity

Optimism	Pessimism
Life satisfaction	Life dissatisfaction
High social support	Low social support
Active lifestyle	Passive lifestyle

Source: Furlong and Cartmel (2003: 30 Table 3.1)

The results from the YUSE survey are in many ways not what one might expect from pessimistic analyses in which young unemployed people are thought of as constituting a socially excluded 'underclass' (cf. MacDonald, 1997): 'the main finding of this study is that few young unemployed people were socially excluded, even in countries such as Italy or Spain with extremely high unemployment' (Hammer, 2003c: 207). However, the fact that social exclusion was not a major problem *per se*, did not mean that exclusionary processes (marginalization) were not in evidence. Across several countries, those young people who had experienced higher levels of economic deprivation were more likely to experience mental health difficulties such as depression or anxiety: 'the most important factor for predicting mental health among the young was economic hardship' (Alvaro and Garrido, 2003: 187). Those young people whose careers were dominated by unemployment were also likely to have slightly lower levels of sociability (Furlong and Cartmel, 2003).

Perhaps of greater significance than cross-country similarities, however, are the differences. Despite having low levels of aggregate unemployment, young people in Scotland experienced more difficult labour market careers, including long-term unemployment, while their own financial difficulties were compounded by unemployment and deprivation among their parents. Their subjective sense of wellbeing was also lower than other countries while they had lower levels of political activity. In contrast, although young people in Spain and Italy experienced a high level of unemployment, this did not necessarily translate into marginalization because they tended to live at home and were supported by their parents. This indicates the relevance of the four-fold welfare regime typology discussed above. Spanish and Italian youth live in a residual welfare system in which they derive considerable parental support, whereas Scottish youth in a liberal regime received neither strong parental nor state support. Unsurprisingly, the best situation, from the standpoint of lower levels of marginalization, was experienced by Danish youth living in the Scandinavian social democratic welfare regime. They had the shortest periods of unemployment as well as the highest probability of re-employment, plus low levels of financial deprivation and 'a higher level of wellbeing than their counterparts in the other countries' (Hammer, 2003c: 208). Nevertheless, the relative success of the Scandinavian universalistic welfare system in preventing social exclusion is tempered by the case of Finland. The young unemployed in Finland displayed economic and social similarities to their Scottish counterparts, including high levels of poverty and deprivation as well as reporting lower levels of mental wellbeing and political activity. The unemployment rate for Finnish young people is particularly high, while the coverage of unemployment benefits is not universal because it does not cover first-time job seekers who receive a minimal income similar to their Scottish counterparts. The example of young people in Finland illustrates how one must be careful in reading off social circumstances from welfare regime typologies given the way that different countries can discriminate on the basis of age, as well as gender and ethnicity.

There are methodological criticisms that can be made of the YUSE findings. As Hammer acknowledges, the study is based on only those young people who were actually registered as unemployed. Those not registered may well face considerably worse situations. The use of a standardized questionnaire delivered via post or telephone may also not be the best method to either access or capture the experiences of vulnerable young people for whom qualitative methods may be more appropriate (MacDonald, 1997; MacDonald and Marsh, 2005).

In-depth biographical interviews were used in the SOSTRIS (Social Strategies in a Risk Society) cross-national exclusion project and one of the groups at risk of social exclusion was unqualified and unemployed youth (Chamberlayne et al., 2002). Box 6.6 illustrates an example of their findings, analyzed by Spano (2002), based on Franco, an unemployed young man from Naples.[35] Italy is included in the Southern European residual regime, which has minimal unemployment support but strong family support. As we saw from the YUSE findings, young people in Italy were not at high risk of social exclusion because of family support. However, Spano (2002) is more critical and emphasizes how Franco's narrative illustrates the increased sense of uncertainty and risk characteristic of social conditions under late modernity (Beck, 1992; Sennett, 1998). In Franco's case, what is particularly lacking is the collective fraternity which is no longer to be found under post-Fordist social conditions.

Box 6.5 **CASE STUDY OF A YOUNG UNEMPLOYED ITALIAN LIVING IN NAPLES (SPANO, 2002)**

Franco is a 19 year-old unemployed Italian who comes from a hard-working family in Naples; his father is a driver for a public transport operator. Following a dispute at school, Franco is suspended from school. His mother gives him the option of returning to school or going to work and he chose work. He then embarks on a series of jobs, ranging from assistant mechanic, flower seller to bar work, which he abandons in the search for higher pay or fewer hours. Eventually he became a painter for a construction firm, a job he want to do with high wage prospects, but the irregular nature of the work and the unscrupulousness of his employers meant that he wound up not being paid for the hours he worked. He considers crime and starts selling hash, but he desists from this because of his family background which had instilled in him the values of honesty. At the age of 19, he was unemployed, with no girlfriend and no long-term prospects:

The 'permanent job' his father managed to find after years of uncertainly now seems like a mirage – you would have to be mad to still want that. Everyone agrees that the era of mass hiring in local/state administrations, used as a social cushion against unemployment, has come to a definite end. The days of the 'movement of organized unemployed', which once allowed many Neapolitans to find stable work, are long gone. The possibility of learning a job is also lost forever: who would ever dream of taking him on as an apprentice? No one, since employers prefer to take on 14- or 15-year-olds, who are satisfied with only 50,000 lire a week. (Spano, 2002: 69)

Franco spends his days getting up at midday, going to the local café for lunch, having a lie down at home, having dinner at home in the evening, and then hanging around outside the café again with his friends until midnight and time to return home.

We go on to examine further examples of qualitative approaches to social exclusion when we discuss the situation of disadvantages young people in North East England in Chapter 7

Migrants

A prominent 'at-risk' group is made up of ethnic minorities, but especially immigrants, refugees and asylum seekers (Bommes and Geddes, 2000; Chamberlayne et al., 2002; Steinart and Pilgrim, 2003; Morissens and Sainsbury, 2005). The conditions of entry of migrants, whether legal or illegal for example, can affect social exclusionary processes, but these also interact with national welfare regimes and labour markets in complex ways.[36] For example, Karazman-Morawetz and Ronneling (2003) found that although illegal migrants in Vienna were excluded from Austrian welfare benefits and services, they could gain employment in the informal sector doing 'off the books' work in an increasingly flexible labour market. By contrast, migrants in Stockholm were legally included and entitled to a range of welfare services and benefits, but they found it extremely difficult to gain access to employment as a result of non-recognition of their qualifications from their countries of origin plus their limited capacity in the Swedish language.[37] This downgrading of qualifications and ultimately class position is illustrated in Box 6.7 based on biographical research by Breckner (2002) from the SOSTRIS project. Although Breckner is concerned not to label all migrants as a 'social problem', her account does illustrate the exclusionary processes affecting migrants in a society which in many ways is more egalitarian than most. Thus even though the Scandinavian social democratic regime seems to provide a level and type of state welfare support that ameliorates and even prevents certain kinds of social exclusion, this does not mean to say that it necessarily inhibits all kinds of exclusionary processes, notably in relation to immigrants (Palme et al., 2002) and especially immigrant women (Knocke, 1999).[38] As mentioned in Chapter 1, the 'feminization of migration' in Europe means that female migrants are subject to specific exclusionary processes as a result of gender inequalities in welfare regimes, labour markets and households (Kofman et al., 2000; Freedman, 2003). We discuss these issues further in Chapter 7 when we come to examine paid domestic employment, an important avenue of employment for migrant women in global cities.

> ## Box 6.6   CASE STUDY OF A BOSNIAN REFUGEE LIVING
> ## IN SWEDEN (BRECKNER, 2002)
>
> Ana was a married 32 year-old Bosnian refugee living in Gothenburg in Sweden. She came from a well-off background, was a graduate and worked as an economist at an import/export company in Bosnia-Herzegovina. The outbreak of war shattered Ana's comfortable life, not least because she was in a 'mixed marriage' since her husband was Serbian. With the help of the Red Cross, Ana escaped to Sweden, a country she has spent holidays in when she was younger. Her husband, mother-in-law and brother followed her, but her parents remained. For the first three years, Ana and her family lived in Varmland as refugees. She learned Swedish and tried, unsuccessfully, to get a job. Following the birth of a second child, Ana and the family moved to Gothenburg in 1995. Neither she, nor her husband, could find regular employment there, however. Ana worked as a cleaner and was attending a course for foreign economists, while her husband, a trained technician, was trying to find work as a taxi driver. They were seeking Swedish citizenship so they could visit Ana's parents in Bosnia, or alternatively so as her parents could come to Sweden. Ana's previous dynamic career and stable life were effectively destroyed:
>
> > 'She now found herself in an uncertain present in Sweden, where she could hardly continue life 'as usual'. This was impossible not least because she was professionally and socially downgraded to the lowest level of the labour market. In addition, her own and her family's future were anything but clear, their attempts to acquire citizenship being stuck in a transitional stage, and her parents still stuck in a threatening war situation'. (Breckner, 2002: 218)

The spatial dimension of poverty and social exclusion

One of the key characteristics of both poverty and social exclusion across European societies is that they have a spatial dimension. As we saw in Chapter 5, this dimension reflects the concomitant hardening of spatial divisions as well as social divisions across western societies, which received extreme form in the shape of the ghetto underclass in the United States (Chapter 5). In continental Europe, attention has focused both on older inner city areas plus the newer peripheral housing estates (Wacquant, 1996; Power, 1997; Byrne, 1999; Marcuse and Van Kempen, 2000a).

Wacquant (1996) has made a direct comparison between the North American ghetto (the Black Belt) and the French suburban housing estates, the banlieues (the Red Belt). This comparison is based on his research in the Woodlawn neighbourhood on the South Side of Chicago, and the Quatre mille, a public housing estate located in the Parisian suburb of La Courneuve. Wacquant names the banlieues the 'Red Belt', referring to the way that the outer suburbs of Paris were characterized by dense networks of working-class organizations in the form of trade unions and the Communist Party during the post-war Fordist period. With deindustrialization and the collapse of male manufacturing jobs, the banlieues around Paris and other French cities have achieved increasing notoriety as zones of social disorder centering on 'lawless' minority ethnic youth who periodically clash with the police (Hargreaves, 1996; Power, 1997). At the time of writing, the banlieues, including La Courneuve, experienced a wave of riots that spread out from Paris to several French cities ('Chirac vows to restore order as riots erupt for eleventh night', *The Independent*, 7 November 2005: 1–2).

Wacquant argues that the banlieue and the ghetto share certain features in common, not least a 'powerful territorial stigma' attached to living in such a place (1996: 237). This stigma results from the poverty and crime that affects the residents in each area: 'they are publicly regarded as dangerous places where delinquency and crime are prevalent, where the rule of law applies but very imperfectly, and that one should shun if at all possible, (1996: 245). Both areas are also perceived as being socially disorganized. However, Wacquant argues that despite these similarities, often ones of perception rather than reality, the Black Belt and Red Belt represent *'different socio-spatial formations, produced by different institutional logics of segregation and aggregation and resulting in significantly higher levels of blight, poverty and hardship in the ghetto'* (1996: 237; original emphasis; see Table 6.7). It would seem that although European societies have experienced similar economic restructuring to the United States, they have not produced equivalent pathologies to those associated with the American inner city.

If the extent and depth of wealth and income inequalities in the United States were underlying factors in creating the extreme social conditions of the inner-city ghetto, another is the extent of racial segregation (Fainstein, 1998; Kaufman, 1998). Comparative studies of ethnic segregation suggest that levels of segregation for African-Americans are far higher than those found among minority ethnic groups in British cities (Peach, 1996). Peach concludes that although ethnic enclaves exist in Britain, they do not take the 'ghetto' form as found in the cities of the United States. Musterd (2003) has compared ethnic segregation in 17 major Northern European and North American cities. Although segregation was significant for certain groups in some European cities, for example Moroccans in Brussels and Asians in London and Birmingham, the highest levels were found for blacks in the major US cities. The intensity of racial segregation and disadvantage in American cities combined with the intensity of poverty and paucity of welfare provision are therefore qualitatively different from the circumstances that can be found in European cities (Musterd and Ostendorf, 1998; Marcuse and Van Kempen, 2000a). The social conditions facing African-Americans living in the 'excluded ghettos' of the major US cities appear, thus far, to be unique: 'only in the United States can we find the awkward combination of economic developments that lead to structural unemployment with racism, and with a private market ideology which in combination legitimate the exclusion of the poor and the concomitant restricted influence of the state' (Marcuse and Van Kempen, 2000b: 261).

Conclusion: towards a liberal welfare convergence?

We have seen how inequality and poverty remain stubbornly resilient features of the landscape in the 'affluent' capitalist societies of Europe and North America. If

Table 6.7 Two socio-spatial formations: the working-class French *banlieue* and the North American ghetto

Aspect of exclusion	French banlieue	American ghetto
Stigma		
Source of stigma	Residential	Racial and residential
Ability to shed stigma	Possible for leaving the territory of the banlieue	Virtually impossible
Subjective impact of stigma on residents	Heightened because of unitarist notion of French citizenship	Lessened because of historical depth and pervasiveness of racial division and American individualist ideology
Crime and insecurity		
Main public safety issue	Petty theft, vandalism	Murder, assault, rape, hand guns, criminal gangs
Public violence	Low	Extremely high
Homicide level	Virtually non-existent: 1.2 per 100,000	Extremely high: 100 per 100,000
Extent and type of drug dealing	Marginal – small quantities of marijuana and opiates in retail	Extensive – heroin and cocaine derivatives for mass market
Common crimes	Car thefts, petty robberies	Homicide
Social organization		
State involvement	Major and multisided, but stigmatized	Virtually non-existent on social welfare front, strong on the penal front
Public health, education and welfare facilities	Extensive, of mixed quality	Limited, of very poor quality
Housing stock	Sections are dilapidated but subject to urban rehabilitation programme	Old, dilapidated, high levels of abandonment in the form of burnt out or boarded up buildings
Cultural facilities	Extensive but limited for young people and insufficient relative to demand	Virtually non-existent
Economy	Wage labour economy low to moderate – high level of unemployment	Wage labour economy superseded by informal and illegal economies
Social divisions		
Sources of exclusion	Class primary, aggravated by ethnicity/immigrant status, but mitigated by state	Race primary and reinforced by class and state
Major fault-line	Age – young v. old	Racial – black v. white
Ethnic mix	Heterogeneous – French and diverse immigrant groups	Homogenous – African-American population

Source: based on Wacquant (1996).[39]

anything, these features have worsened during the last 30 years alongside economic restructuring and neo-liberal welfare policies. Increased poverty is intertwined with class, gender, age and ethnicity inequalities to form new complex patterns and processes of social exclusion. A cross-national perspective based on welfare regime theory can help to illuminate the differential nature of poverty and social exclusion, even if the explanatory 'fit' between regime type on the one hand and poverty and exclusion on the other is by no means always symmetrical.

One major problem with using welfare regime typologies is that they can become out-of-date given the rapid pace of contemporary social change including that within welfare states themselves. Any typology can therefore ossify into a static way of understanding dynamic welfare systems that are in various stages of transition, restructuring and reform (Alcock and Craig, 2001; Clarke et al., 2001). As Esping-Andersen (1999) admits, the three worlds typology emerged out of the 'Golden Age' of post-war welfare capitalism, a phase that has effectively come to an end via the emergence of post-industrial economies. To what extent, therefore, can welfare state typologies accommodate the more recent changes associated with advanced capitalist societies, notably deindustrialization, globalization, the feminization of the workforce, declining fertility rates, aging populations and increased immigration, to name just some of the most significant (Esping-Andersen, 1996, 1999, 2002; Mishra, 1999; Alcock and Craig, 2001; Clarke et al., 2001)?

It has been suggested by some commentators that the European 'social model', in either its social democratic or conservative variants, is struggling to compete under conditions of increased global competitiveness that require the introduction of flexible, deregulated labour markets with far less state provision and protection mechanisms (Hemerijck, 2002). Even that bastion of Scandinavian social democracy, Sweden, abandoned its full employment policy and introduced cuts in its previously generous state benefits and welfare programmes under pressure from Swedish business responding to globalization (Wilks, 1996; Mishra, 1999; Ginsburg, 2001; Palme et al., 2002). Thus instead of 'decommodification', one can point to the 'recommodification' of welfare across many contemporary European welfare states (Murie, 1998; Gray, 2004). European Union policies, notably the deflationary goals inherent in the Maastricht Treaty and European Monetary Union, are furthermore exacerbating such recommodification trends (Burkitt and Baimbridge, 1995). As Gray (2004) argues, the widespread pursuit of 'workfare' policies by European governments to pressurize the unemployed into taking low-paid jobs also contributes towards the recommodification of welfare. Such trends will lead to increased socio-economic inequalities and a reduction in the levels of state welfare provision that continental Western Europeans have grown to expect in the post-war period. At the extreme, this could lead to a liberal convergence in welfare state regimes towards the model of market-based welfare and residual public provision dominant in the United States.

Debates about welfare state restructuring are often bound up with ideological arguments about whether welfare *ought* to be delivered by the state or the market or the family, in other words traditional debates between socialists, liberals and conservatives. Without wishing to engage with this debate here, there are nevertheless several grounds for thinking that a liberal convergence has not, thus far, occurred. While the 'European social model' in both its social democratic and conservative guises is experiencing a degree of strain, both from globalization and from neo-liberal political advocates of globalization, it is far from clear that it is exhausted as a viable alternative to the liberal model represented by the United States (Mishra, 1999; Esping-Andersen, 2002; Hemerijck, 2002). Despite globalization rhetoric from the left as well as the right, cross-national studies of poverty, social exclusion and labour markets indicate that there is considerable variation along welfare regime lines, as seen above (Mishra, 1999; Gray, 2004).[40] Moreover European and United States' models of welfare are deeply rooted in long-standing differences in political institutions and ideologies which are themselves linked to divergent historical trajectories and demographic differences (Alesina and Glaeser, 2004). If there has been a liberal welfare state restructuring, this has gone further in some European countries than others, notably Britain since the 1970s, a country which has also experienced extensive labour market deregulation (Mishra, 1999; Lewis, 2002; Gray, 2004). These factors have undoubtedly contributed towards the widening socio-economic inequality and poverty that has been so prominent in Britain compared with other Western European countries. Whether this widening inequality and liberal restructuring is now being reversed under New Labour (Hills and Stewart, 2005) or whether Blairism represents the 'Trojan horse of Americanization', as Wacquant suggests (cited in Gray, 2004: 154), threatening the European social model from within, are matters of considerable sociological and political import.

Further reading

For useful edited collections on the changing nature of welfare states in a cross-national framework which draw upon regime theory see Esping-Andersen (1996), Alcock and Craig (2001), and Cochrane et al. (2001). One highly relevant study from the standpoint of the themes raised in both this and the following chapter is by Zuberi (2006) on hotel workers in Seattle and Vancouver; in this book he demonstrates how cross-national variations in social policy make a profound difference to the lives of the working poor. Byrne (1999) represents a vigorous attempt to analyze social exclusion in relation to contemporary processes of economic restructuring by drawing upon the Marxist reserve army of labour theory. Mingione (1996) contains several important articles on urban poverty, social exclusion and the underclass. Appelbaum et al. (2003) is an excellent edited book which examines a wide range of low-wage industries and occupations in the United States and gives due consideration to the roles of employers and unions. Hills and Stewart (2005) is an up-to-date audit on the impact of New Labour on poverty, exclusion and inequality in Britain. See Body-Gendrot and Martiniello (2000) for an insightful analysis of the multi-faceted nature of social exclusion at the neighbourhood level in relation to migrants in European cities.

For social exclusion in Britain, see the Social Exclusion Unit website at http://www.socialexclusion.gov.uk/. URBEX (The Spatial dimensions of Urban Social Exclusion and Integration: A European Comparison) is an excellent cross-national urban studies research project examining social exclusion in several European countries and cities – the downloadable reports can be found at http://www2.fmg.uva.nl/urbex/.

CHAPTER SEVEN

New Work and
New Workers

Introduction

As we have seen in previous chapters, there are grounds for arguing that a novel form of flexible capitalism has developed, a 'new economy' characterized by greater insecurity and risk, short-termism, non-standardized employment patterns and disidentification with work itself (Sennett, 1998; Beck, 2000; Smith, 2001). This 'new work' has penetrated the middle classes, as we saw in Chapter 5, but many of the negative characteristics associated with this new work are most acutely experienced by those employed at the lower end of the labour market in low-skilled and low-paid jobs (Allen and Henry, 1997). Although some of these jobs are in the manufacturing sector, as seen in sweatshops, increasing proportions are in post-industrial service jobs, sometimes referred to as 'McJobs'. Many of the employees in these types of jobs are female, while young people and minority ethnic groups are also well represented. Our focus in this chapter is on the new forms of work in contemporary post-industrial societies and on the 'new workers' who carry it out.

We begin with the archetypal post-industrial 'McJob', the burger flipper, focusing on the role played by fast food restaurant employment in New York City. We then move on to examine another major recent growth area of post-industrial employment, call centres. We summarize debates about what kind of work employment in call centres involves and we also consider forms of worker resistance in call centres, both informal and formal via trade union organization. Another recent development in 'new work' has been the increase in the (very old) sector of paid domestic work typically under-taken by migrant women in the homes of the metropolitan middle classes. We exam-ine reasons for this expansion and also provide an illustration of such employment based on research into Filipina paid domestic workers in Los Angeles and Rome. Some of this paid domestic labour takes place on a cash-in-hand basis and in the following section we examine informal economic activity. Finally, we examine work and leisure activities among young people in North East England. This restructured region, once noted for its heavy industry, is now dominated by post-industrial service employment. We outline two main approaches to young people in British sociology, youth transi-tions and cultural studies, and look at exemplars of these based on ethnographic research.

New work

We have indicated in previous chapters how the various dimensions of the new work are predicated on a shift from an industrial manufacturing-based economy, in which males dominated paid employment, towards a service-based economy in which the pro-portion of women in paid employment has increased, i.e. a feminization of the labour market. Many of the expanding employment areas, in caring, cleaning and serving, are those which have traditionally been undertaken by women (Crompton, 1997).

Other aspects of the new work include, firstly, a reduction in standard employ-ment, where employers provide a full-time contract, and an increase in 'non-standard' forms of employment or what Beynon (1997: 31) has called 'hyphenated workers': 'part-time workers, temporary-workers, casual-, even self-employed workers'. This has been seen as part of the move towards a 'flexible' workforce which is something that management gurus have trumpeted. There has been considerable scepticism expressed about the notion of 'flexibility' *per se*, both about whether it involves a radical break with the past, and especially about its supposed benefits for workers (Pollert, 1991). Certainly one should be wary of assuming that the move towards non-standard employment is as all-encompassing as argued by Beck's (2000: 2) 'Brazilianization of the West' thesis in which he warns that 'attractive, highly skilled and well-paid full-time employment is on its way out'. Some forms of non-standard employment seem to have expanded more than others in Britain. Thus whereas part-time employment and self-employment have increased substantially during the last 20 years, the expan-sion in temporary employment is relatively modest in comparison (Gallie et al., 1998; Bradley et al., 2000). The 2003 Labour Force Survey indicated that non-permanent employment (fixed-term, casual and agency working) had increased by only two per cent from 1988 to stand at seven per cent in total (cited in Worth, 2005). This total is less than in many other European countries (Gray, 2004). However, there are sig-nificant age and sectoral differences in Britain whereby non-standard employment is substantially higher among young people and in the public sector (Conley, 2002;

Worth, 2005), as well as among the jobs that the unemployed are likely to enter (Gray, 2004).

Secondly, there is evidence that the British labour market is polarizing, generating more well-paid, high-skilled 'MacJobs' but also more badly paid, low-skilled 'McJobs' (Goos and Manning, 2003). The former MacJobs (signified by Apple Macintosh) are those in the professions and management, whereas the latter McJobs (signified by McDonald's) can be found in several industries, but many are in the expanding private service sectors such as retailing, hotels and catering, personal services and call centres. Low pay is not randomly distributed, as indicated in Box 7.1.

Box 7.1 WHICH WORKERS ARE MORE LIKELY TO BE LOW PAID THAN OTHERS IN BRITAIN?

Those in certain social categories – women, ethnic minorities, young people, people with low levels of qualifications, people with little work experience, long-term sick and disabled, older people.

Those employed in certain industries – textiles, hotels and catering, retail, residential care, agriculture.

Those working in particular occupations – cleaners, sewing machinists, waiters, bar staff, sales assistants, check-out operators, hairdressers, catering assistants, security guards.

Those employed on non-standard contracts (part-time, temporary) *or in non-standard environments* (for example, homeworkers).

Sources: Brown and Scase (1991), Stewart (1999), McKnight (2002), Goos and Manning (2003).

Thirdly, as we saw in Chapter 4, Sennett (1998) has given expression to the insecurity that has permeated work in the new capitalism, as the short-term is the only time frame that matters and occupation no longer provides a coherent sense of identity. While greater insecurity has affected professional workers (Burchell, 2002), the negative impact of heightened risks and uncertainties is more severe on those at the bottom of service labour markets in low-paid, non-standard jobs, as Allen and Henry found in their study of contract labour in the cleaning, catering and security industries: 'employment risk is something which traps, whereas for those with tradeable skills higher up the income scale, risk may open up more opportunities than it closes down' (1997: 194). There is also a noticeable synergy between job insecurity and unemployment at the lower end of the labour market as the unemployed are far more likely to re-enter paid work via a temporary job; whereas the latter constitute nearly seven per cent of all jobs, they represent one in five jobs taken by unemployed people in the UK (Gray, 2004: 125). As Gray argues, given the lack of promotion prospects inherent in such 'bad jobs', many of the unemployed who take them go back onto 'the dole' after the job has ended. Many temporary jobs are also low paid, and hence this contributes towards the 'low-pay/no-pay cycle' that we highlighted in Chapter 6.

Fourthly, although trade unions were an important feature of the post-war manual working class, as we saw in Chapters 3 and 4, union membership and density have fallen dramatically since the late 1970s in most European and North American societies (Western, 1997; Visser, 2002). Along with Ireland, the UK experienced one of the largest declines in union density during the 1980s consequent upon rapid deindustrialization plus vigorous anti-union legislation (Western, 1997: 24). At its peak in 1979, there were over 13 million union members in the United Kingdom, but during the following two decades there was a haemorrhaging of 5.5 million members (Metcalf, 2003). By 2002, union density among employees was down to 29 per cent, but this was far higher in the public sector (three in five) compared to the private sector (less than one in five): 'union members are now disproportionately well educated and in professional, often public sector, occupations' (Metcalf, 2003: 170). The contrast between the post-war period, when trade unions had a firm base, not only in male manufacturing and extractive industries but also in the surrounding community, as in mining villages (Dennis et al., 1956), could not be stronger. The challenge facing unions in Britain is a daunting one:

> ... the growth areas of the economy – business and personal services, retail and distribution, hospitality and leisure – and the growing workforces associated with them – women, minority ethnic workers, part-time and agency staff – are those least associated with trade union organization. Unless they find new ways to appeal to at least some of these private sector service workers, trade unions look set to continue their steady decline. (Wills, 2005a: 139)

As noted above, the growth areas of the economy are also those that are producing the low-paid McJobs that are less likely to be unionized. In the following chapter, we will see that there are signs of renewal and resurgence among unions, especially in the United States.

In conclusion, we can see that there has been a considerable shift in the patterns of work. Whilst the changes are by no means monopolized by those at the lower end of the labour market, it is those same workers who have the least resources to cushion themselves against any 'risks' if, or rather when, they occur. As we saw in Chapter 6, low-paid post-industrial jobs are not evenly distributed geographically since their prevalence varies according to the welfare regime in operation. At the aggregate level they are more prevalent in societies with liberal welfare regimes and flexible labour markets, such as the United States and Britain, rather than in continental European societies (Esping-Andersen, 1993, 1996). The flexible de-regulated labour markets of the United States and Britain have encouraged the expansion of low-paid jobs, both in the formal and informal sectors, and many of these jobs are to be found in global and globalizing cities (see Chapter 5). However, there are also trends towards 'flexibiliza-tion' of employment patterns across EU countries, as seen in the growth of temporary employment contracts, as well as increased state pressure on the unemployed to take up such work 'opportunities' via the importation of North American style 'workfare' policies (Gray, 2004). Gray has provided an impressive critique of the way EU governments are falling into line with employers' demands to have more flexible and cheap labour forces, along North American lines, and thereby create more jobs:

> The 'flexibilisation' of labour markets impacts most on those with least bargaining power as individuals – the low-paid, less well-educated and less experienced workers. 'Flexibilisation', for them, means an intensification of exploitation – *flexploitation'* (2004: 3; original emphasis).

In what follows, we will see various aspects of this growing flexibilization and flexploitation of new workers in a variety of socio-spatial contexts.

Fast food workers – flipping burgers in the globally branded restaurant

If the Ford Motor Company was the archetypal exemplar of industrial production, McDonald's, the fast food franchisee, is the archetypal post-industrial corporation. Currently it employs over two million people in 18 countries. Four new McDonald's restaurants are opened every day somewhere on the planet, and it aims to have 50,000 restaurants by 2010, doubling its 2000 figure (Royle and Towers, 2002a). While McDonald's is the largest fast food company, the industry as a whole represents a significant chunk of the global economy containing many multinational corporations with familiar high street brands such as KFC, Pizza Hut and Burger King. It's estimated that there are 2.5 million fast food workers in the United States (Leidner, 2002), while seven of the largest fast food operators in the European Union employ over half a million workers (Royle and Towers, 2002a). As Royle and Towers note, the success of the fast food companies is achieved at the cost of workers' rights, pay levels and employment conditions:

> The key to the success of fast-food revolves around limited menus and highly standardized product offerings, which permit the use of low skilled and easily replaceable labour. Fast-food companies are at the vanguard of companies demanding ever more 'flexibility' of working conditions and have frequently been involved in lobbying governments to introduce lower rates of pay for young workers. (2002a: 1–2)

Although there have been some successful bids for union recognition in continental European countries, labour relations in the fast-food industry in both the UK and United States are characterized by either no or very limited trade union involvement; in fact, no union recognition has been achieved in the UK (Royle and Towers, 2002b). In examining the fast food industry and its workers, we will refer to two ethnographic studies, both undertaken in New York City (Newman, 1999; Talwar,

2004). These studies took place at non-unionized globally branded restaurants at which, as Talwar (2004: 203, n4) notes, labour costs are substantially less than at independent unionized restaurants.

Katherine Newman's focus in *No Shame in My Game* (1999) is on the working poor in ghetto areas. The book is based on interviews with 200 fast food workers employed in four 'Burger Barn' restaurants in Harlem, as well as around 100 interviews with rejected workers plus participant observation. The interviewees were either African-Americans or Latinos, mainly Dominicans. The employees were often burger-flippers, the emblematic low-wage job. Newman's main point is that many African-American and Latino inner-city residents are not on 'welfare', the curse of all decent Americans, but are actually employed in entry-level jobs for poverty pay for years on end. In other words, the value system of many ghetto-dwellers is not so dissimilar from that of 'middle Americans'; the main difference lies in their economic conditions.

Nationally, fast food work is predominantly female and often undertaken by young people. However, in Harlem 70 per cent of Newman's sample were over 19 and half were male. Although Hispanics made up around half of the fast food workforce, with blacks the other half, there were no white workers at all. At the same time, African-Americans also had a greater risk of being rejected for jobs in comparison with Latinos. One point emphasized by Newman is that the burger flippers in Harlem often lived in households in which one or more members are on welfare. In other words, the polarity between welfare-dependent households and employed households is not necessarily clear-cut. Instead, the problems identified by Newman were that the fast food workers' wages were simply not high enough to raise them out of poverty, while their limited social networks and qualifications meant that they were unlikely to experience any major upward mobility. Nevertheless, Newman thought that the McJobs her respondents had did offer some benefits. For example, they allowed them to gain a range of work-relevant skills such as inventory management, team working and people skills. Importantly the workers themselves demonstrated the value of work and as such maintained a strong belief in the American Dream of individual achievement via hard work. Although the working poor had to negotiate the day-to-day hazards of living in ghetto neighbourhoods, including gangs, violence and drugs, their presence guaranteed an alternative value structure for young people growing up in such conditions.

As we mentioned in Chapter 6, a key question in relation to the working poor is whether or not they are able to move out of poverty over time. During the 18 months of her research, Newman found that only a small number managed to 'move up', in some cases to management-level positions in the fast food business and others to better jobs outside the industry. Public sector jobs have played a key role in raising black employment prospects in many US cities (Fainstein, and Fainstein, 1996) and it is noteworthy that many of the parents of the Burger Barn workers worked at such unionized jobs in New York. Getting one of these diminishing number of 'union jobs', with benefits and health insurance, was a goal among some of the young burger flippers.

Newman went back to interview a sub-sample of her original respondents four years after the original research (Newman and Lennon, 2004). By this time, in the late

1990s, urban labour markets had tightened and there were more job opportunities available even in areas like Harlem despite the fact that it still had above average unemployment levels. However, contrary to negative expectations, Newman and Lennon (2004) reported that among both the 'hires' and 'rejects' from the original sample, the majority were in employment, they had gained substantially more education, and they had also moved towards independent living arrangements. However, those employed in 1993–4 were significantly more likely to be employed four years later than the original 'rejects'. Among those in work, Newman and Lennon found substantial improvements in wage rates, since nearly half of the sample had 'clearly moved up, earning higher wages' (2004: 126). Around 28 per cent earned $5 an hour or more than they did originally and so had 'truly broken free' from low-wage jobs. Many of these were fast food workers who had been internally promoted into managerial positions. At the same time, Newman and Lennon note the worrying position of those who were unemployed or still working in low-wage jobs in the late 1990s.

In *Fast Food, Fast Track*, Jennifer Talwar (2004) paints a more pessimistic picture than Newman and Lennon. She undertook ethnographic research at seven fast food restaurants in three neighbourhoods of New York City: Chinatown in Manhattan, the 'Little Dominican Republic' in Washington Heights, and Downtown Brooklyn. She found a massively diverse ethnic workforce made up largely of immigrants from a variety of countries, but especially from the Dominican Republic, China and the West Indies. Most workers lived outside the neighbourhood the restaurant was located in, necessitating lengthy commutes from similar ethnically mixed poor neighbourhoods, 'the ghetto you don't know' (Newman, 1999: 239), which suited both employers and employees:

- Employers did not want the workers' friends coming in as customers and expecting free meals.
- Employees wished to avoid managers' distrust regarding the 'friends' issue, and they also sought to avoid the stigma associated with being a 'burger flipper', a stigma that would have been exacerbated by working in a neighbourhood where people knew them.

Box 7.2 UPWARD AND HORIZONTAL MOVEMENT IN FAST FOOD

Socially mobile working class – Fabiola is a 24-year-old assistant manager at McDonald's from the Dominican Republic. She began working at McDonald's when she was 18 and moved up the management chain via gaining additional qualifications. Her husband is also a fast food manager. They live with their one-year-old son at Fabiola's parents' apartment in the Bronx. Fabiola can only work because her mother, who is retired, looks after her son.

The new poor – Marco is a 35-year-old crew member at Burger King from Cuba. He is an ex-Marine who has moved around from one low-wage job to another. Lacking a college degree, Marco has little real prospect of moving into management. He is divorced and shares an apartment with a stranger. Although he works most days, he struggles to pay his share of the rent. Without parental support in times of crisis, Marco would be in danger of living on the streets.

Source: adapted from Talwar (2004: 175–6 and 180–1)

While noting that some of the managers she interviewed had moved up from being burger flippers themselves, Talwar also comments that the average fast food manager's salary is relatively low and does not necessarily guarantee independent living (see *Fabiola* in Box 7.2). Furthermore, without additional support from family, it was difficult for crew members to gain training or educational experience because of the unpredictable hours, lengthy commutes and low wages.[41] Workers such as Marco (Box 7.2) were therefore engaged in 'horizontal mobility' as they cycled between a series of low-wage jobs:

> ... the amount of job experience one accumulates at the bottom rungs of the service and retail economy has little influence on vertical mobility in the service and retail sectors at large. No matter how many years of experience they had, or how many jobs they had previously held, my employee respondents began working every new job at the entry level, and, by and large, at minimum wage. (Talwar, 2004: 181)

Talwar highlights how employers preferred immigrants to Americans because they were thought to have 'less attitude'. Thus although foreign-born West Indians were sought after by managers in the Brooklyn restaurants, African-Americans were not.[42] The latter were at the end of the 'hiring queue' of sought-after workers, as Newman (1999) also found in Harlem. This exclusionary process contributes towards the overall disadvantages faced by African-Americans in urban labour markets (Waldinger and Lichter, 2003), as well as their supposed ghetto 'underclass' status (see Chapter 5).

--------- **Call centres – taking calls in the interactive service factory** ---------

The massive and rapid expansion in call centre operations and in the numbers employed in them has been one of the main developments within the changing nature of employment in Western Europe and North America during the 1990s and beyond. This expansion has meant that call centres have been subject to a great deal of media and political speculation as well as academic attention in their short lives (Glucksmann, 2004). Call centres were first used in Britain during the late 1980s in the financial services industry and then later spread with amazing rapidity to telecommunications and consumer products. During the 1990s, they were widely regarded as the post-industrial panacea for manufacturing job losses in deindustrializing regions, and they have certainly been a significant source of new jobs in areas like the North East of England, as we discuss below (Richardson et al., 2000; Perrons, 2004). A few years into the new century and call centres have again received considerable publicity, but this time for their rerouting to less developed countries, notably India, so soon after they were installed in the British post-industrial landscape (Deb, 2004; Taylor and Bain, 2005). Such 'offshoring', whereby familiar British firms such as Prudential, Lloyds-TSB and British Telecom take advantage of relative labour costs, represents a classic example of the economic interconnectedness arising from globalization but one that is not without recurrent problems of worker alienation and resistance, as Taylor and Bain (2005) indicate.[43] In this section, we will examine what call centre operations say about white-collar work and workers today.

A call centre is defined by the integration of telephone and computer technologies or, more precisely, as 'a dedicated operation in which computer-utilising employees receive inbound – or make outbound – telephone calls, with those calls processed and controlled either by an Automatic Call Distribution (ACD) or predictive dialling system' (Taylor and Bain, 1999: 102). Despite media talk about the 'call centre industry', call centres do not constitute an industry in the traditional sense since they exist across a range of different existing industries; hence the preferred academic term 'call centre sector'. The fact that call centres can be found in several industries means that estimates about the number of call centres and their employees are less than definitive. In Germany, for example, it is thought that there were 3,000 call centres employing between 300,000 to 400,000 employees (Bittner et al., 2002). Other countries show similarly large estimates (cited in Bain and Taylor, 2002: 42):

- USA – 4 to 9 million employees (three to six per cent of the total workforce);
- UK – 600,000 employees (over two per cent of the total workforce);
- Netherlands – 200,000 employees (nearly three per cent of the total workforce).

The financial services industry, especially banking, has been paramount in the development and expansion of call centres in the United States and Western Europe; it accounts for 30 per cent or more of all call centre employment in Britain and Germany (Shire et al., 2002).

Professional service interfacers or electronically tagged sweatshop drones?

Bain and Taylor (2000) suggest that two contrasting popular images of call centres have emerged, each of which has some support in the burgeoning academic literature:

Optimistic – based around the notion that centres involve quasi-professional, team-working staff who exercise considerable interpersonal skills in dealing with customers. Unsurprisingly this image is the one trumpeted by industry representatives and employers.

Pessimistic – based upon the view that the regimented workers in these white-collar factories are subject to previously unheard of levels of managerial control via the application of new technology to employee monitoring and surveillance.

Much of the research on the nature of work in call centres has been explicitly concerned with assessing the veracity of these starkly drawn optimistic and pessimistic images that can be regarded as representing the polar ends of a spectrum. At the optimistic end of the spectrum are Frenkel et al. (1999) in their cross-national study of 'front-line work', including call centres. They were concerned with elucidating 'workflows', or the structured set of tasks which lead to a specified output pertinent to a particular market. Frenkel and colleagues conclude that call centre work is not particularly regimented, but instead offers considerable possibilities for discretion and creativity since employees must customize their servicing tasks to customers' wants and needs. The pessimistic end of the spectrum image is represented by Fernie and Metcalf (1998) who regard call centres as the 'new sweatshops' based upon the operation of an 'electronic panopticon' in Foucauldian terms. Employees are simultaneously watched, assessed and controlled via their work stations which function as all-seeing electronic monitoring devices for management. According to Fernie and Metcalf, employees internalize management norms under the ever-watchful eye of the electronic supervisor.

Box 7.3   CALL CENTRES AND THEIR EMPLOYEES

Relatively large workplaces – 150+ employees

'Flat' organizational structure – few managerial and supervisory positions

Limited promotion prospects

Emphasis upon 'soft skills' (communications and team working)

Employees predominantly female and young (under 35)

Mixture of full-time and part-time contracts

Low paid

High labour turnover

Sources: adapted from Taylor and Bain, 1999; Bain and Taylor, 2000; Taylor et al., 2002, 2003; Belt et al., 2002; Hyman et al., 2003)

'The typical call centre operator is young, female and works in a large, open plan office or fabricated building, which may well justify the white-collar factory description. Although probably full-time, she is increasingly likely to be a part-time permanent employee working complex shift patterns which correspond to the peaks of customer demand. Promotion prospects and career advancement are limited ... work consists of an uninterrupted and endless sequence of similar conversations with customers she never meets. She has to concentrate hard on what is being said, jump from page to page on a screen, making sure

---

> that the details entered are accurate and that she has said the right things in a pleasant manner. ... The pressure is intense because she knows her work is being measured, her speech monitored, and it often leaves her mentally, physically and emotionally exhausted.' (Taylor and Bain, 1999: 115)

Recent case study research on the call-centre sector in Britain has tended to cast a sceptical eye on both the optimistic and pessimistic images *per se* (Taylor and Bain, 1999; Bain and Taylor, 2000; Taylor et al., 2002, 2003; Belt, 2002; Belt et al., 2002; Hyman et al., 2003).[44] This research has highlighted the rationalization embedded in call centre work and therefore offers either an explicit or an implicit critique of the optimistic image that the sector itself promotes. Box 7.3 provides an ideal type of call centres and their employees based on this research and it also offers 'a day in the life' of a typical call centre operator. The degree of intensity and regimentation Taylor and Bain (1999) highlight suggests that call centre workers exercise relatively little discretion, but are instead subject to the demands of an intensely competitive market place. Some researchers have argued that call centres highlight 'soft skills', such as communications and team working, which are valued by employers (Richardson et al., 2000; Belt et al., 2002). At the same time, these skills are not highly paid, not least because they are associated with feminized labour and are hence 'naturalized', while women's exercise of these skills only takes place within the narrow constraints imposed by the regimented work organization.

While call centres do not appear to offer the levels of creativity sometimes claimed for them, neither is the pessimistic scenario outlined above supported either. Instead of total domination and smooth functioning in the 'electronic panopticon', managers are beset by a number of ongoing labour problems, such as lack of motivation, excessive levels of stress, exhaustion and absenteeism because of sickness, and high staff turnover (30 per cent plus) (Taylor and Bain, 1999; Bain and Taylor, 2000; Richardson et al., 2000; Hyman et al., 2003; Taylor et al., 2003; Mulholland, 2004). These kinds of labour problems have necessitated management to introduce an array of employee involvement techniques, such as team working. As Taylor and Bain (1999) comment, managers would not need to employ such techniques if electronic monitoring were as dominant as the 'electronic panopticon' view suggests.

Neither the optimistic image (empowered knowledge professionals) nor the pessimistic image (quiescent electronically tagged drones) equates with the more mundane reality of call centre employment. This reality seems to be that such employment is characterized by an interactive customer service version of Taylorized monotony and regimentation. While call centre work is partly concerned with enhancing customer satisfaction, in practice this emphasis on the 'quality' of service is often subordinated to the 'quantitative' logic of standardization and cost-minimization whereby workers have to meet targets in a routine repetitive fashion (Bain and Taylor, 2002; Taylor et al., 2002).

Trade unions and worker resistance

Writers following in the labour process tradition of industrial sociology have stressed that call centre employment routinely involves 'worker resistance' on the part of employees to conditions that are not of their own choosing, as we saw in Chapter 4 when discussing Fordist factory workers. There is considerable space at call centres for the development of both informal and formal collective action against managers and employers. This ranges from employees sneaking breaks on the job to unionization and collective bargaining (Taylor and Bain, 1999; Bain and Taylor, 2000). Box 7.4 illustrates a study of informal resistance by Kate Mulholland.

Box 7.4   WORKER RESISTANCE IN AN IRISH CALL CENTRE

In her study of PhoneCo, a telesales company employing 300 staff (two-thirds female) in Belfast, Mulholland (2004) identified four informal resistance strategies on the part of the workers:

Slammin' – workers cheated by pretending to make sales over the phone.

Scammin' – workers avoided work, for example by absenteeism, taking sick leave, and leaving work before the shift ended.

Smokin' – even if workers did not actually smoke, they took an extra 'smoke' break.

Leavin' – the firm was beset by resignations and high labour turnover.

Unlike poststructural explanations for such resistance that stress the individualized nature of such responses, Mulholland adopts a more traditional labour process approach to argue that they are the outcome of the structural employment relationship and collective worker grievances over pay and work intensification. However, Mulholland also accepts that this informal resistance has not thus far translated into traditional sustained union activism, even though between one-half and one-third of the staff were members of the Communications Workers Union (CWU).

Union membership in the call centre sector in the UK is around 30 per cent, which is similar to some continental European rates (28 per cent in the Netherlands), but is more than double the 14 per cent in the United States (Bain and Taylor, 2002: 50). Call centres are embedded within existing national industrial relations systems, for example the corporatist and more regulated systems found in continental Western Europe compared to the neo-liberal and deregulated systems characteristic of the United States and the UK (Holtgrewe et al., 2002). These systems can have significant impacts on working practices in call centres via the presence, extent and nature of collective bargaining arrangements. However, the establishment of call centres can itself be a factor in managerial strategies to bypass existing collective bargaining arrangements, as, for example, seems to be occurring in the German case (Shire et al., 2002).

A key issue in new post-industrial workplaces, such as call centres, is the capacity of workers to organize themselves collectively in trade unions, even in the face of anti-union employers. A case study by Taylor and Bain (2003) examined the struggle for union recognition among a group of workers employed at a non-unionized call centre in Scotland. This study relied on 'mobilization theory', as originally developed in the social movement literature but applied to the field of industrial relations by Kelly (1998). This theory provides a framework within which workers' actions can be understood via analyzing the conditions and processes of interest formation and how workers come to construct collective forms of organization. The case study was undertaken at Excell Multimedia, an outsourced telecommunications call centre in Glasgow. The company was resolutely hostile to trade unions. Nevertheless, a collective sense of grievance gradually emerged out of the following factors.

1. Persistent sources of dissatisfaction. These emerged from the labour process itself with the over-riding priority to take the maximum number of calls, up to 900 per shift, involving a rigidly enforced series of measurements and targets. Agents on directory enquiries, for example, had to answer calls every 30 seconds: 'my flatmates used to laugh at me because I'd shout in my sleep, "which name please, which town please, thank you, here's your number now" and I'd only been working there a month (Maddy)' (Taylor and Bain, 2003: 157).
2. The lack of breaks, minimal concessions for operators who experienced abusive customers or health problems themselves, and 'bullying managers' added to the overall sense of dissatisfaction. However, this dissatisfaction by itself is insufficient to lead workers to collective action; many of the Excell workers left after only short periods or they sought solace in alcohol or drugs.
3. Injustice, interest identification and leadership. Out of the widespread dissatisfaction, a small group of workers began to develop a sense of injustice, individually at first but gradually this took a collective form as a leadership group emerged. This group coalesced at informal meetings in the smoking room at work and in local pubs. Eventually a member of this group joined the CWU and began a recruitment drive on his shift. Key leaders demonstrated a style that gelled with the concerns of fellow workers, helping to thereby create what Fantasia (1988) has called a 'culture of solidarity'.

Following a transfer of the call centre to another company, a union was eventually recognized following a successful ballot. The case study demonstrates the significance of 'bottom-up' mobilizing activities that were in many ways adversarial. The success was qualified, however, since even at its peak 70 per cent of the workforce were non-members. This can be explained by fears of reprisals by the company, fatalistic views that the union would not be able to enact change, and the expectation that working at the call centre was only a temporary measure. The latter factor highlights the ongoing problems of organizing unions among transient post-industrial workforces (Wills, 2005a) – see Chapter 8.

--------- **Paid domestic workers – caring and cleaning in global cities** ---------

Throughout the nineteenth century and into the early twentieth century, domestic employment was the single most important category of paid employment for all women in both Britain and the United States (Cox, 2000; Hondagneu-Sotelo, 2001). Ironically the pre-capitalist distinction in British Edwardian households between 'upstairs', dominated by the employing middle-class family, and the 'downstairs' which was the terrain of their domestic servants, was one of the most profound socio-spatial divides of nineteenth and twentieth century industrial capitalism. This indicator of class privilege and exploitation, allied to a clear status demarcation, began to break down in the period following the First World War leading to 'the servant problem' as domestic servants became far harder to find (Cox, 2006). Opportunities for working-class women opened up in factories and offices, while middle-class families reduced in size. By the 1970s, sociologists were writing obituaries for domestic service, describing it as 'obsolescent' given its strict status demarcation and hence supposed incompatibility with industrialization and modernization (Coser, 1973). Given this 'incompatibility', one of the most remarkable aspects of the late twentieth century social structure has been the revival of paid domestic work (Cox, 2006). In the affluent homes of the middle-classes in many Western cities, the employment of paid domestic workers, usually women from less developed countries, has become commonplace. These women, typically nannies and cleaners, carry out domestic service functions of maintaining cleanliness, domestic well-being and childcare.

Several writers have identified an expansion in this kind of employment. Based upon an analysis of adverts placed in magazines and newspapers, Gregson and Lowe (1994) found a near-doubling of demand for waged domestic labour during the 1980s in Britain. This demand encompassed a wide variety of occupational categories, including the Victorian-sounding 'butlers' and 'maids', but two-thirds related to the care of young children, primarily 'nannies'. Gregson and Lowe argue that, despite its overall expansion, waged domestic labour is not widespread among the middle classes. Instead, their survey of employing households indicated that it was far more common in dual-career households containing two employed professionals or managers. Gregson and Lowe estimated that as many as one third of such households employed waged domestic labour of one kind or another, mainly cleaners, nannies and gardeners. Other research has also found considerable expansion of paid domestic work. One survey found that the amount spent on household workers in Britain went up from £1.1 billion in 1987 to £4.3 billion in 1997, while it is estimated that there were between 700,000 and one million employers of domestic workers in Germany in 1996 (cited in Anderson, 2001). Journalists have estimated that there are around two million domestic workers in Britain, more than in Victorian times, and that 2.7 million British households employ some form of domestic help (cited in Cox, 2006).

On the other hand, some studies have queried whether or not there has been such a prominent 'domestic outsourcing' as these kinds of statistics imply. Bittman et al. (1999) conclude that while the outsourcing of gardening has occurred, there has been no real change in the employment of cleaners according to Australian Household Expenditure Survey data from 1983–94. Childcare outsourcing has increased substantially, but this has taken the form of institutional rather than private childcare. Bittman and colleagues conclude that Gregson and Lowe's argument for expansion does not hold in Australia. Other research in Britain based on expenditure survey data has concluded that there has been no 'boom' in demand for nannying or house cleaning (Gardiner, 1997).

How can we reconcile these conflicting interpretations? We believe that one way to do so is to inject a spatial perspective into the analysis. It may well be that at the national level there is not a 'boom' in paid domestic work. However, there seems to be substantial evidence that the vectors of demand and supply for domestic workers, primarily social polarization and migration flows, come together in global cities. As a result, it is also in such cities that the expansion in this kind of work is most likely to have occurred (Sassen, 1991, 2003). Paid domestic employment declined in most cities in the United States from 1980–90, but increased substantially in the three major metropolises of Southern California (Milkman et al., 1998). Los Angeles is the metropolitan area with the largest proportion of women in paid domestic employment, followed by Miami, Houston and New York. All of these cities have large populations of Latina and Caribbean immigrant women, while Los Angeles is the main destination for Mexicans, Salvadoreans and Guatemalan arrivals in the United States (Hondagneu-Sotelo, 2001). As Hondagneu-Sotelo found, Latina nannies even joke about how many days it would take for Los Angeles to shut down if they went on strike. Gregson and Lowe (1994) found that most demand for paid domestic labour in Britain came from London and the affluent Southeast of England. London alone accounted for 55 per cent of all demand in 1990 which represented an increase over the 1980s. The 1991 Census recorded over 30,000 working in paid domestic jobs in London alone (Cox and Watt, 2002).

Moreover, the social invisibility and private nature of paid domestic work (Ehrenreich and Hochschild, 2003), plus the fact that it is often undertaken by non-citizens on an informal basis for cash-in-hand, means that measuring the precise numbers of paid domestic workers is problematic. Again the concentration of Third World migrants in First World cities is likely to mean that paid domestic workers will be found in the latter, even if the conditions of their entry to the country mean that they will not necessarily appear in the official statistics (Cox and Watt, 2002): 'speak to any recently arrived, undocumented female migrant in the European Union, and the likelihood is that she is working in domestic or sex work' (Anderson, 2001: 18).

Explaining the expansion of paid domestic work

According to Cox (2000, 2006), there are three main sets of factors that can account for the increase in paid domestic work.

1. Changing gender relations within Western capitalist societies. There has been an increasing feminization of professional and managerial positions and these are

disproportionately found in global cities, such as London (Hamnett, 2003). Not only have the absolute and relative levels of female middle-class employment increased, but also, as Gregson and Lowe (1994) point out, service-class careers entail considerable time commitment which can cause strain within households containing two professionals. This arises because of the conflict over domestic labour. While they accept that some forms of domestic labour are increasingly shared, there is nevertheless a continued resistance regarding the sharing of certain routine tasks:

> ... it is the labour-intensive tasks of cleaning and ironing in particular which are the major problem. And, given the gendered nature of these tasks, it is women in service class occupations who, for the most part, have to try to synchronize the time-space demands of paid employment with those of household needs for these particular domestic services. (1994: 89)

Since middle-class men have not taken these domestic tasks on board, buying in 'help', in the guise of a nanny or cleaner, may therefore represent the solution to the domestic labour burden. It affords middle-class men and women the opportunity to offload their domestic household labour to an outsider.

2. Social polarization – widening income inequality provides the material bedrock for wealthier households to be able to employ domestic workers, again a trend which is most acute in global cities (see Chapter 5). One study of the largest cities in the United States found that household income inequality was a significant factor in predicting what proportion of the female labour force was employed in domestic work (Milkman et al., 1998). It is not only that increased incomes at the top end of the distribution that facilitate this out-sourcing of domestic labour. Many work-rich middle-class households are time-poor as working hours have elongated due to public and private restructuring and the middle classes are spurred into working longer hours to avoid the next crop of redundancies. Social polarization also impacts on the poor with an increasing number of workless households in the sense of having no members employed in the formal economy. Welfare benefits have been cut in real terms, while some households may not be entitled to benefits as a result of their members' migrant status (Cox and Watt, 2002). The low paid jobs available to women in the formal labour market may also prompt the turn to informal means of supplementing either wages or benefits, as we discuss below. Studies of paid domestic work, both in the UK and United States, have found that such work can take place on an informal cash-in-hand basis (see Box 7.5). It is noteworthy that in Sweden, with its universal childcare system, high level of unemployment benefits and low income inequalities, the number of paid domestic workers is extremely low (Milkman et al., 1998).

3. Globalization and migration (see Chapters 2 and 5): 'the lifestyles of the First World are made possible by a global transfer of the services associated with a wife's traditional role – childcare, homemaking, and sex – from poor countries to rich ones' (Ehrenreich and Hochschild, 2003: 4). Some female migrants are sex workers enmeshed in global networks of sex tourism and commodification which can take the form of bonded 'sex slavery', as in the case of Thai women brutalized in Japanese, European and American brothels (Bales, 2003). More prosaically, female migrants take up employment as domestic workers.

Box 7.5 CASE STUDY OF A DOMESTIC CLEANER IN NORTH LONDON

Zoe was a single parent in her 30s and lived with two teenage children on a council estate in Camden, North London. She had lived with the children's' father for several years until he left. After then, Zoe did the occasional cleaning job to supplement the meagre £72 a week she received in benefits for her and her children. She walked from her estate to clean the 'big houses' in Hampstead. Childcare demands meant that being able to work fairly close to where she lived was important for Zoe, as it is for many working-class women. 'However, she was worried about working "off the cards" and going beyond the amount of hours she could legally work because some of her friends had been caught "fiddling" by the DSS. Zoe was effectively caught in the poverty trap. The low wages on offer for unskilled women in the local [north London] labour market, plus the loss of housing benefit, made sole reliance on formal employment an unrealistic option for Zoe and others like her':

'I mean a lot of my friends do the cleaning because it's money in the hand, and they get more money doing the cleaning than what they would if they was working full-time, and it's cash, but I suppose you've got to do it. [...] Even when you pick up the local paper and look through for jobs and that, when you look at the money sometimes, you think "is it worth doing?" But then I suppose if you want the money, you want nice things you've got to do it. A lot of my friends they have worked on the cards and left the Social, but they've had to go back on because of the money they get. [...] It seems just pointless working, you'd have to really earn a fortune to be able to pay full rent, your poll tax, everything. At the moment you get benefits, reductions off of it'.

Source: Watt (2003: 1781–2)

There is evidence from a variety of cities that there is a 'hierarchy of desirable nationalities' (Cox and Watt, 2002: 42) in relation to paid domestic labour with certain ethnic and migrant groups preferred by employers and employment agencies over others for particular jobs. In London, cooks and housekeepers were most often sought among women from Spain, Portugal and the Philippines, while nannies tended to be British, Australian or New Zealanders (Cox and Watt, 2002). Research in Toronto suggests that the actions of domestic worker placement agencies can reinforce notions that certain nationalities are 'best-suited' to certain kinds of work (England and Stiell, 1997). In Los Angeles, Latinas were preferred as domestic workers since, unlike whites, they were seen as less likely to reveal family secrets, while unlike African-Americans they were seen as unthreatening (Hondagneu-Sotelo, 2001). This kind of ethnically based distinction therefore takes an explicit moral form drawing upon and reinforcing racist stereotypes: 'in Italy, the division between the "good" and the "bad" migrant is incarnated in the figures of the Nigerian prostitute and the Filipino domestic worker' (Scrinzi, 2003: 85). Let us now turn to examine a case study of the latter undertaken in Rome and Los Angeles.

Globalization and Filipina paid domestic workers in Los Angeles and Rome

In Chapter 6 we saw how social exclusion has multiple dimensions and an excellent illustration of this can be found in a compelling study of Filipina paid domestic workers in Rome and Los Angeles, *Servants of Globalization* by Rhacel Salazar Parrenas (2001). Unlike many other studies that have looked at domestic workers, Parrenas concentrates upon excavating the experiences of the workers themselves and does not examine the employers' perspectives.[45] Parrenas' research was primarily based upon in-depth interviews with 46 female Filipina domestic workers in Rome and 26 in Los Angeles. They were engaged in three kinds of domestic work: cleaning, child-care and elderly care. Whereas most of the Los Angeles sample were 'live-in' workers, staying with their employers during the week and returning to their own homes at weekends, only half of the Italian sample lived in.

Parrenas uses the concept of 'contexts of reception' to articulate the very different social circumstances the domestic workers found themselves in. In Los Angeles, there has been an established Filipino community of both men and women since the 1920s, and Filipinos qualify for permanent residency in the United States. In labour market terms, they are spread across the occupational spectrum with many in professional work. By contrast, Filipinos in Rome were mainly female domestic workers. They had settled in Rome much later, since the 1970s, and their stay in Italy was limited to temporary visas. Scrinzi (2003: 88) cites official statistics that indicate that only 200,000 of the 1.2 million paid domestic workers in Italy were employed legally with a contract in 1997; migrants made up half of the overall total domestic workers.

Drawing inspiration from poststructuralist theories of subjectivity, Parrenas rejects a fixed essentialist view of identity. Instead she is concerned with elucidating the 'multiple subject-positions' which the Filipina domestic workers took (2001: 31). These subject-positions were focused upon the workers' involvement in 'four key institutions of migration: nation-state, family, labour market and migrant community' (2001: 243). Given their subordinate position in each institution, the end-result for the Filipana migrants was one of multiple dislocations: 'partial citizenship, the pain of family separation, contradictory class mobility, and non-belonging' (2001: 23). An important aspect of Parrenas' analysis is that despite the very different 'contexts of reception', she found that the domestic workers lived 'parallel lives' in Rome and Los Angeles with a good deal of similarity vis-à-vis the dislocations. We will discuss each institutional dislocation in turn.

1. Partial citizenship (nation-state) – Parrenas notes the workers' lack of full rights not only in the Philippines but also in the Filipino diaspora. The workers she interviewed still regarded the Philippines as 'home' but this contributed towards their marginalization from full rights in the host country. If anything, partial citizenship was worse in Rome than Los Angeles with the Filipinos in Rome being restricted to domestic labour.
2. Pain of family separation (family) – transnational households were characterized in both cities by splintered families; many of the workers did not see their children for long periods of time as in the case of Rosemarie in Rome:

When the girl that I take care of calls her mother 'Mama', my heart jumps all the time because my children also call me 'Mama'. I feel the gap caused by our physical separation especially in the morning, when I pack (her) lunch, because that's what I used to do for my children. (Parrenas, 2001: 119)

3. Contradictory class mobility (labour market) – while domestic work increased their financial status, it represented a reduction in their social status. The Filipina domestic workers did not come from poor rural backgrounds. Instead, they were often educated women who had been previously employed in professional and white-collar jobs; over a third of the Los Angeles sample were teachers in the Philippines. Unsurprisingly the women regarded domestic work as socially inferior and as deskilling, describing it as *nakakabobo* or making someone stupid. Finally, they also saw it negatively since it did not utilize their educational qualifications. Set against these aspects of downward social mobility is the upward mobility via increased earning power to levels well beyond those they could achieve in their middle-class jobs in the Philippines, as described by Michelle in Rome.

    I came right after graduation. I could have worked but my salary would have just been enough for me. I would not have been able to help my parents. At first, I regretted coming here. I cried a lot. I could not accept being a maid. ... It was only after a year when I could finally look at my situation as something good. I thought about how my income here is pretty good compared to what it would have been in the Philippines even though I am a college graduate. (Parrenas 2001: 173)

4. Non-belonging (migrant community) – in both Rome and Los Angeles, Parrenas found that the migrant Filipino communities were constituted by coexisting cultures of competition and collectivism. The place of the domestic workers was similarly ambivalent comprising elements of both anomie and solidarity, even if the basis of these elements varied between the two cities. In Rome, the Filipina workers were essentially 'guest workers' with marginal citizenship rights. As such, they were segregated in domestic service work. In their 'pockets of gathering', at churches, bus stops and at friends' apartments, solidarity was displayed in which workers gave each other mutual support. At the same time, this solidarity was also undercut by the workers' goal of accumulating capital, their reason for migration, which resulted in a commercialization of social relations, for example, as in the case of day workers renting out access to their apartments to friends and relatives who were live-in workers on the latter's day off. If anomie results from what Parrenas (2001: 245) calls the 'hypercapitalist state of the migrant community in Rome', in Los Angeles it results from class segmentation with the well-off Filipinos pitted against the poorer domestic workers.

While Parrenas' analysis is grounded in her subjects' accounts of their involvement in four institutions of migration, she is at pains to provide a macro-social explanation for what she calls their 'parallel lives' in the two very different contexts. Her explanation for this is in global capitalist restructuring processes, primarily the creation of post-industrial societies in the West, the global feminization of labour, the unequal development of nations, and the contradictions of nationalism under global capitalist conditions in which economies are 'denationalized' but their polities are 'renationalized'. Parrenas' book is an outstanding example of how forms of stratification are generated by the interlinkage of private lives with global conditions.

———— Cash-in-hand jobs – informal work in marginal localities ————

Informal economic activity refers to that 'economic activity which is not recorded in official statistics and which operates in the absence of administrative monitoring and control' (Leonard, 1998b: 2). It is too simplistic to claim that such activity takes place in an entirely separate realm apart from the workings of the formal economy. If anything, the links between the formal and informal economies have strengthened. Sassen (1991) has identified processes of 'informalization' in global cities whereby a range of firms in both manufacturing and services use informal employment mechanisms to enhance labour flexibility. We saw above how informalization is a significant factor in the burgeoning paid domestic sector. A common perception is that such informal economic activity is higher among low-income neighbourhoods and especially among the unemployed, a view that accords with right-wing media stereotypes about 'welfare scroungers' (Golding, 1999). This view has been challenged by Pahl (1984) who emphasized that it was actually those people employed in the formal labour market who were more likely to engage in informal economic activity because they had the tools, skills and contacts necessary for this type of work. Similarly Williams and Windebank (2002) found a concentration of paid informal work among higher income populations living in suburban areas rather than among poor inner-city populations.

If informal economic activity is not concentrated in deprived areas, this does not mean to say that it plays *no* role in the lives of the urban poor (see Box 7.5). Working for cash-in-hand while in receipt of unemployment benefits, what MacDonald (1994) refers to as 'fiddly jobs' and Leonard (1998a) calls 'doing-the-double', can provide an additional source of income for some of those who are formally unemployed. Informal economic activity is also prompted by UK benefits regulations in the sense that a woman with an unemployed or sick husband maybe better off carrying out domestic work informally than seeking a low paid formal job (Gregson and Lowe, 1994). Doing-the-double is also generated from employer practices that enhance informalization, for example, as Leonard (1998a) found in relation to the expansion of sub-contracting firms in the commercial cleaning and construction industries of West Belfast. From the standpoint of the urban poor themselves, informal economic activity can be regarded as a 'survival strategy' (Leonard, 1998b), a strategy that is better associated with staving off the worst effects of welfare dependent poverty rather than providing luxury lifestyles. 'Fiddly jobs' are characterized by their short-term nature, insecurity, exploitative payment and working conditions (MacDonald, 1994; Leonard, 1998a; Watt, 2003).

'Survival strategies', informal economic activity and the operations of the labour market alongside punitive welfare systems are the subjects of ethnographic research by David Smith (2005) in a south London council estate. Although the area had been a centre of light manufacturing in the inter-war and early post-war periods, this sector had dramatically contracted by the 1990s.[46] The demand for manual labour reduced and was replaced by low-wage employment in retail, hotels and catering and personal services. However, these jobs by themselves did not offer a reasonable standard of living in the sense that they did not pay a 'family wage', and nor did they offer any prospect of career advancement. Small businesses and self-employment expanded in the local area, a process facilitated by employers seeking a flexible pool of labour, one that could be employed on a cash-in-hand basis, as one small retailer explained:

> I wouldn't survive unless I cut corners – you've got cab offices competing with taxis, Indians [restaurants] competing with pizza shops, wine bars competing against pubs. You've got small shops competing against big shops and if we didn't use them [cash workers] we'd go under. (2005: 152).

The increased use of self-employment contracts on the part of small businesses was a means by which they could avoid the consequences of minimum wage and employment legislation and so gain a competitive edge.

Smith found that undeclared work on a cash-in-hand basis was common among the estate residents, mainly as a supplement to formal wages but to a lesser extent involving working while officially unemployed. Access to both formal and informal work was largely contingent on an individual's network of contacts. Undeclared micro-businesses permeated social life on the estate, as one resident commented: 'I could get my hair cut, have my clothes cleaned and ironed, my building work done, my car fixed, or buy cheap fags or booze without ever going half a mile from my front door and without a penny going through any books' (2005: 147). The estate's residents maintained a strong work ethic, but they operationalized this within the local opportunity structures open to them, notably the low wages and insecurity associated with many of the available jobs in the formal labour market. Those on welfare benefits also expressed considerable anxiety about losing the security offered by housing benefit if they left the unemployment register. Smith emphasizes that blanket notions of 'welfare dependency' and permanent exclusion from paid employment are overly simplistic notions to apply to those who entered the world of work during the 1980s and 1990s in London. Although some estate residents were unemployed and not working at all, either formally or informally, many moved in and out of formal employment, informal work and reliance on state benefits at different points during their lives.

Watt (2003) found similar patterns of intermittent employment trajectories in a study of working-class council tenants in North London, again involving occasional informal cash-in-hand work (see Box 7.5). However, Watt also identified greater labour market disengagement, in the form of long-term sickness and disability, than Smith. These disengaged tenants tended to be older than those in Smith's study (cf. Alcock et al., 2003). In North London, the middle-aged and elderly male tenants in particular had great problems adjusting to the 'flexible' patterns of employment open to the low skilled in London. Age and generational differences, as well as gender and ethnicity, make a profound difference as to how work is experienced and viewed by those at the lower end of urban labour markets (Jordan et al., 1992). We will now turn to explore how young people make the transition to work and adulthood generally.

Young people – working and playing in a restructured region

'Two tribes' of youth sociologists[47]

Over the last 25 years, youth sociology in Britain has developed along two divergent 'traditions' or approaches based around different theoretical, methodological and thematic concerns: youth transitions and youth cultural studies (Cohen and Ainley, 2000; Hollands, 2002; MacDonald and Marsh, 2005).

1. *Youth transitions* – this approach is primarily concerned with empirical and policy-oriented accounts of school-to-work transitions among young people. It focuses on mapping and explaining the various routes that young people take once they have left school and enter the world of paid employment, or rather as they try to enter paid work since many moved into unemployment and training schemes during the 1980s and 1990s (Banks et al., 1992; Furlong, 1992). Although it has tended to focus on the school-to-work or no-work transition, this approach has also extended its remit to cover other transitions notably around housing and leaving the parental home (Jones, 1995). It has engaged with debates around social exclusion, as discussed in Chapter 6, and addresses the needs of disadvantaged youth in the spheres of employment, training, education and housing. As well as class, gender and ethnicity have also been included as structural variables in order to explain the various transitions young people take (Furlong, 1992). Furlong and Cartmel (1997) have also incorporated the work of Beck on individualization and risk into the transitions approach.

2. *Youth cultural studies* – this approach can be traced back to the influential work of the CCCS during the 1970s (see Chapter 3), who used a combination of Marxism, notably Gramsci's theory of hegemony, with ethnography to show how sub-cultures of mods, rockers and skinheads represented symbolic attempts by working-class youth to counter the hegemonic cultural forms of the ruling class via 'resistance through rituals' (Hall and Jefferson, 1976). For example, the style of the skinhead, cropped hair, big boots and extreme territorialism, represented an attempt by young males to symbolically recreate a form of working-class community at the same time that real working-class communities were declining in areas such as East London (Cohen, 1972). More recently, this cultural studies tradition has taken a postmodern turn via an emphasis on the fragmented and episodic nature of young people's leisure and consumption activities which it is claimed has rendered the notion of class-based sub-cultures redundant (Redhead, 1993; Miles, 1995, 2000; Bennett and Kahn-Harris, 2004).

Instead of post-war youth sub-cultures representing counter-hegemonic rituals, they can be re-read as the result of disparate groups of young people trying different types of clothes, music and drugs according to consumer preferences. In the postmodern world of the marketplace, older loyalties, such as class and the neighbourhood, are regarded as of limited importance for fleeting contemporary youth cultures which, according to Miles (2000), are better captured by the term 'youth lifestyles'. Such lifestyles are a product of the dialectic between the global mass media and young people's use and subversion of such mass marketed products. In this dialectic, class and place are no longer regarded as significant, if they had ever been in the first place. Miles also takes issue with the youth transitions approach for failing to take young people's own agency and perspectives seriously: 'the most damaging problem with the "transition debate" is that it has tended to take young people as troubled victims of economic and social restructuring without enough recourse to the active ways in which young people negotiate such circumstances in the course of their everyday lives' (2000: 10).

Studies of young people's leisure activities and social identities in a variety of locations, including Northern post-industrial cities such as Manchester and Sheffield (Taylor et al., 1996) as well as suburban towns in Southeast England (Watt and Stenson, 1998), have challenged the postmodern notion, exemplified above by Miles, that place and the local neighbourhood are no longer significant: 'the everyday lives of many young people living in cities are far more place-bound and prosaic than postmodern theory might suggest' (Watt, 1998: 692). In the rest of this section, we examine how locality and place shape opportunity structures and young people's responses to such structures via their actions and identities. We do so with reference to two exemplar studies of the above approaches, each of which is concerned to move beyond the narrow confines of the traditions that they exemplify: firstly youth transitions represented by Johnston et al. (2000) and MacDonald et al., (2001), and secondly cultural studies represented by Nayak (2003). Each is based on qualitative research undertaken in the same region, the North East of England.

North East England

North East England is a good example of an 'old' industrial region characterized by early industrialization and a historical reliance on heavy industries such as coal mining, iron and steel production, ship building, chemicals and engineering. These industries offered highly skilled and relatively highly paid manual employment for men, while trade unionism in such industries was strong.[48] Family life was based around a traditional patriarchal gender division of labour with relatively low levels of female paid employment. The North East was a centre of traditional working-class solidarity in the early post-war period (see Chapter 3).

In common with many other old industrial regions or 'rustbelts', North East England has suffered from deindustrialization. From 1975–95, there was a net loss of

179,000 jobs or 14 per cent of the 1975 total. Despite the region being a recipient of manufacturing branch plants in electrical goods and clothing during the 1960s and 1970s, there was nevertheless a loss of over 200,000 manufacturing jobs from 1975–95 or 48 per cent of the 1975 total (Hudson, 2000, cited in Castree et al., 2004: 142–3). Jobs have been created in further rounds of branch plant developments, prominently the Nissan car factory which opened in 1984 near Sunderland and employs 4,500–5,000 people (Perrons, 2004). At the same time global competitiveness has also meant the closure of other branch plants, for example Fujitsu and Siemens both in 1998. The public sector has witnessed long-term growth, partly as a result of government decentralization of tax and social security, while more recently jobs have expanded in cultural industries and call centres (Richardson et al., 2000; Perrons, 2004). The cultural industries include crafts, football and tourism, while the major cities, especially Newcastle upon Tyne but also Middlesborough and Sunderland, have become centres of the 'night-time economy', that congery of pubs, bars and clubs that have come to make up the commercial heart of many deindustrialized, now post-industrial, cities (Chatterton and Hollands, 2003). The transition from the 'old' to the 'new' economy in the North East is symbolically signified by the fact that the Stadium of Light, the new home to Sunderland Athletic Football Club, is built on the sight of the former Wearmouth Colliery.

The restructuring of the North East economy is a result of a complex set of circumstances operating at a range of spatial scales including enhanced global competition, national industrial policies, long-term regional deindustrialization and local regeneration initiatives (Bradley, 1999; Bradley et al., 2000: 24–30; Castree et al., 2004: 140–6; Perrons, 2004: 142–55). If the exact weight of these various explanatory factors is debatable, what is less debatable are the shifting patterns of employment and gender relations including the feminization of employment, increased numbers of low paid service sector jobs, greater job insecurity across the private and public sectors, and higher levels of male unemployment (although this can take the form of economic inactivity and labour market withdrawal among older males). Trade unionism has declined in strength in the region with reductions in union membership and reluctance on the part of employers in new branch plants to recognize unions. Nevertheless, there remains a strong 'union culture' in the region alongside higher than average levels of union membership (Bradley, 1999; Bradley et al., 2000).

Snakes and ladders: youth transitions in North East England

Against this background, how have young people in the North East made the transition from youth to adulthood? The youth transitions approach has emphasized how deindustrialization has resulted in increasingly hazardous school-to-work routes for young people in the North East (Coffield et al., 1986; MacDonald and Coffield, 1991; MacDonald and Marsh, 2000). These transitions include an increased risk of unemployment, as well as cycling between low-skilled jobs, government schemes and benefits. For a minority of young people, these inherently risky transitions have resulted

Table 7.1 Potential career routes and exemplar interviewees amongst young people

Potential career routes	Exemplar interviewees
'Traditional' careers – regular employment in the economic mainstream	Employed in a full-time job
Careers involving repeated periods of unemployment and little engagement with employment or education	Unemployed
Careers involving informal economic activity	Cash-in-hand worker
Educational and training careers	Trainee on vocational programme
Domestic and home-centered careers	Single parent
Criminal careers	Prisoner

Source: adapted from Johnston et al. (2000: 5–7)

in long-term social exclusion and immersion in illegal economies based around the usage and sale of illicit drugs. For many young working-class people in North East England, the transition from youth to adult is highly problematic.

In order to understand exactly how such problematic transitions manifested themselves to create social exclusion, a team of researchers examined youth transitions, 'snakes and ladders', in one particularly disadvantaged locality (Johnston et al., 2000; MacDonald et al., 2001). This was the 'Willowdene' neighbourhood in Teeside, a residential area of approximately 10,000 people dominated by large council housing estates. Alongside the deindustrialization of Teeside more generally, Willowdene has suffered from especially high levels of joblessness, educational under-achievement and poor health. Although Willowdene was regarded as a desirable place to live in the 1950s, by the early 1990s it had become notorious for crime, especially drug-related offences.

The researchers undertook interviews with stakeholder organizations from the public and voluntary sectors and also participant observation with young people. The main data, however, came from semi-structured interviews with nearly 100 young people aged 16–25 from Willowdene. The interviewees, nearly half of whom were female, were virtually all white and from working-class backgrounds. The sample of young people was not statistically representative, but was instead chosen purposively to represent six hypothetical potential career routes, as seen in Table 7.1.

The interviews took a biographical form, but a broad concept of transition was utilized which moved well beyond the traditional youth transitions emphasis on school-to-work and instead aimed to capture young people's biographical movements across four careers:

- School-to-work careers – including experiences of school, training, employment and informal economic activity.
- Family and housing careers – including leaving the parental home, family formation, housing and homelessness.

- Criminal careers – offending patterns and involvement with the criminal justice system.
- Drug careers – involvement with illicit drugs.

As it turned out, the hypothetical career routes devised were too simple to represent the complex nature of the transitions that the young people actually took (Table 7.1). For example, Holly, aged 24, was nominally representative of the 'educational or training career'. At the time of the interview, she was a trainee placed on a vocational course via the New Deal programme. However, Holly's school-to-work career prior to the interview incorporated a multiplicity of changing statuses over time which did not follow any kind of neat linear fashion:

> Holly had been a youth trainee, employed in a part-time job, unemployed, a further education student, self-employed, involved in illicit and informal economic activity and a 'New Dealer'. Some of these statuses were recurrent. Moreover, not only had Holly experienced fast changing and multiple training, educational and labour market statuses *over time*, she has also been involved with some of these different activities *at the same time*. (MacDonald et al., 2001: 4.3; original emphasis)

The kinds of jobs Holly had during her school-to-work career were mainly shop work, although she also worked in a nightclub and had sold fake perfume for periods of time. The kinds of jobs the young people took in the study were typically of the McJobs type, low-wage and low-skilled service sector jobs, although some of them reported having been turned down for archetypal youth labour market jobs such as working in fast food outlets. In addition, several had worked in 'fiddly jobs' in the informal economy at one time or another, while others made money illegally selling drugs or stolen goods. Apart from the complexity of the transitions, MacDonald and colleagues stress a number of different analytical issues arising from their findings:

- The unpredictability, insecurity and contingency of the transitions – freeze framing a biography at any point made it difficult to predict what happened next to an individual. The wider point is the inherently insecure nature of many contemporary labour market opportunities for many young people.
- The significance of life events as turning points in individual biographies – encounters with sympathetic or unsupportive professionals (for example, teachers) could make a difference, as could an unexpected change in family circumstances such as the death of a parent.
- The importance of understanding the inter-related nature of the different youth transitions – in an area like Willowdene, and potentially in similar areas, both criminal and drug careers could impact on school-to-work and family/housing careers.
- The relevance of tracing youth transitions over a long-term time period – focusing on the 16–19 year age band was considered too narrow to fully encapsulate the nature of youth transitions.
- The complex relationship between structural constraints and personal agency in shaping youth transitions – the young people made choices but within heavily circumscribed opportunity structures. Thus many had experienced spells of unemployment despite their efforts to find work.

- The importance of culture in youth transitions – there were a plurality of youth cultural forms operating in Willowdene. Thus even though there was a strong local drug culture that could play a part in school disengagement, many of the young people adhered to conventional values and identities about the importance of education and work.
- The significance of the locality in shaping youth identities and transitions – most of the young people had spent all their lives in Willowdene. Both their worldviews and their opportunity structures, for example in relation to job search activities, were highly localized.

The 'snakes and ladders' research reported here offers one way of seeing how class formation takes place among young working-class people living in one disadvantaged locality. It successfully broadens out the concept of youth transitions beyond a narrow school-to-work focus, and it does not flatten young people into being merely the passive victims of structural disadvantage but instead recognizes the role of individual agency. At the same time, it also situates this agency within heavily circumscribed opportunity structures, structures with a distinct spatial locus. However, from the standpoint of traditional class analysis, the study could be criticized for offering a series of individual life histories which ultimately support the notion of individualization put forward by Beck and Giddens. On the other hand, postmodern youth cultural analysts could argue that despite broadening out the notion of transitions to include criminal and drug careers, it remains a relatively thin notion of culture that does not really engage with the breadth of young people's leisure activities. Let us now turn to a study that does indeed focus on leisure.

White ethnicities: youth cultures in North East England

As we have seen in previous chapters, issues of ethnicity are central to how class is formed and lived. However, the emphasis tends to be placed very much on the ethnicity of minorities, an emphasis which not only exoticizes minorities, but also erroneously assumes that 'white' is not an ethnicity (Bonnett, 2000). One study which has examined the formation of white ethnicities is that of Anoop Nayak (2003) in his innovative *Race, Place and Globalization*, a study of young people and leisure in North East England. Nayak sets out what he calls a historical ethnography rooted in a 'discursive materialism'. This approach is predicated upon an attempt to engage with the complexity of cultural relations as raised by postmodernism, but situated within a light-touch materialism that on the one hand recognizes the relevance of shifting class relations but on the other does not try to simplistically read off culture from economy. Moreover, place is not rendered irrelevant in Nayak's account, but instead has a range of real and symbolic meanings that are in a process of constant flux shifted by global economic and cultural forces.

The core of Nayak's ethnography is an analysis of three alternative ways of doing 'whiteness' in North East England, a region that is usually portrayed as part of an exclusively 'white hinterland'. Nayak is concerned to demonstrate on the contrary that the

North East has had a minority ethnic presence for a very long time, albeit one that is geographically localized in the present. Nayak identifies three local youth subcultures among white young people: the *'Real Geordies'*, *'Charver Kids'* and *'B-Boyz'*.

The *Real Geordies* are a group of young white men who were concerned to symbolically uphold the values of their fathers and older generation based around hard work, male bonding and mutual respect. However, while the older generations could demonstrate these values in reality, via the strictures of skilled manual work in the shipyards and other local heavy industries, the present generation could only nostalgically recreate these values in the very different post-industrial world they faced. Given that their labour market prospects centered on 'learning to serve' rather than 'learning to labour', the locus of their Geordie identities shifted from the world of work and production to that of leisure and consumption. They demonstrated a masculine pride in being *'Real Geordies'* not by hard graft in the shipyards but by hard drinking in the pubs and clubs of Newcastle upon Tyne city centre. If drinking copious amounts of alcohol was one way that being a *Real Geordie* was proved, another was via support for Newcastle United and 'gannin the match'.

The *Charver Kids* were a group of mixed males and females living on one of the inner-city council estates. Unlike the *Real Geordies*, the *Charver Kids* were positioned by others around them as not quite white. This was exacerbated by the presence of minority ethnic groups on their estate. The *Charver Kids* had a distinctive urban street style based on wearing trainers, tracksuits and chunky gold jewellery.[49] Many of them were into Jungle and Rave music. If the *Real Geordies* had an uncertain relationship with the contemporary world of work, the *Charver Kids* were living in a world that was at best marginal and at worst excluded from the world of formal employment. Instead, their families and friends on the estate tended to be involved in informal and illegal economies.

The *B-Boyz* (alternatively *Wiggers*, *Wannabes* and *White Negroes*) were a group of young men and women with an outward-looking conception of style rooted in reorienting 'whiteness' around black culture. In contrast to the other two groups, the *B-Boyz* had a far deeper and accepting immersion in multi-ethnic global cultures, notably via their preference for various forms of black music, black sports such as basketball, as well as black fashions. Whereas the *Real Geordies* offer a vision of exclusive white masculinity, the *B-Boyz* represent a hybrid notion of whiteness/blackness that drew upon 'global mass media images of black American "cool" [which] have become desirable models for many young people to follow' (Nayak 2003: 120) despite the limited presence of a local black population.

Nayak's book offers a spatially sensitive approach to youth cultures which does not lose sight of material inequalities. In particular, he has grounded his account of the *Real Geordies* and *Charver Kids* within economic and cultural divisions which are increasingly important for the working class. The *Real Geordies* are from suburban homes and represent the better off, 'respectable' working class, whereas the *Charver Kids* are the 'rough' lower working class from the sink estates, the putative 'underclass' of marginal British urban spaces, places like Willowdene discussed above.

Despite its merits, there are several hiatuses within Nayak's account. Firstly, it is notable that whereas the first two groups, the *Real Geordies* and *Charver Kids,* are located within intra-working class divisions, there seems to be no material underpinning to the *B-Boyz* or at least we are not told whether there is or not. Postmodernists would respond that this demonstrates that youth cultures are far fuzzier and less grounded in class and material inequalities than Nayak asserts. Secondly, in discussing the *Charver Kids,* Nayak has focused on the exotic deviant elements of lower working-class youth. As such he has not grasped the diverse ways that young people can grow up even in disadvantaged estates as the 'snakes and ladders' study emphasizes. Finally, while Nayak has demonstrated the local roots of football support and drinking in Newcastle, it is also the case that these two activities are core to the development of working-class masculinities across many British towns and cities which have never had any heavy industry at all (Chatterton and Hollands, 2003).

Conclusion

In this chapter, we have examined several groups of post-industrial workers in a variety of spatial settings. These workers do not represent the working class *in toto* since even in societies, such as Britain and the United States, a minority of the workforce remains in manufacturing employment, while the industrial sector is more significant in corporatist societies such as Germany (see Chapter 6). Nevertheless, low-paid service jobs of the kind we have discussed above do represent a major growth pole of the 'new economy', especially in the United States and Britain with their liberal welfare regimes and flexible labour markets. That much of the service work we have discussed is undertaken by women, minority ethnic groups, immigrants and young people, indicates how far we have moved from the early post-war period when the working class was effectively equated, not least by sociologists, with white adult male factory workers.

At the end of the chapter we discussed two different approaches to the study of young people, youth transitions and youth cultural studies. This raises an issue we will return to in Chapter 8, that is the relationship between production relations (employment) and consumption relations (leisure). Although both the case studies we examined on youth in the North East of England did make this part of their research brief, it is noteworthy that the literature we discussed above on call centre workers tended to focus on their employment experiences. We know relatively little about their lifestyles in relation to families, neighbourhoods and leisure activities, or about their social and political attitudes in general. In other words, although call centre workers seem to be quintessential post-industrial proletarians at work, we know relatively little about how this relates to wider social processes concerned with subjective identities and culture. This hiatus is striking, especially in comparison to earlier post-war studies in class and industrial sociology, such as the 'affluent worker' study (see Chapter 3).

Further reading

Bourdieu et al. (1999) is a wide-ranging collection of stimulating essays based on interviews with those people experiencing 'the weight of the world' who are at the receiving end of contemporary processes of economic and social restructuring. Dickens et al. (2003) provides an overview of the recent main developments in the British labour market. Gray (2004) offers a forceful Marxist-inspired critique of current welfare and labour market policies in Europe and in particular welfare-to-work policies. Van Gyes et al. (2001) is an international collection of essays that address questions of class solidarity notably in relation to the role of trade unions. Milkman (2000) examines union organization among migrants in California, while Gall (2003) provides a cross-national perspective on union organization. On labour relations in the global fast food industry, see the edited collection by Royle and Towers (2002b). Anderson (2000) provides a Marxist-feminist account of paid domestic employment with material drawn from several European cities. Cox (2006) is a useful overview of the development of paid domestic employment in Britain and also includes data on au pairs, an often overlooked group. Two overviews of informal employment in a cross-national perspective are Leonard (1998b) and Williams and Windebank (1998). MacDonald and Marsh (2005) is an extremely valuable recent study in the youth transitions tradition which examines various aspects of social exclusion in relation to British young people living in a deprived area of North East England. Hollands (2002) is a good example of an article which offers a bridge between the youth transitions and youth cultures approaches in the context of research on urban nightlife.

Three research centres which examine work and workers from an explicit class perspective are: the Working Lives Research Institute at London Metropolitan University – http://www.workinglives.org/; the Center for Study of Working Class Life at State University of New York (SUNY) at Stony Brook – http://naples.cc.sunysb.edu/CAS/wcmnsf; and The Center for Working-Class Studies at Youngstown State University – http://www.as.vsu.edu/~cwcs/.

CHAPTER EIGHT

Class Identity
•••••••••

- Introduction
- Class interests
- From class consciousness to class identity
- The French connection – Bourdieu
- Debating class identity
- Identity and organization
- Final thoughts

─────────────────────────── **Introduction** ───────────────────────────

In 2005 a riot took place in Edmonton, North London. Nothing particularly surprising about that you might think. In 1976 the workers – mainly Asian women – at a photo lab called Grunwicks, also in North London, had gone on strike and had been locked out by the management. Every morning thousands of supporters got themselves up in time for a 7 a.m. mass picket and relations with the police proved frosty and led to inevitable confrontations (Dromey and Taylor, 1978). In 1985 there was a riot on a North London housing estate, Broadwater Farm in Tottenham, that led to the murder of a police constable for which a black man (Winston Silcott) was charged, convicted and subsequently freed (Power, 1997: 195–218). These events could be seen as analogues for our changing times and the nature of social conflict. The riot on 10 February 2005 occurred at the opening of a new IKEA store and led to massive newspaper coverage including the editorial in Box 8.1.

Box 8.1   THE SOFA RIOTS

A familiar scene on the high streets of today's Britain? Well after midnight, an unruly mob on the streets, with police and security guards losing control. The rampaging pack was a vivid illustration of the dangers of 'happy hour' prices, designed to lure in the punters and beggar their neighbours. The scene – a booze barn? No. Was the rampaging mob drunk on cheap alcopops? Again, no. The 6,000 or so who gathered in Edmonton, North London, in the early hours of yesterday morning were intoxicated all right, but more by the prospect of buying £45 sofas, rather than cut-price gin. Never mind the 24-hour binge drinking – after the mayhem of IKEA's megastore opening, when is the government going to act against binge shopping?

As anyone who has visited an IKEA on a busy day – that is to say most weekdays, weekends or bank holidays – will be aware, it is hard enough to resist the violent urges brought on by the depressing conditions at any time. But when goaded by the prospects of cheap tables and wardrobes, a mini-riot took place, as customers climbed over each other to reach the promised land of the £30 bed. This was no laughing matter: six people were hospitalized, a man was stabbed, and dozens more crushed in the seething mass. Thankfully, things were not as bad as the last IKEA event that led to violence: a special offer at an outlet in Jeddah, Saudi Arabia led to three deaths during a stampede in September last year.

Violent incidents of mob rule are not uncommon, but tend to occur in times of scarcity or panic, over food or water rather than discount vouchers. Historians may look back on the IKEA outbreaks as the precursor of fundamentalist consumerism, marking the start of guerrilla shopping wars as the nation state weakens. This is the sort of dystopian future portrayed in films such as Soylent Green, where every consumer good is fought over. But yesterday's events should remind us that no wardrobe, no matter how cheap, is worth a riot. Human dignity is more valuable than a £45 sofa. Shoppers of the world unite – you have nothing to lose but your chaise-longue. (*The Guardian*, 11 February 2005)

Has the world gone full circle from the food riots against the Corn Laws in the early nineteenth century (leading to the 1819 Peterloo Massacre in Manchester) by the dispossessed of the early years of industrialization and the birth of the working class in Britain, to the 'sofa riots' of the relatively possessed nearly two centuries later? If so, what, if anything, does this tell us about the power of social class? In the late nineteenth century the Bishop of London welcomed the 1889 dock strike because the sight of dockers marching through the East End indicated to him that the trade unions were now able to offer discipline and leadership over the famously undisciplined East Enders who, during the 1880s, had often camped out over the summer in the West End and, on more than one occasion, trashed St James' in Piccadilly. Do the various riots of the last 30 years – at Saltley Coke depot in 1974, at Grunwick in 1976, in Brixton and Toxteth in 1981 and St Paul's in Bristol the previous year, at Orgreave colliery in 1984, Broadwater Farm in 1985 and the 'poll tax' riot in London in 1990 – tell us a story? Labour historians of the nineteenth century, such as Hobsbawm and Rudé (1969), argued that the riot was the means of expression of the dispossessed whilst the strike expressed the organized working class. If we are now witnessing this in reverse, is the IKEA riot symptomatic of the new fault lines in consumption-based society (Ransome, 2005)? In the rest of the chapter, we examine the changes that have occurred in relation to social class – those of consciousness, identity, politics and the apparent shift from divisions around the means of production to those around the icons and places of consumption.

Class interests

Traditionally, the British working class has been typified as being collectivist in its behaviour whilst the middle class has been seen as individualistic, the contrast being between the working-class job and the middle-class career.[50] The relationship of these class groups to production and consumption practices is complex. The working class was traditionally identified in terms of its occupational position in the system of production – mainly as manual workers in manufacturing or in primary production. In relation to consumption, the working class was seen – somewhat stereotypically – as practising 'immediate' (as opposed to) 'deferred' gratification – 'the live today, for tomorrow you may die' philosophy promulgated by the 1950s' working class (Zweig, 1952; Dennis et al., 1956). A more sophisticated version of this argument was advanced in other studies of the working class which distinguished between the 'rough' and 'respectable' (for example Bott, 1964 on family networks; Jackson and Marsden, 1962 on education; and Stacey, 1960 on neighbourhood). These distinctions not withstanding, the working class as a whole had relatively little by way of discretionary income over and above that needed to meet immediate subsistence needs. In terms of cultural reproduction, several studies pointed to the cultural factors that kept the two class worlds apart (see *inter alia* Hoggart, 1958; Bernstein, 1975).

In contrast to the working class, the middle class was defined both in terms of its occupational position and its strategic approach to social reproduction and occupational mobility. 'Deferred gratification' meant that time and resources were invested in training and education (human capital) in order to gain or at least maintain long-term advantage across the life course. The intergenerational mission of the middle class, it might be claimed, has been to pass its comparative advantage on to its children – education therefore is a vital 'field' for the middle class. This has been attested to by a long line of sociological studies and official reports which demonstrated how middle-class advantage was achieved and reproduced (see inter alia Benn and Simon, 1970; Silver, 1973; Savage et al., 1992; Egerton and Savage, 1997; Ball, 2002; Power et al., 2003; Devine, 2004a). Unlike the working class, which was regarded as a homogenous group in which any divisions were either normative (rough versus respectable) or based on distinctions of skill (which it could be argued are also normative), the middle class has tended to be seen as normatively homogenous (for example, with its commitment to deferred gratification) but otherwise heterogeneous – divided occupationally between managers, professionals and the self-employed or small employers (Savage et al., 1992; Roberts, 2001).

The argument about the middle class became encapsulated in the debate over what to call it: in the 1980s – the preferred term being the service class (Goldthorpe, 1982; Abercrombie and Urry 1983; Goldthorpe, 1987; Lash and Urry, 1987). The choice of the term service class reflected the concern of these authors at the time, despite other differences they might have had, with the organization of industrial society and its occupational structure. The broad assumption was that it 'serviced' the running of society, at a time when society and economy were in deep crisis and allegiances were primarily constituted by class.

The debate about the service class can crudely be divided between those concerned with identifying its class position within the overall class structure, and those who have been concerned with the process of class formation within the overall development of capitalist society. The most consistent attempts to synthesize these positions on class structure and formation into a coherent understanding of social class have been led by Mike Savage and those working with him (see inter alia Savage et al., 1992; Butler and Savage, 1995; Savage, 2000; Savage et al., 2004, 2005a, 2005b). This approach, which we discuss below, has drawn on the neo-Marxism of Erik Olin Wright (1985) and particularly Pierre Bourdieu (1984, 1987).

The definition of the middle class involves all sorts of boundary issues and is not particularly new – as Michael Mann (1993) pointed out in his work on class and political power.

> Defining of the middle class has always been contentious. The rise of 'middling groups' immediately presented conceptual problems for nineteenth century observers. Most used the plural 'middle classes', impressed by their heterogeneity ... contemporaries left definitions to us, but our historians have been no great help ... Sociologists provide more concepts – the petit bourgeoisie with its old, new and traditional fractions; the middle class, old, new and decomposed; the new working class; the service class; the professional and managerial class – all of these may be in 'contradictory class locations'... this plethora embodies five alternative theories. Middling groups are:
>
> 1. In the working class – the conclusion of orthodox Marxism
> 2. Part of the ruling bourgeois or capitalist class – an occasional, pessimistic Marxian response
> 3. In an ambiguous, contradictory class location (Wright, 1985: 42–57)
> 4. 'Decomposed', as various middling groups fall into different classes, or Stande – the most common view (e.g. Dahrendorf, 1959)
> 5. A separate middle class (e.g. Giddens, 1973).
>   (Mann, 1993: 547)

Mann opts for what he terms an impure middle class:

> Three variably 'impure' relations of production impinge on middling groups: (1) capitalist property ownership, (2) hierarchies specific to capitalist corporations and modern state bureaucracies, and (3) authoritative state-licensed professions. (Mann, 1993: 549)

Mann locates these within a wider concept of the distinction which he draws between 'authoritative' and 'diffused' power relations and notes that capital does not consist just of authoritative employment organizations but also other 'diffused circuits of capital, including consumption' (1993). These in turn are embedded in his model of social power which comprises networks of ideological, economic, military and political power:

> All three of these criteria – employment relations, diffused power relations, and all the sources of social power – confer an additional common quality on middle-class persons: they have predominantly segmental relations with dominant classes above, reinforcing their loyalty – if for some generating a worrying 'superloyalty'. Thus they are fractions of a single middle class defined by the formula: segmental middling participation in the hierarchies of capitalism and nation state. (Mann, 1993: 549–50)

Much of the work that was undertaken in the 1980s tended to see this group as a service class operating in the long-term interests of the dominant economic class. More recent work has distanced itself from this somewhat functionalist view in favour of a more 'pluralist' approach to the middle classes and argues against seeing them (or it) as a unitary grouping with a common set of interests.

The adoption of the term 'middle classes' in place of the 'service class' during the 1990s implies that intra-class differences are of considerable significance; place and gender come to take on important meanings whilst occupation is somewhat relegated to but one aspect of understanding, and explaining, the various forms of 'habitus' that its members occupy. This approach argues that people come to occupy different positions in the class structure in different ways (Savage et al., 2005a). It shares with Goldthorpe (1980) a concern about social mobility and class structure but argues that, to some extent at least, class structure is an outcome of the mobility strategies pursued by individual members of the middle class. It shares Urry's (Lash and Urry, 1994) assumption that the structures and actions of the middle class will change with the developments taking place in capitalism (notably deindustrialization and the fetishization of consumerism) and recognizes that sections, at least of the middle classes, are responsible for managing this change process within which individual careers are shaped. Savage has developed this approach to argue that whilst class is important in a sociological sense it does not imbue and determine notions of identity in the ways in which it used to (Savage et al., 2001, 2005a). It is not the primary reference point for people in understanding and making sense of their social position nor of the cultural imperatives flowing from that. Savage suggests that place performs a greater sense of belonging than occupational class (Blokland and Savage, 2001; Savage et al., 2004, 2005a, 2005b).[51] Class remains, as it were, as a benchmark against which people calibrate their social position; only in the professional middle class is there any strong sense of 'being' middle class. Otherwise people refer to their background, their cultural activities and their occupation to make sense of themselves against a perceived sense of what class means (Savage et al., 2001).

For the middle classes, the problem has always been how to ensure relative advantage and privilege intergenerationally. Savage et al. (1992) resolve the problem of how skills are transmitted intergenerationally by adopting Bourdieu's concept of cultural capital (exemplified, for example, by the possession of higher educational qualifications) which can be 'stored' and then realized in the occupational structure.

The education system is therefore crucial for the professional middle class; managers, dependent on their organizations' assets, can attempt to advantage their children either by passing on property and/or providing them with the cultural capital they themselves might lack, although in this strategy they are likely to be at a disadvantage compared with the professionals who are more adept at gaining benefit from the education system. On the other hand, managers have more assets to purchase these advantages through private education. In more recent work, Savage has focused rather less on the detailed divisions of these assets and rather more on how their overall possession of these resources in general contributes to individuals' sense of their stock of 'capital'. This has become known as the CARs (Capitals, Assets and Resources) approach and provides a theoretical counterweight to the dependency on rational action theory in both Marxist and Weberian accounts (Savage, Warde and Devine, 2005).

> ...it is possible to re-energise local studies through a greater attention to issues of habitus and capital, through their relationship to place and space – rather than through occupation or the division of labour, as has been the standard approach to class analysis. Bourdieu sees social distinction as being inherently spatial in character: the powerful depend on being spatially distinct from the powerless, and situations which bring these classes into interaction are dealt with through the ritualization of encounter, in which the structuring of interaction usually allows the powerful to retain control ... Conflicts over space are in fact rare, a point which can be related to the power of the habitus to act as a regulating device. Where people feel comfortable in places, they tend to populate such places, either through permanent residence or through revisiting, but where they do not, they tend to avoid them. Hence a complex process of sorting of people's habitus to certain kinds of zones allows a social *which is also a spatial* structure to be defined. (Savage et al., 2005b: 101)

The general point about the relationship between spatial and social structures has been an underlying concern of this book and we welcome this incorporation of a sense of place into an understanding of 'how class works' as a highly significant and important advance. Savage has suggested that there is an elision here between Bourdieu's work and Massey's (1984) concept of the spatial division of labour. However, the claim that conflicts over space are rare is more contentious; much of the literature on gentrification assumes a tension with the phenomenon of displacement (Smith, 1979; Atkinson, 2000). This process of displacement is, however, difficult to chronicle and it may well be that the conflict over space points to the fact that choice is so often constrained – usually by possession of economic assets. Nevertheless, there is a danger that researchers on the middle class have 'gone native' and failed to see that conflict can be present but suppressed.

From class consciousness to class identity

A concern with 'class consciousness' implied that there is a singular true (or false) representation of reality tied to an overarching grand historical narrative, as particularly associated with Marxism (Bradley, 1996). However, despite the huge amount of sociological work on class by Marxists, Weberians and others, the only conclusion that can be reached with any degree of confidence is that there did not appear to be any kind of consistent class consciousness amongst the working classes of the industrialized nations (Mann, 1973; Savage, 2000). The result of the sociological endeavour in this field was an impasse in relation to class consciousness in the sense that the latter could not simply be regarded as a 'reflex' of class position (Devine and Savage, 2005: 12; see also Savage, 2000). One prominent consequence flowing from this impasse has been that the focus on class consciousness within mainstream sociology has gradually been supplanted by an interest in 'identity', as part of the wider 'cultural turn' in the social sciences (Devine and Savage, 2005). The study of social identity emerged in response to the failure of class theory to take adequate account of gender and ethnicity as sources of inequality, as argued by feminists and anti-racists. The emphasis on social identity also reflects processes of postmodernization and globalization in which identities are increasingly complex, contested and no longer singularly reducible to class or occupation in any straightforward fashion:

> … although in an earlier period 'bank manager' connoted authority, conservatism, discretion, the 'bank manager' in the twenty-first century might connote something quite different (young, IT-skilled, entrepreneurial innovator). When added to the fact that 'bankmanagernous' is now only one source, rather than all of, the identity of a person who has that occupational role, the permutations multiply very considerably. The disabled, ethnic-minority, urbanite bank manager occupies a very different position in the sign system of social identity than does that mature-age, white male heterosexual treasurer of Backwoods, Virginia. (Ransome, 2005: 103)

Ironically, the shift away from class consciousness to identity has proved fruitful in reinvigorating class analysis since it allows for greater methodological and theoretical innovation, not least since 'identities are not labels of your position, but "claims for recognition" … which are both contested and fraught' (Devine and Savage, 2005: 12). Devine and Savage trace three inter-related influences that have played a part in this shift away from consciousness to identity and which inform recent research:

- *Methodological* – a move away from surveys towards a reliance on qualitative research, notably in-depth interviews and ethnographies, which allow for a more holistic and complex account of the various nuances of class identifications.
- *Contextual* – a concern to locate class awareness to the context of people's everyday lives, rather than considering it in abstract terms in relation to what class awareness *should* be like.
- *Anti-reductionism* – an emphasis on understanding the ambiguities and complexities of class awareness on its own terms rather than attempting to explain it away via recourse to dominant ideology or forms of political organization.

It is striking that the shift from class consciousness to identity has occurred even among sociologists who remain committed to retaining an emphasis on the material economic dimensions of class (see *inter alia* Bradley, 1996, 1999; Skeggs, 1997; Reay, 1998a, 1998b; Savage et al., 2001; Devine et al., 2005). In all of these studies, the term 'class identity' has now effectively supplanted 'class consciousness'. Even in recent texts that highlight the continued salience of capital/labour relations and demonstrate an explicit left-wing political commitment to furthering the interests of workers, there is a shying away from the use of 'consciousness' towards 'identity' (Zweig, 2000; Castree et al., 2004). Towards the end of this chapter, we return to these debates around identity and class. Before doing so, we need to examine briefly the ways in which the work of Pierre Bourdieu has been incorporated in Britain into work on social class.

The French connection – Bourdieu

The work of the French sociologist Pierre Bourdieu, who died in 2002, has been the subject of considerable discussion since his death – for example, both the *British Journal of Sociology* and *Sociological Review* have devoted special issues to his work in the period since his death. His influence on British sociology and particularly thinking about class during the last 20 years, stemmed from the English language translation of *Distinction* (Bourdieu, 1984), his study of taste and the French class structure.[52] This work, alongside his other writings on class, form part of Bourdieu's wider sociological project, one characterized by theoretical innovation, close attention to empirical research, and often a challenging even obscure writing style (Jenkins, 1992; Swartz, 1997; Wacquant, 1998). In theoretical terms, Bourdieu is concerned to challenge typical dualisms that are found in sociology, notably structure and agency, and between the material and symbolic dimensions of social life.

As Swartz (1997) demonstrates, Bourdieu's work on class is strongly influenced by Marx and Weber. Like both Marx and Weber, his vision of class relations is an antagonistic one characterized by conflicts of interest between classes. Drawing on Marx, but especially Weber, class for Bourdieu is a phenomenon of power whereby there are dominant and subordinate classes. Again similar to both Marx and Weber, class for Bourdieu has a material element rooted in the economic inequalities of wealth and income distribution. However, Bourdieu also differs in important ways from both Marx and Weber. As well as containing a material element, class for Bourdieu also has a powerful symbolic and cultural component; in other words it has a cultural dimension. This separates Bourdieu from Marxism which tends to focus on material inequalities. However, unlike Weber, who separates class from status, Bourdieu effectively joins class (economic) and status (social) power together. Bourdieu is probably more similar to Weber than Marx on the ontological status of classes. While not denying the material reality of classes, Bourdieu (1987) is careful to stress that classes only come into social being, as opposed to just classes 'on paper', when people themselves come to act and think in subjective class terms.

Bourdieu (1984) stresses that class is not a unidimensional category in which people are allocated a position on a pre-existing class map. Instead, Bourdieu views class relationally and dynamically as being concerned with the ways in which individuals and groups utilize a range of resources in their dealings with others who similarly do likewise. These resources take the form of various kinds of 'capital', and it is the distribution of these capitals in social relations of power which provides the basis for the class structure in Bourdieu's work. According to Bourdieu, unlike in the case of Marx, economic capital is only one form of capital. Rather, classes are formed by the social distribution of three main types of capital:

- *Economic capital* – resources in the form of material and financial assets such as income and wealth.
- *Cultural capital* – resources in the form of scarce symbolic goods, skills and titles, for example linguistic skills or educational qualifications.
- *Social capital* – resources accrued by virtue of membership of a network in the form of social connections.

In addition to these three, Bourdieu (1987: 4) also makes reference to a fourth type, 'symbolic capital' as 'the form the different types of capital take once they are perceived and recognized as legitimate'. In other words, symbolic capital represents an additional resource boost granted to possession of the other kinds of capital once they are legitimated as *not* being based around interests; their interest basis is thus hidden.[53]

Class position is charted by two co-ordinates: the volume and composition of capital. The volume of capital is determined by the total amount of economic, cultural and social capital which classes have, whilst the composition of capital is determined by the relative sizes of the three types of capital.[54] However, one cannot treat the possession of such capital statically, since it changes its composition over time via the notion of 'trajectory'. Instead of understanding mobility on a single plane, or social space, Bourdieu argues that the relationship between the forms of capital changes over time within the trajectories of social space, and this is effected by what Bourdieu calls 'reconversion strategies' in which it is possible to switch assets from one form of capital to another over time:

> The strategies which individuals and families employ with a view to safeguarding or improving their position in social space are reflected in transformations which modify both the volume of the different class fractions and the structure of their assets ... The reconversion of economic capital into educational capital is one of the strategies which enable the business bourgeoisie to maintain the position of some or all of its heirs ... (Bourdieu, 1984: 135–7).

It is the combination of capitals that is significant in relation to how the various classes are socialized, both by the family and in the educational system. The socialization process imbibes a distinctive class 'habitus'. The habitus is the system of durable and transposable dispositions through which we perceive, judge and act in the world. Such dispositions consist not only of learned thought and attitudes, but also modes of feeling – in other words, dispositions have both cognitive and affective components. The system of dispositions people acquire, their habitus, depends on the positions they occupy in society, that is on their particular endowment in capital. The habitus is unconscious and is learned by us via exposure to particular social conditions – hence we internalize external constraint within our bodies: 'the habitus as the feel for the game is the social game embodied and turned into a second nature' (Bourdieu, 1990: 63).

The dispositions associated with a particular habitus are shared by people subjected to similar experiences even if each individual has an individual variant – that is why people of similar classes, genders and nationalities feel 'at home' with people who share their social space. The habitus is the mediation between past influences and present stimuli – as such it is at once *structured*, by the patterned social forces that have produced it, and *structuring*; it gives form and coherence to the activities of individuals across the various spheres of life or 'fields'. In relation to social class, a person from a working-class background will carry the influence of their background around with them and it will be expressed in terms of speech patterns, types of attitudes, ways of comporting one's body, etc.[54]

In *Distinction* (1984), Bourdieu provides a detailed analysis of the French class structure based around the relative weights of economic and cultural capital held by various occupational groups. At one extreme is the dominant class characterized by possession of a large volume of capital, but fractured along the lines of their location within economic capital and cultural capital hierarchies. Thus, for example, artistic producers, such as artists or writers, are high on cultural capital but low on economic capital, whereas the opposite is the case for industrialists (Ley, 2003). At the other extreme is the working class, consisting of manual workers and farm labourers, defined by its relative lack of either economic or cultural capital. In between the working and dominant classes is the middle classes, for example primary school teachers, junior executives and clerical workers, who have intermediate levels of economic and cultural capital.

These various classes define themselves in cultural terms in relation to the various kinds of leisure activities they pursue including such things as the types of music they listen to, the food and places they eat, the sports they play and the holidays they take. Indeed, the major argument of *Distinction* is that the cultural tastes exhibited by different social classes define themselves in oppositional terms: 'taste is first and foremost the distaste of the tastes of others' (Wacquant, 1998: 223). The preference for playing tennis and going to the opera among the dominant class is valorized by them precisely because it is *not* that of the working class who instead like watching sport on TV and going to public dances (Bourdieu, 1984: 128–9). However, the capacity of the various classes to make distinctions in the first place is determined by the overall volume of capital they possess. Thus Bourdieu characterizes the working-class relation to culture as the 'choice of the necessary': 'economic constraints and the dispositions of the working-class habitus produce an adaptive response which is distinguished by the relative absence of aesthetic choice-making' (Jenkins, 1992: 145), unlike the case of the dominant class who can make choices based upon possessing large amounts of economic and/or cultural capital.

Bourdieu's theoretical oeuvre and empirical analysis of the French class structure in *Distinction* have proved rich sources of inspiration for many class analysts, notably those who wish to incorporate a cultural dimension into their work (Devine et al., 2005). Bourdieu's influence is especially marked in relation to the analysis of the middle classes (Savage et al., 1992), notably in relation to gentrification and the new middle class living in inner-city locales (Butler with Robson, 2003; Watt, 2005; see Chapter 5). In addition, class analysts have also made fruitful use of Bourdieu in relation to the contemporary working class (see Rupp, 1997; Charlesworth, 2000), as we discuss below in relation to the work of Bev Skeggs.

Why has Bourdieu's work proved so influential? Bourdieu introduces a complexity missing from many accounts of class in his suggestion that class is a multi-dimensional phenomenon incorporating different forms of capital. Bourdieu therefore provides a model of class analysis which avoids the economic reductionism and, arguably, political anachronism associated with Marxism which sees capital in purely economic terms. Bourdieu's complexity is also invoked in his concern to demonstrate the ways in which class is lived out through cultural and lifestyle distinctions. This is very different from the 'employment aggregate' survey-based approach to class which can forget that occupation is only an indicator of class and not the thing itself (see Mills, 1995, for an example). The overall result is that there is a sociological richness to Bourdieu's account of class, a richness which is eminently suited to understanding the dynamics of class formation via case studies. At the same time, Bourdieu's work on class has also been the subject of intense criticism.

First, although some find the multi-dimensional nature of Bourdieu's class analysis appealing, others find this to be a source of great frustration since it means that there is no easily identifiable class structure: 'there is no attempt to define a class structure and it is argued that the boundaries between classes are constantly changing' (Bridge, 1995: 24).

Secondly, Bourdieu lacks an over-arching theory of society and history, as can be found for example in Marxian political economy. Unlike Marx who situates his analysis of class and capital within a historically grounded theory of capitalism, Bourdieu has no such theory and 'sees capital simply as a resource (that is, a form of wealth) which yields power' (Calhoun, 1993: 69). Marxists also argue that the various capitals are not equivalent, as Bourdieu tends to imply. The fact that workers might possess social capital through their networks of contacts does not allow them the same degree of power as capitalists who possess economic capital.

Thirdly, Bourdieu's treatment of the working class is said to be inadequate since it is effectively a deficit model in which they are simply treated as an absence lacking both economic and cultural capital (Jenkins, 1992; Swartz, 1997), and he also fails to examine divisions *within* the working class (Rupp, 1997; Watt, 2006).

Fourthly, Bourdieu's theory of social class over-emphasizes social reproduction and under-emphasizes the role of social mobility. This can be seen, for example, in his account of cultural capital and educational attainment. Since the education system depends on cultural capital, this means that it is very difficult for working-class pupils to succeed in the field of education. This is quite a deterministic theory which seems to downplay the extent to which working-class pupils gain qualifications and are upwardly mobile into middle-class positions in British society (Halsey et al., 1980; Swartz, 1997: 182–4).

Fifthly, Bourdieu's original research for *Distinction* was undertaken during the 1960s and it is possible to argue that cultural practices around consumption no longer take the relatively fixed form characteristic of France at that time as a consequence of both globalization and postmodernism (Longhurst and Savage, 1996). The collapsing of high/low cultural boundaries associated with postmodern cultural forms, for example the inclusion of Act III of Wagner's opera *The Valkyrie* performed by the English National Opera at the Glastonbury rock music festival in the summer of 2004, erodes the rigid hierarchies of the kind Bourdieu analyzed.

Sixthly, although Bourdieu's account of class is a conflictual one, like that of Marx and Weber, it is a conflict that is largely individualistic rather than collective; people try to maximize their various capitals as individuals or as families alongside others who are doing likewise. In this sense, it has sympathetic parallels to Weber's individualistic, market focused concept of class sitting alongside status and party as aspects of the distribution of power. Class struggle, in its Marxist variant of workers trying to collectively mobilize against exploitative employers, is largely absent in Bourdieu's work: 'Bourdieu's portrayal of social conflict as almost exclusively one of market competition seems odd in a country that produced the French Revolution' (Swartz, 1997: 188).

Working-class women in North West England

Bourdieu's work has been particularly influential on the so-called 'Manchester' school of work on class comprising the work of scholars such as Fiona Devine, Michael Savage and Alan Warde. Much of this work takes its theoretical inspiration from the work of Bourdieu. Although Bourdieu himself paid insufficient attention to working-class cultural practices (Jenkins, 1992), a number of British sociologists have attempted to take Bourdieu's ideas and apply them in ways that bring out the subtleties and richness of working-class cultural dispositions, at the same time as not losing sight of the limited economic resources and social power which the working class has (Reay, 1998a, 1998b; Charlesworth, 2000).

Prominent amongst these accounts is that of Bev Skeggs (1997) who, in *Formations of Class and Gender,* has constructed an innovative account of class and gender relations by using a combination of Bourdieu's multi-capital approach to class, feminist theory and Foucault's poststructural approach to the construction of subjectivity via discourses. The book is a feminist ethnography based on an extended period of research with 83 young white working-class women in an anonymized town in North West England.[55] One of the central analytical themes in Skeggs' book is that of 'respectability'. Historically 'the display of respectability became a signifier of *not* being working class' (1997: 47; original emphasis), an emphasis the women in

Skeggs' research continued. Using Bourdieu's theoretical toolkit, Skeggs interpreted class via processes of *dis-identification* rather than identification, in which class was revealed by what the women chose *not* to identity with. In dis-identifying with the working class, who they considered as uniformly rough and undesirable, the women stressed their own respectability via their clothes and bodily appearance. The women strove to prove their respectability in the light of the culturally hegemonic 'middle-class gaze' (1997: 93) by wearing the 'right' clothes, living in the 'right' houses, and adopting the 'right' standards of heterosexual femininity:

> The working class are never free from the judgements of imaginary and real others that position them, not just as different, but as inferior, as inadequate. Homes and bodies are where respectability is displayed but where class is lived out as the most omnipresent form, engendering surveillance and constant assessment of themselves. (1997: 90)

However, despite their best efforts the women in Skeggs' study did not manage to 'get it right' in middle-class terms because they lacked the kinds of cultural and economic capital taken for granted by the middle class – that capital which had the power of 'symbolic capital' in Bourdieu's terms:

> Legitimation is the key mechanism in the conversion to power. Cultural capital has to be legitimated before it can have symbolic power. [...] Symbolic capital is powerful capital: it brings power with it. If one's cultural capital is delegitimated then it cannot be traded as an asset; it cannot be capitalized upon (although it may retain significance and meaning to the individual) and its power is limited. (Skeggs, 1997: 8 and 10)

One of the key arenas in which cultural capital is converted into symbolic capital is the education system. The possession of higher education qualifications both delivers the kind of symbolic legitimation that the working-class women's own bodily form of cultural capital simply could not, as well as provides access to the economic capital associated with the middle class. The women in Skeggs' study were limited to displaying those forms of cultural capital with the least generalized legitimacy and power, their femininity, bodily appearance and 'respectability'.

Skeggs provides both a theoretically sophisticated and empirically rich account of social identities and inequalities vis-à-vis working-class women. Her book has been very influential and has effectively formed a bridge between cultural and sociological accounts of the working class. However, at the same time there is a theoretical tension in the book between an emphasis on the 'real' and the 'discursive', a tension which reflects her marrying of Bourdieu with Foucault's poststructural approach to subjectivity. On the one hand, Skeggs uses Bourdieu's framework to provide a detailed analysis of the ways in which the various forms of capital intertwined in the women's lives. She places great store on the notion that the women in her study were defined by various forms of exclusion, from the labour market, from education, etc., and that such exclusions had real impacts on their lives. She explicitly refers to class, 'race' and gender as 'structurally organized social positions [that] enable and limit our access to cultural, economic, social and symbolic capital and thus the ability to recognize ourselves as the subject positions we occupy' (1997: 12–13).

On the other hand Skeggs also argues that 'class is a discursive, historically specific construction, a product of middle-class political consolidation, which includes elements of fantasy and projection' (1997: 5). The women's own subjectivity is therefore a discursive construction, in the manner of Foucault, subject as they are to the power of the middle-class gaze which operates via 'frameworks of regulation, knowledge and discourse' (1997: 12). There is therefore a limited space in which the women can *themselves* construct their own identities. The absence of any notion of independent working-class politics in Skeggs' book inevitably means that her respondents are always and everywhere the objects of others' gazes. Furthermore, Skeggs plays down the role of 'rough/respectable' status divisions *within* the working class; see Watt (2006) for a discussion of such intra-class distinctions.

Debating class identity

In the early post-war period, surveys indicated that most people in England could readily identify themselves as either working or middle class (see *inter alia* Benney et al., 1956; Willmott and Young, 1960; Zweig, 1961; Runciman, 1966). The majority of manual workers thought of themselves as 'working class', while most non-manual professionals, managers and clerical employees considered themselves to be 'middle class'. Working-class identification was further enhanced by trade union membership and being a tenant rather than a home owner.[56] There were also links between subjective class identity and politics, since working-class identifiers were more likely to support the Labour Party. As mentioned in Chapter 3, the affluent worker study found high levels of working-class identification and Labour support among factory workers in Luton, a town that was not associated with strong Labour traditions or heavy industry (Goldthorpe et al., 1969). During the last two decades, class identity has come to be regarded as far less straightforward and instead characterized by ambivalence, uncertainty and embarrassment, even by writers generally sympathetic to class analysis (Bradley, 1996; Savage et al., 2001; Sayer, 2005). It is possible to identify three broad approaches to class identity and in particular working-class identity.

---

1. Class identity has weakened and become more ambivalent (postmodern and late modern theorists)

Theorists of postmodernity and late modernity have argued that class identity has declined in importance and become increasingly ambivalent. As already mentioned, postmodernists point to the notion that class is simply one identity among many hence it should not be surprising that it is characterized by far greater uncertainty. Theorists of late modernity, such as Beck and Giddens, are similarly unsurprised by the increased ambivalence surrounding class identity. Giddens (1996) argues that collectivized class identities based on working-class communities have weakened as a result of macro-social changes associated with globalization and advanced modernity; individuals increasingly reflexively monitor their identities in a self-conscious fashion. Class may still hold purchase, but merely as part of an individual's biographical narrative and not as an expression of any social collectivity. Someone could thus say, 'I come from a working-class background because my dad was a coal miner', even if their class means little in the sense of acting as any kind of mobilizing force.

The strength of this approach to class identity is that it directs attention towards general social trends which suggest that 'class' is less significant than it once was. Theoretically it provides a coherent explanation as to why these trends might have occurred and why class identity is increasingly weak and ambivalent. The shift from the study of 'class consciousness' to 'identity' by sociologists who remain committed to class analysis suggests that elements of this postmodern/late modern critique apply since class no longer has the purchase on the sociological (or social) imagination that it once had.

2. Class identity has remained significant ('traditional' class analysts)

If postmodernists and theorists of late modernity have indicated why class is increasingly weak and ambivalent, 'traditional' class analysts have argued that the evidence base for such wide-ranging theoretical claims is lacking. Traditional class analysts are most associated with Marxism and Weberian theory and have a tendency to rely on the 'employment aggregate' methodology (Marshall et al., 1988; Wright, 1997). Survey research is used to indicate that not only are people generally well aware of class inequalities, but that they can also readily identify themselves as members of particular social classes (Reid, 1998). Despite the dominant view from the mass media and opinion leaders that the United States is an overwhelmingly 'middle-class' society, recent survey evidence indicates that the *majority* of Americans self-identify as working class rather than middle class (cited in Zweig, 2000: 57–9). Box 8.2 provides similar evidence based on a major survey of class undertaken in Britain. It is this kind of evidence that buttresses the argument that notions of a secular decline in class identity are predicated on an unwarranted 'dualistic historical thinking whereby a communitarian and solidaristic proletariat of some bygone heyday of class antagonism is set against the atomized and consumer-oriented working class of today' (Marshall et al., 1988: 206).

Box 8.2   CLASS IDENTITY IN BRITAIN

The 'Essex' Class Survey found that:

- 60 per cent of people thought of themselves as belonging to a particular social class;
- Over 90 per cent could place themselves in a class category when asked to do so;

- of the latter, 58 per cent identified as 'working class' and 42 per cent as 'middle class';
- class identity was associated with the Nuffield class schema since the majority of service class men and women self-identified as 'middle class' whereas the majority of manual working-class men and women self-identified as 'working class';
- affiliation to the working class increased the proportion of Labour voters among all social classes;
- 79 per cent overall could think of no other salient group identity *apart* from social class.

Source: Marshall et al. (1988: 127–8, 143–6 and 246–7)

A variant on the traditional approach is Devine's (1992a, 1992b) re-study of affluent manual workers in Luton based on semi-structured interviews. Devine found that when she initially asked her respondents directly about their class identity, they were not very forthcoming. However, this changed when she introduced the topic of politics in the sense that being 'working class' was more likely to be articulated in relation to support for the Labour Party. She concludes that class identity has particular salience in relation to politics and voting, a view that has congruence with the findings from Marshall et al. (1988) that workers' class identity is affected by the way that those organizations representing workers, the Labour Party and trades unions, articulate a form of class politics themselves. In emphasizing the role played by organizations, the traditional approach rightly draws attention to the institutional context within which people's identities are created, a point we return to below.

The traditional approach to class analysis cautions against simplistic notions of a secular decline in class identity that draw upon a historical romanticized notion of the working class. Groups that are regarded as archetypal traditional 'workers' with clearly established and unproblematic working-class identities were not always thus. Richards (1996) shows how the distinction between striking and non-striking miners in the 1984 coal dispute was predicated on a historical regional sectionalism, for example between Yorkshire and Nottinghamshire, that has long divided coal miners in Britain. Similarly, a historical study of the Becontree council housing estate in East London shows how privatism and non-unionism flourished in the inter-war period (Olechnowicz, 1997).

This approach to class identity has been subject to several criticisms, many of which are methodological. It is argued that class identity is a complex phenomenon which is not easily amenable to analysis via structured questionnaires; the latter have problems in capturing context which is all important in relation to research on identity, a criticism that leading analysts associated with the 'traditional' approach have themselves made (Marshall, 1988; Devine, 1992b). More specifically, critics have suggested that the questions employed in many class surveys *lead* the respondents to self-identify as members of classes. One example is the criticism levelled at the Essex researchers that they primed their respondents to think of themselves in class terms since they had been 'bombarded with questions about class right from the start of the interview' (Saunders, 1989: 4).[57] Nevertheless despite this 'bombardment', it is notable that only 60 per cent of respondents said that they belonged to a class when directly asked, whilst 40 per cent did not (Box 8.3). The percentage of positive class identifiers is considerably less than was found in previous surveys on class in Britain dating back to the 1950s and 1960s (see *inter alia* Benney et al., 1956; Zweig, 1961; Runciman, 1966). Marshall et al. (1988: 166–7) conceded this point themselves, although they suggested that the difference between their and Runciman's results, for example, was probably due to the fact that they employed a less directive question than he did which meant that the difference was artefactual and not indicative of a decline over time between the two surveys. Devine (2004b) has suggested that, on the other hand, it could well be that sociologists, both in the early post-war period and later, simply did not pay sufficient attention to the complexity of people's views, a point recently developed by Savage (2005) in his re-analysis of the 'Affluent Worker' data.

Certainly there are issues about exactly how one asks questions in surveys about something as complex as class identity. It is noteworthy that the evidence that Zweig (2000) cites about the prevalence of working-class identity in the United States was based on a survey question which said 'what class are you?' and gave respondents a fixed choice of four different options. Box 8.3 below provides an exercise on asking different kinds of questions about class awareness and class identity.

Box 8.3 EXERCISE: ASKING QUESTIONS ABOUT CLASS AWARENESS AND IDENTITY

Work in pairs for this exercise

Listed below are two different versions of the same short interview schedule about class identity. One person in the pair chooses version one and the other person, version two. Each person in the group should then try out their version of the interview schedule on 10–12 people. Read the questions out to the respondents and note down their answers. As far as possible, each person in the pair should try to ask the questions to similar kinds of people (similar proportions of men and women and of similar ages).

When the schedules are completed, each person should then examine the responses to the three questions and consider what the responses might mean for how people think about social class. Compare the results with those of Bradley (p. 184 below).

In pairs, compare the responses across the two different versions of the schedule. What are the similarities and what are the differences? Discuss why these similarities and differences might have occurred?

What are the limitations of this exercise? How would you improve it if you were doing a real piece of sociological research?

Version One

In this version, you will be using closed questions. These are questions in which you ask the respondent to choose from the list that you give them. Tick the box that they indicate.

Q1. Do you think that social class exists in [YOUR SOCIETY] today?

Yes   ☐

No   ☐

Don't know   ☐

Q2. Do you think of yourself as belonging to any particular social class?

Yes   ☐

No   ☐

Don't know   ☐

Q3. Suppose you were asked to say which class you belonged to, which would you say?

Upper class   ☐

Middle class   ☐

Working class   ☐

Underclass   ☐

Version Two

In this version, you will be using open-ended questions. Write down exactly what the respondent says in answer to each question.

Q1. Do you think that social class exists in [YOUR SOCIETY] today?

Q2. Do you think of yourself as belonging to any particular social class?

Q3. Suppose you were asked to say which class you belonged to, which would you say?

---

3. Class identity has become more ambivalent but is still significant ('revisionist' class analysts)

The limitations of standardized surveys have prompted stratification researchers to increasingly use qualitative methods, such as semi-structured interviews or even participant observation (see *inter alia* Skeggs, 1997; Bradley, 1999; Reay, 1998a, 1998b; Charlesworth, 2000; Savage et al., 2001, 2005a). This body of research is far more guarded about the salience and supposed unambiguous nature of class as a form of social identity than survey findings would suggest, a finding that particularly applies to 'working-class' identity. In these studies, far greater attention is paid to monitor reflexively what 'class' means within the interview context itself; thus the exact location of class questions in the interviews is itself an aspect of the research findings with questions increasingly placed at the end of the interviews to see if the language of class is used prior to the researcher asking direct questions about class. One study that extends this more open-ended approach is that of Lamont (2000) in her research on American and French workers' views on social hierarchy.

Alongside such methodological developments, there has also been a concerted effort made to rethink what ambivalent and weak class identities might tell us about social class inequalities. Diane Reay examined children's education in London by interviewing young mothers at two dissimilar schools, one largely working class and one middle class. She noted that only a minority of her interviewees referred to social class prior to being asked to self-identify in class terms, although they did refer to concepts such as 'people like us' and 'people unlike us'. Using Bourdieu's theoretical framework, Reay interpreted these phrases as *meaning* class. Even though only a minority of Reay's respondents spontaneously referred to class, many managed to place themselves in class terms when explicitly asked to do so, although considerable ambivalence was also evident (1998b: 41–3).

The work of the 'revisionist' class analysts has helped to reinvigorate class analysis within both sociology and geography in Britain and elsewhere. By drawing inspiration from an eclectic mixture of theoretical developments, notably Bourdieu's conceptual architecture, but also feminism and poststructuralism, this work has helped to reconnect class to the rest of the disciplines rather than ploughing on regardless in the manner of the traditional approach to class. Bourdieu's theoretical framework offers a subtle basis for understanding class identity that allows researchers to steer a path between the polarity of the 'all change/no change' debate that characterizes the first two approaches discussed above (Devine et al., 2005).

There appear to be two main directions that the revisionist approach to class identity is leading. The first is towards an emphasis on place, as discussed above in relation to the recent work of Savage et al. (2004, 2005a, 2005b). They have argued that affiliations to a sense of place have perhaps replaced those of occupation in the understanding of the process of class allegiance and, contra to Lockwood's notion of occupational communities, these are essentially communities of consumption (Wynne, 1998; Florida, 2002). The second revisionist direction is towards emphasizing how class identity is constituted by the making of moral judgements about self-worth and the worth of others. Skeggs' (1997) work on 'dis-identification' and respectability has highlighted the way that class identity is bound up with moral boundary making. She develops this theme in her latest book via an analysis of representations of the working class by the middle class: 'any judgement of the working class as negative (waste, excess, vulgar, unmodern, authentic, etc.), is an attempt by the middle-class to accrue value' (Skeggs, 2004: 118). Hence the working class are routinely pathologized by the middle class as a way of shoring up their own fragile sense of moral superiority, as seen in Germaine Greer's comment on 'Essex girls': 'she used to be conspicuous as she clacked along the pavements in her white plastic stilettos, her bare legs mottled patriot red, white and blue with cold, and her big bottom barely covered by a denim mini-skirt' (cited in Skeggs, 2004: 112). If Skeggs tends to focus on representations, other sociologists are more concerned to examine how lay actors express the moral connotations of class identity (see *inter alia* Lamont, 2000; Watt, 2001, 2006; Sayer, 2005). As social identities become increasingly linked to the global mass media (see the discussion of youth cultures in Chapter 7: Nayak, 2003), so the representational/lay distinction can itself become increasingly blurred. This can be seen, for example, in the recent case of the 'chav' phenomenon which has ushered in a media-driven form of 'new snobbery' against the working class, according to John Harris ('Bottom of the Class', *The Guardian*, 11 April 2006).

Identity and organization

Whilst recognizing that the revisionist approach to class identity, and in particular that the work inspired by Bourdieu has reinvigorated class analysis, it has also been suggested that this 'cultural turn' has gone too far in its neglect of traditional issues such as work, employment and politics (Crompton and Scott, 2005). As Savage et al. (2001: 889) note, 'when people talk about class they tend to talk about politics'. Skeggs and Reay, for example, are concerned with the role of class identity in relation to consumption and education respectively and as such have little to say about the potential role played by political parties and trade unions in shaping class identities, both among women as well as men. Of course, it is important to note how the main organizations traditionally involved in working-class formation, trade unions and the Labour Party, historically marginalized women's concerns and interests, a marginalization which has been ameliorated if not eradicated in the contemporary period (Cunnison and Stageman, 1995; Bradley, 1999).

Bradley (1999) has highlighted the role played by organizations in the formation of class identity in her study of class and gender relations in North East England (see Chapter 4). She found that four-fifths of the female and male respondents (blue and white-collar employees) thought class inequalities still existed, but only just over half identified as belonging to a class *themselves*, mainly as working class. Bradley therefore suggests that there is an element of stigmatization surrounding being 'working class' as Skeggs (1997) highlighted. At the same time, Bradley argues that there was also a 'counter-discourse' of positive class identity among her respondents rooted in close-knit working-class families and communities. This discourse moreover was stronger in unionized workplaces, particularly among trade union activists: 'at work a link between class and trade unions still exists; a strong union presence promotes active or politicized class identification' (1999: 159), as the post-war studies on class identity also indicated (see above). Trade union activists therefore demonstrated what she has called elsewhere a 'politicized class identity' (Bradley, 1996: 26) in the sense that class played a more or less permanent role in their social identities and contributed to their own activism. Trade unions and politics therefore remain significant in the constitution of class identities, albeit more so for some people than others. Bradley concludes that some of the increased ambiguity around class identity can be explained by the shift towards post-industrial employment patterns in which manual/non-manual (and 'collar') distinctions no longer have the social and economic salience they once had – see Chapter 4.

It would seem that workplace organizations, such as trade unions, potentially make a difference to people's identities and perceptions of class. However, the majority of private post-industrial workplaces are not unionized (see Chapter 7). Does this therefore imply a catch-22 position in which class identity only exists in unionized workplaces, but that in order for unions to exist in workplaces then workers must have a sense of class identity? Perhaps one way out of this dilemma is to simply sidestep the notion of class identity altogether and instead focus on the conditions under which workers come together and organize collectively, as Castree et al. (2004) suggest. The primary concern among the Scottish call centre workers we discussed in Chapter 7 was with expressing a sense of injustice rather than with any class-based identity *per se*. A concern with the language of justice and injustice might therefore prove more fruitful for labour activists rather than with the language of class identity; the latter is of limited use given the widespread acceptance of postmodern arguments that class identity is only one among several competing identities:

> ... today it is abundantly clear that a 'working class' identity ignores and excludes all those important non-class elements of worker identity that make working people what they are. So class is a limited and exclusive basis for any form of global struggle founded on a common worker identity. Indeed it is fair to say that virtually *all* attempts to locate such an identity risk falsely 'essentializing' workers, which is to say they risk mistaking a part of their identity as *the* fundamental element of that identity. (Castree et al., 2004: 242; original emphasis)

The potential exists for 'worker resistance', as we saw in Chapter 7. Moreover such resistance can still take collective forms, even if the source of that collective coming together is no longer around a specific 'working-class' identity – an identity that for many workers is either at best partial or at worst anachronistic.

In fact, collective organization can even involve mobilizing along social identities *other than* class, notably around the concerns of women, migrants and other minority ethnic groups. This is broadly the position advocated by a group of North American and British sociologists, geographers and labour activists who have highlighted the success of union mobilization campaigns among immigrants in California, especially Los Angeles, one of the epicentres of social polarization and accelerating ethnic diversity as we saw in Chapter 5 (Waldinger et al., 1998; Milkman, 2000; Holgate, 2005; Wills, 2005a, 2005b; Tufts, 2006). Instead of bemoaning the collapse of the white male constituency for trade unions as found in post-war industrial society, the prominence of women and minority ethnic groups in the post-industrial service economy can be regarded as a source of potential strength as labour activists focus their organizing efforts on the ethnic or immigrant community across the city instead of just at the workplace. This can be seen in the famous *Justice for Janitors* campaign in Los Angeles, which was the subject of the film *Bread and Roses* directed by Ken Loach (Waldinger et al., 1998). Another less well-known example is the HERE Local 75 union's efforts to transform the image of the ethnically diverse hotel workforce in Toronto away from mere service providers to 'cultural workers' who are key to culture and tourism in the multi-ethnic global metropolis (Tufts, 2006). Whether this innovative form of community-based union activism can be effectively deployed in Britain, with its narrow industrial relations agenda, is a moot point, as recent studies of organizing among minority ethnic factory and hotel workers indicate (Holgate, 2005; Wills, 2005a).

Nevertheless, the above illustrates a fundamental issue in relation to the new work discussed in Chapter 7. The workers undertaking the many McJobs and/or 'bad jobs' that are being generated in the post-industrial economy have essentially two possibilities. The first is to do such jobs for as short a period of time as possible and then leave for a MacJob or 'good job'. Many immigrants in globalizing cities around the world are doing just this, as illustrated in Box 1.1 on page 2. There are two problems with this 'escape route' scenario, however. The first is whether or not such upward mobility is likely or even possible given the lack of promotional possibilities, or 'ladders', many such jobs have, as we saw in the case of both fast food and call centres. Furthermore, there are also profound structural barriers in place, not least racial discrimination, which could prevent ethnic minorities from moving up (Wrench et al., 1999). As we saw in Box 7.2 on page 141, 'horizontal mobility' might well prove the norm. The second possibility is that if such escape routes are either not available or achievable, then the workers doing those jobs will be virtually permanently materially disadvantaged as well as socially stigmatized. This is clearly the possibility that the 'youth transitions' literature is warning about. In a recent paper, Wills (2005b) has emphasized that major attention should be given to considering how 'bad' jobs can be turned into, not necessarily 'good 'jobs', but at least 'better' jobs, which can confer a sense of dignity, justice and even rewards. This might well seem utopian, but as socio-historical studies have shown, many of the bad jobs from the industrial past were only transformed into 'better jobs' via the actions of groups of workers themselves, not least via trades unions, as in the case of the much lamented coal miners (Richards, 1996). It is worth remembering that employment in the inter-war non-unionized car assembly plant at Ford Dagenham was characterized by little personal contact between workers, high rates of labour turnover and little experience of unions on the part of young workers (Olechnowicz, 1997); such conditions are redolent of much service sector employment today.

Final thoughts

There has been a continuing pattern since the end of the Second World War in which as capitalism becomes more powerful, people appear to become more tied up with their own private lives. Goldthorpe and Lockwood first noted this phenomenon in their work in Luton in which they identified a privatized, home centred working class. Giddens and Beck, as we have seen, argue that this is now the dominant experience in social consciousness. As capitalism moved into crisis during the 1970s, there was perhaps a brief resurgence in working-class communalism and radical political action but this rapidly retreated once more into privatism and consumption as the neo-liberal medicine dosed out to the economy by the Thatcher Government began to take effect. People are now invited to view the public realm in individual consumer terms rather than those of class allegiance and have generally responded to this positively, if not enthusiastically. In this centre ground, classes are – for most people – something they use to 'triangulate' their social position. They used to be working class because that was what their father was – but his job no longer exists and they have moved on, own their home and have a couple of cars; they are not middle class because they are not a doctor, dentist or director, nor do they speak like that and nor do they live next to them. They are somewhere in between in a neither/nor land in which they are doing OK (better than their father) but not as good as they might (living in a better area). This situation, in which people deploy their various assets and resources – cultural, social and economic – according to their aspirations, feelings and abilities, describes the middle mass of a society whose boundaries are patrolled by the ghosts of classes past and fantasies for the future. Even for those in secure professional and managerial employment it is hard to rejoice because of endless performance reviews and organizational restructurings. This of course is, at best, only half the story. For many, but particularly in the United States and Britain as we have shown, increasing socio-economic inequality has meant that they are living at the margins of poverty reliant on alternating combinations of McJobs and welfare benefits. Social exclusionary processes embrace a significant segment of Western populations as they experience the vicissitudes of 'flexible capitalism' and 'flexploitation' in post-industrial workplaces.

What people sought, and got, at the end of the Second World War was a measure of security in which, when all was said and done, you were either working class or middle class and that determined 'who' you were. Where you might aspire was for your children. The neo-liberal transformations of the 1980s offered the possibility of exciting alternatives but at the cost of removing the comfort blanket provided by social class membership. Social class may still be out there but it is no longer the sole provider of culture and belonging which has been outsourced – to various forms of identity providers which have mediated cultural and social if not economic forms of capital by which people construct their social position. 'Class of itself', while still out there, is less good an indicator of 'class in itself' than it was.

Further reading

The book by Savage et al. (2005a) based on research in and near Manchester is a major intervention in the debate about the role of class and space in approaches to stratification. Two recent valuable sources on the 'cultural turn' in class analysis, especially in relation to questions of identity, are the edited book by Devine et al. (2005) and the special issue of *Sociology* (2005). Bourdieu's work is notoriously difficult to read, but we would recommend that every student of social class has a look at *Distinction* (Bourdieu, 1984). For an exceptionally clear example of how Bourdieu's theory of capital and class can be applied empirically, see the chapter by Elliott

(1997) based upon his research on Scottish migrants in Canada. Drawing both upon Bourdieu and the phenomenology of Merleau-Ponty, Charlesworth (2000) offers a compelling, if one-dimensional, account of the contemporary 'working-class habitus' in deindustrialized Rotherham in Northern England. Lamont (2000) is an insightful comparative study of the subjective identities of male workers, in the United States and France. Two recent North American ethnographies which emphasize the role of place in relation to class and race are a study of a white working-class enclave of Chicago by Kefalas (2003), and Low's (2004) study of 'gated communities'.

.... Bibliography

Abel-Smith, B. and Townsend, P. (1965) *The Poor and the Poorest*. London: G. Bell & Sons.

Abercrombie, N. and Urry, J. (1983) *Capitalism, Labour and the Middle Classes*. London: Allen & Unwin.

Abercrombie, N., Hill, S. and Turner, B.S. (2000) *Dictionary of Sociology*. London: Penguin.

Abrahamson, M. (2004) *Global Cities*. Oxford: Oxford University Press.

Abrams, F. (2002) *Below the Breadline: Living on the Minimum Wage*. London: Profile Books.

Aglietta, M. (2000) *A Theory of Capitalist Regulation*. London: Verso.

Alcock, P., Beatty, C., Fothergill, S., Macmillan, R. and Yeandle, S. (2003) *Work to Welfare: How Men Become Detached from the Labour Market*. Cambridge: Cambridge University Press.

Alcock, P. and Craig, G. (eds.) (2001) *International Social Policy*. Basingstoke: Palgrave.

Alesina, A. and Glaeser, E.L. (2004) *Fighting Poverty in the US and Europe*. Oxford: Oxford University Press.

Allen, J. and Henry, N. (1997) 'Ulrich Beck's *Risk Society* at work: labour and employment in the contract service industries', *Transactions of the Institute of British Geographers (New Series)*, 22(2): 180–96.

Allen, J. and Massey, D. (eds.) (1988) *The Economy in Question*. London: Sage

Althusser, L. (1969) *For Marx*. London: Allen Lane.

Alvaro, J.L. and Garrido, A. (2003) 'Economic hardship, employment status and psychological wellbeing of young people in Europe', in T. Hammer (ed.) *Youth Unemployment and Social Exclusion in Europe: A Comparative Study*. Bristol: The Policy Press, pp. 173–92.

Amersfoort, H. van and Cortie, C. (1996) 'Social polarisation in a welfare state? Immigrants in the Amsterdam region', *New Community*, 22(4): 671–87.

Amin, A. (1994a) 'Models, fantasies and phantoms of transition' in A. Amin (ed.), *Post-Fordism: A Reader*. Oxford: Blackwell, pp. 1–39.

Amin, A. (ed.) (1994b) *Post-Fordism: A Reader*. Oxford: Blackwell.

Amin, A. and Thrift, N. (2002) *Cities: Reimagining the Urban*. Cambridge: Polity Press.

Andall, J. (2000) *Gender, Migration and Domestic Service: The Politics of Black Women in Italy*. Aldershot: Ashgate.

Andersen, J. (1999) 'Social and system integration and the underclass', in I. Gough and G. Olofsson (eds.) *Capitalism and Social Cohesion*. Basingstoke: Macmillan Press, pp. 127–48.

Anderson, B. (2000) *Doing the Dirty Work: The Global Politics of Domestic Labour*. London: Zed Books.

Anderson, B. (2001) 'Why madam has so many bathrobes: demand for migrant domestic workers in the EU', *Tijdschrift voor Economische en Social Geografie*, 92(1): 18–26.

Anisef, P. and Lanphier, M. (eds.) (2003) *The World in a City*. Toronto: University of Toronto Press.

Apospori, E. and Millar, J. (2003) *The Dynamics of Social Exclusion in Europe*. Cheltenham: Edward Elgar.

Appelbaum, E., Bernhardt, A. and Murnane, R.J. (eds.) (2003) *Low-Wage America: How Employers are Reshaping Opportunity in the Workplace*. New York: Russell Sage Foundation.

Armstrong, P., Glyn, A. and Harrison, J. (1984) *Capitalism since World War II*. London: Fontana.

Atkinson, R. (2003a) 'Domestication by Cappucino or a revenge on urban space? Control and empowerment in the management of public spaces', *Urban Studies*, 40(9): 1829–44.

Atkinson, R. (2003b) 'Introduction: misunderstood saviour or vengeful wrecker? The many meanings and problems of gentrification', *Urban Studies*, 40(12): 2343–50.

Atkinson, R. and Bridge, G. (eds) (2005) *Gentrification in a Global Context: the new urban colonialism*. London: Routledge

Avila, E. (2004) *Popular Culture in the Age of White Flight: Fear and Fantasy in Suburban Los Angeles*. Berkeley: University of California Press.

Bagguley, P. and Mann, K. (1992) 'Idle thieving bastards? Scholarly representations of the "underclass"', *Work, Employment and Society*, 6(1): 113–26.

Bain P. and Taylor, P. (2000) 'Entrapped by the electronic panopticon? Worker resistance in the call centre', *New Technology, Work and Employment*, 15(1): 2–18.

Bain P. and Taylor, P. (2002) 'Consolidation, "cowboys" and the developing employment relationship in British, Dutch and US call centres', in U. Holtgrewe, C. Kerst and K. Shire (eds.) *Re-Organising Service Work: Call Centres in Germany and Britain*. Aldershot: Ashgate, pp. 42–62.

Bales, K. (2003) 'Because she looks like a child', in B. Ehrenreich and A.R. Hochschild (eds.) *Global Woman: Nannies, Maid and Sex Workers in the New Economy*. London: Granta Books, pp. 207–29.

Ball, S.J. (2002) *Class Strategies and the Education Market: the Middle Classes and Social Advantage*. London: Routledge Falmer.

Banham, R. (1971) *Los Angeles: The Architecture of Four Ecologies*. London: Allen Lane: Penguin Press.

Banks, M., Breakwell, G., Bynner, J., Emler, N., Jamieson, L. and Roberts, K. (1992) *Careers and Identities*. Buckingham: Open University Press.

Baran, P.A. and Sweezy, P.M. (1968) *Monopoly Capital; An Essay on the American Economic and Social Order*. Harmondsworth: Pelican.

Barnes, M., Heady, C., Middleton, S., Millar, J., Papadopoulos, Room, G. and Tsakloglou, P. (2002) *Poverty and Social Exclusion in Europe*. Cheltenham: Edward Elgar.

Baudrillard, J. (1988) *America*. London: Verso.

Bauman, Z. (1998) *Work, Consumerism and the New Poor*. Buckingham: Open University Press.

Beaverstock, J.V., Smith, R.G. and Taylor, P.J. (1999) 'A roster of world cities', *Cities*, 16(6): 445–58.

Beck, U. (1992) *Risk Society*. London: Sage.

Beck, U. (2000) *The Brave New World of Work*. Cambridge: Polity Press.

Beck, U., Giddens, A. and Lash, S. (1994) *Reflexive Modernization: Politics Tradition and Aesthetics in the Modern Social Order*. Cambridge: Polity Press.

Beechey, V. (1987) *Unequal Work*. London: Verso.

Bell, C. and Newby, H. (1971) *Community Studies*. London: Allen & Unwin.

Belt, V. (2002) 'Capitalising on femininity: gender and the utilization of social skills in telephone call centres', in U. Holtgrewe, C. Kerst and K. Shire (eds.) *Re-Organising Service Work: Call Centres in Germany and Britain*. Aldershot: Ashgate, pp. 123–45.

Belt, V., Richardson, R. and Webster, J. (2002) 'Women, social skill and interactive service work in telephone call centres', *New Technology, Work and Employment*, 17(1): 20–34.

Benn, C. and Simon, B. (1970) *Half Way There: report on the British comprehensive school reform*. London: McGraw Hill.

Bennett, A. and Kahn-Harris, K. (eds.) (2004) *After Subculture: Critical Studies in Contemporary Youth Culture*. Basingstoke: Palgrave Macmillan.

Benney, M., Gray, A.P. and Pear, R.H. (1956) *How People Vote: A Study of Electoral Behaviour in Greenwich*. London: Routledge & Kegan Paul.

Berghman, J. (1995) 'Social exclusion in Europe: policy context and analytical framework', in G. Room (ed.) *Beyond the Threshold: The Measurement and Analysis of Social Exclusion*. Bristol: The Policy Press, pp. 10–28.

Bernstein, B. (1975) *Class Codes and Control*. London: Routledge.

Berry, B. (1985) 'Islands of renewal in seas of decay', in P. Preston (ed.) *The New Urban Reality*. Washington, DC. Brookings Institute, pp. 69–96.

Berthoud, R. (2004) *Patterns of Poverty Across Europe*. Bristol: The Policy Press.

Beynon, H. (1984) *Working for Ford*, 2nd edn. Harmondsworth: Penguin.

Beynon, H. (1997) 'The changing practices of work', in R.K. Brown (ed.) *The Changing Shape of Work*. Basingstoke: Macmillan Press, pp. 20–53.

Beynon, J. and Dunkerley, D. (eds.) (2000) *Globalization: the Reader*. London: The Athlone Press.

Bittman, M., Matheson, G. and Meagher, G. (1999) 'The changing boundary between home and market: Australian trends in outsourcing domestic labour', *Work, Employment and Society*, 13(2): 249–73.

Bittner, S. Schietinger, M., Schroth, J. and Weinkopf, C. (2002) 'Call centres in Germany: employment, training and job design', in U. Holtgrewe, C. Kerst and K. Shire (eds.) *Re-Organising Service Work: Call Centres in Germany and Britain*. Aldershot: Ashgate, pp. 63–85.

Blackburn, R.M. and Mann, M. (1979) *The Working Class in the Labour Market*. London: Macmillan.

Blackman, S.J. (1997) 'Destructing a giro: a critical and ethnographic study of the youth "underclass"', in R. MacDonald (ed.) *Youth, the 'Underclass' and Social Exclusion*. London: Routledge, pp. 113–29.

Blauner, R. (1964) *Alienation and Freedom: the Factory Worker and his Industry*. Chicago: University of Chicago Press.

Blokland, T. (2003) *Urban Bonds*. Cambridge: Polity Press.

Blokland, T. and Savage, M. (2001) 'Network, class and space', *International Journal of Urban and Regional Research*, 25: 221–26.

Body-Gendrot, S. (1996) 'Paris: a "soft" global city?', *New Community*, 22(4): 595–605.

Body-Gendrot, S. and Martiniello, M. (eds.) (2000) *Minorities in European Cities: The Dynamics of Social Integration and Exclusion at the Neighbourhood Level*. Basingstoke: Macmillan.

Bommes, M. and Geddes, A. (eds.) (2000) *Immigration and Welfare: Challenging the Borders of the Welfare State*. London: Routledge.

Bondi, L. (1999) 'Gender, class and gentrification: enriching the debate', *Environment and Planning D: Society and Space*, 17: 261–82.

Bonnett, A. (2000) *White Identities: Historical and International Perspectives*. Harlow: Prentice Hall.

Bonoli, G. (1997) 'Classifying welfare states: a two-dimension approach', *Journal of Social Policy*, 26(3): 351–72.

Bott, E. (1964) *Family and Social Network*. London: Tavistock Publications.

Bottero, W. (2005) *Stratification: Social Division and Inequality*. London: Routledge.

Bottomore, T. (1965) *Classes in Modern Society*. London: Allen & Unwin.

Bourdieu, P. (1984) *Distinction: A Social Critique of the Judgement of Taste*. London: Routledge.

Bourdieu, P. (1987) 'What makes a social class? On the theoretical and practical existence of groups', *Berkeley Journal of Sociology*, 32: 1–17.

Bourdieu, P. (1990) *In Other Words*. London: Sage.

Bourdieu, P. et al. (1999) *The Weight of the World: Social Suffering in Contemporary Society*. Cambridge: Polity Press.

Bourgois, P. (1995) *In Search of Respect: Selling Crack in El Barrio*. Cambridge: Cambridge University Press.

Bourne, L.S. (1993a) 'Close together and worlds apart: an analysis of changes in the ecology of income in Canadian cities', *Urban Studies*, 30(8): 1293–317.

Bourne, L.S. (1993b) 'The demise of gentrification? A commentary and prospective view', *Urban Geography*, 14(1): 95–107.

Bradley, H. (1996) *Fractured Identities: Changing Patterns of Inequality*. Cambridge: Polity Press.

Bradley, H. (1999) *Gender and Power in the Workplace*. Basingstoke: Macmillan Press.

Bradley, H., Erickson, S., Stephenson, C. and Williams, S. (2000) *Myths at Work*. Cambridge: Polity Press.

Braverman, H. (1974) *Labor and Monopoly Capital*. London: Monthly Review Press.

Breckner, R. (2002) 'Migrants: a target-category for social policy? Experiences of first-generation migration', in P. Chamberlayne, M. Rustin and T. Wengraf (eds.) *Biography and Social Exclusion in Europe: Experiences and Life Journeys*. Bristol, The Policy Press, pp. 213–28.

Breen, R. (2005) 'Foundations of a neo-Weberian class analysis', in E.O. Wright (ed.) *Approaches to Class Analysis*. Cambridge: Cambridge University Press, pp. 31–50.

Brennan, A., Rhodes, J. and Tyler, P. (2000) 'The nature of local area social exclusion in England and the role of the labour market', *Oxford Review of Economic Policy*, 16(1): 129–46.

Brenner, N. (1998) 'Global cities, glocal states: global city formation and state territorial restructuring in contemporary Europe', *Review of International Political Economy*, 5(1): 1–37.

Bridge, G. (1995) 'The space for class analysis? On class analysis in the study of gentrification', *Transactions of the Institute of British Geographers, New Series*, 20: 236–47.

Bridge, G. (2003) 'Time-space trajectories in provincial gentrification', *Urban Studies*, 40(12): 2545–56.

Bruegel, I. (1996) 'Gendering the polarisation debate: a comment on Hamnett's "social polarisation, economic restructuring and welfare state regimes"', *Urban Studies*, 33(8): 1431–39.

Brown, P. and Scase, R. (eds.) (1991) *Poor Work*. Milton Keynes: Open University Press.

Buck, N. and Gordon, I. (2000) 'Turbulence and sedimentation in the labor markets of late twentieth century metropoles', in G. Bridge and S. Watson (eds.) *A Companion to the City*. Oxford: Blackwell, pp. 181–91.

Buck, N., Gordon, I., Hall, P., Harloe, M. and Kleinman, M. (2002) *Working Capital: Life and Labour in Contemporary London*. London: Routledge.

Buckingham, A. (1999) 'Is there an underclass in Britain?', *British Journal of Sociology*, 50(1): 49–75.

Bulmer, M. (ed.) (1975) *Working-Class Images of Society*. London: Routledge & Kegan Paul.

Burchardt, T., Le Grand, J. and Piachaud, D. (1999) 'Social exclusion in Britain', *Social Policy & Administration*, 33(3): 227–44.

Burchardt, T., Le Grand, J. and Piachaud, D. (2002) 'Degrees of exclusion: developing a dynamic, multidimensional measure', in: J. Hills, J. Le Grand and D. Piachaud (eds.) *Understanding Social Exclusion*. Oxford: Oxford University Press, pp. 30–43.

Burchell, B. (2002) 'The prevalence and redistribution of job insecurity and work intensification', in B. Burchell, D. Lapido and F. Wilkinson (eds.) *Job Insecurity and Work Intensification*. London: Routledge. pp. 61–76.

Burgers, J. (1996) 'No polarisation in Dutch cities? Inequalities in a corporatist country', *Urban Studies*, 33(1): 99–105.

Burgess, S. and Propper, C. (2002) 'The dynamics of poverty in Britain', in J. Hills, J. Le Grand and D. Piachaud (eds.) *Understanding Social Exclusion*. Oxford: Oxford University Press, pp. 44–61.

Burkitt, B. and Baimbridge, M. (1995) 'The Maastricht Treaty's impact on the welfare state', *Critical Social Policy*, 14: 100–11.

Burtenshaw, D., Bateman, M. and Ashworth, G. (1991) *The European City: A Western Perspective*. London: David Fulton Publishers.

Butler, A.M. and Ford, B. (2003) *Postmodernism*. Harpenden: Pocket Essential Ideas.

Butler, T. (1992) 'People Like Us': Gentrification and the Service Class in Hackney in the 1980s. Unpublished PhD thesis, Department of Geography, Open University, Milton Keynes.

Butler, T. (1997) *Gentrification and the Middle Classes*. Aldershot: Ashgate.

Butler, T. and Hamnett, C. (1994) 'Gentrification, class and gender: some comments on Warde's "gentrification of consumption"', *Environment and Planning D: Society and Space*, 12: 477–93.

Butler, T. and Hamnett, C. (forthcoming) *Urban Studies* special issue on the Geography of Education.

Butler, T. and Robson, G. (2003a) 'Negotiating their way in: the middle classes, gentrification and their deployment of capital in a globalizing metropolis', *Urban Studies*, 40(9): 1791–809.

Butler, T. with Robson, G. (2003b) 'Plotting the middle classes: gentrification and circuits of education', *Housing Studies*, 18(1): 5–28.

Butler, T. with Robson, G. (2003) *London Calling: the middle classes and the remaking of inner London*. Oxford: Berg.

Butler, T. and Savage, M. (eds.) (1995) *Social Change and the Middle Classes*. London: UCL Press.

Byrne, D. (1998) 'Class and ethnicity in complex cities – the cases of Leicester and Bradford', *Environment and Planning A*, 30: 703–20.

Byrne, D. (1999) *Social Exclusion*. Buckingham: Open University Press.

Calhoun, C. (1993) 'Habitus, field and capital: the question of historical specificity', in C. Calhoun, E. LiPuma and M. Postone (eds.) *Bourdieu: Critical Perspectives*. Cambridge: Polity Press, pp. 61–88.

Callinicos, A. (1989) *Against Postmodernism: a Marxist Critique*. Cambridge: Polity Press.

Cannadine, D. (1982) 'Residential differentiation in nineteenth century towns: from shapes on the ground to shapes in society', in J.H. Johnson and C.G. Pooley (eds.) *The Structure of Nineteenth Century Cities*. London: Croom Helm. pp. 235–251.

Cannadine, D. (1998) *Class in Britain*. London: Yale University Press.

Castells, M. (1996a) *The Power of Identity*. Oxford: Blackwell.

Castells, M. (1996b) *The Rise of Network Society*. Oxford: Blackwell.

Castells, M. (1997) *End of Millennium*. Oxford: Blackwell.

Castles, S. and Kosack, G. (1973) *Immigrant Workers in the Class Structure in Western Europe*. Oxford: Oxford University Press.

Castles, S. and Miller, M.J. (2003) *The Age of Migration*, 3rd edn. Basingstoke: Palgrave Macmillan.

Castree, N., Coe, N.M., Ward, K. and Samers, M. (2004) *Spaces of Work: Global Capitalism and Geographies of Labour*. London, Sage.

Caulfield, J. (1994) *City Form and Everyday Life: Toronto's Gentrification and Critical Social Practice*. Toronto: University of Toronto Press.

Chamberlayne, P. (2002) 'Conclusions: social transitions and biographical work', in P. Chamberlayne, M. Rustin and T. Wengraf (eds.) *Biography and Social Exclusion in Europe: Experiences and Life Journeys*. Bristol: The Policy Press, pp. 269–88.

Chamberlayne, P., Rustin, M. and Wengraf, T. (eds.) (2002) *Biography and Social Exclusion in Europe: Experiences and Life Journeys*. Bristol: The Policy Press.

Champion, A. and Ford, T. (1998) 'The social selectivity of migration flows affecting Britain's larger conurbations: an analysis of the regional migration tables of the 1981 and 1991 Censuses', Department of Geography, University of Newcastle upon Tyne.

Charlesworth, S.J. (2000) *A Phenomenology of Working-Class Experience*. Cambridge: Cambridge University Press.

Chatterton, P. and Hollands, R. (2003) *Urban Nightscapes: Youth Cultures, Pleasure Spaces and Corporate Power*. London: Routledge.

Clapson, M. (1998) *Invincible Green Suburbs, Brave New Towns: Social Change and Urban Dispersal in Postwar England*. Manchester: Manchester University Press.

Clapson, M. (2003) *Suburban Century: Social Change and Urban Growth in England and the United States*. Oxford: Berg.

Clark, E. (1992) 'On blindness, centrepieces and complementarity in gentrification theory', *Transactions of the Institute of British Geographers NS*, 17: 358–62.

Clarke, J., Langan, M. and Williams, F. (2001) 'Remaking welfare: the British welfare regime in the 1980s and 1990s', in A. Cochrane, J. Clarke and S. Gewirtz (eds.) *Comparing Welfare States*, 2nd edn. London: Sage Publications, pp. 71–111.

Cochrane, A. (1993) 'Looking for a European welfare state', in A. Cochrane and J. Clarke (eds.) *Comparing Welfare States*. London: Sage Publications, pp. 239–68.

Cochrane, A., Clarke, J. and Gewirtz, S. (eds.) (2001) *Comparing Welfare States*, 2nd edn. London: Sage Publications.

Cockburn, C. (1983) *Brothers: Male Dominance and Technological Change*. London: Pluto.

Coffield, F., Borill, S. and Marshall, S. (1986) *Growing Up at the Margins*. Milton Keynes: Open University Press.

Cohen, P. (1972) 'Sub-cultural conflict and working-class community'. *Working Papers in Cultural Studies* No. 2. Birmingham, Centre for Contemporary Cultural Studies, University of Birmingham.

Cohen, P. and Ainley, P. (2000) 'In the country of the blind? Youth studies and cultural studies in Britain', *Journal of Youth Studies*, 3(1): 79–95.

Colatrella, S. (2001) *Workers of the World: African and Asian Migrants in Italy in the 1990s*. Trenton: Africa World Press.

Conley, H. (2002) 'A state of insecurity: temporary work in the public services', *Work, Employment and Society*, 16(4): 725–37.

Cooke, P. (1989) 'Locality, economic restructuring and world development', in P. Cooke (ed.) *Localities*. London: Unwin Hyman, pp. 1–44.

Coser, L. (1956) *The Functions of Social Conflict*. Glencoe: The Free Press.

Coser, L.A. (1973) 'Servants: the obsolescence of an occupational role', *Social Forces*, 52(1): 31–40.

Cox, R. (2000) 'Exploring the growth of paid domestic labour: a case study of London', *Geography*, 85(3): 241–51.

Cox, R. (2006) *The Servant Problem*. London: I.B. Tauris.

Cox, R. and Watt, P. (2002) 'Globalization, polarization and the informal sector: the case of paid domestic workers in London', *Area*, 34(1): 39–47.

Craig, G., Derricourt, N. and Loney, M. (eds.) (1982) *Community Work and the State. Towards a Radical Practice*. London: Routledge & Kegan Paul.

Crompton, R. (1997) *Women and Work in Modern Britain*. Oxford: Oxford University Press.

Crompton, R. (1998) *Class and Stratification*, 2nd edn. Cambridge: Polity Press.

Crompton, R. (ed.) (1999) *Restructuring Gender Relations and Employment*. Oxford: Oxford University Press.

Crompton, R. (2000) 'The gendered restructuring of the middle classes', in R. Crompton, F. Devine, M. Savage and J. Scott (eds.) *Renewing Class Analysis*. Oxford: Blackwell: 165–83.

Crompton, R. and Jones, G. (1984) *White Collar Proletariat: Deskilling and Gender in Clerical Work*. London: Macmillan.

Crompton, R., Devine, F., Savage, M. and Scott, J. (eds) (2000) *Renewing Class Analysis*. Oxford: Blackwell.

Crompton, R. and Scott, J. (2005) 'Class analysis: beyond the cultural turn', in F. Devine, M. Savage, J. Scott and R. Crompton (eds.) *Rethinking Class: Culture, Identities and Lifestyles*. Basingstoke: Palgrave Macmillan, pp. 186–203.

Crosland, A. (1956) *The Future of Socialism*. London: Jonathan Cape.

Crow, G. (1997) *Comparative Sociology and Social Theory: Beyond the Three Worlds*. Basingstoke: Macmillan.

Cunnison, S. and Stageman, J. (1995) *Feminizing the Unions*. Aldershot: Avebury.

Dahrendorf, R. (1959) *Class and Class Conflict in an Industrial Society*. London: Routledge & Kegan Paul.

Danziger, S. and Lin, A.C. (eds.) (2000) *Coping With Poverty: The Social Contexts of Neighborhood, Work and Family in the African-American Community*. Ann Arbor: University of Michigan Press.

Davis, K. and Moore, W. (1945) 'Some principles of stratification', *American Sociological Review*, 10: 242–9.

Davis, M. (1990) *City of Quartz*. London: Verso.

Davis, M. (1998) *The Ecology of Fear: Los Angeles and the Imagination of Disaster*. London: Picador.

De Clercq, E., *et al*. (2000) *Belgium/Brussels and Antwerp: URBEX Series, No. 2*. Amsterdam, Amsterdam Study Centre for the Metropolitan Environment.

Dear, M. (2002) 'Los Angeles and the Chicago School', *City and Community*, 1(1): 5–32.

Dear, M.J. (2000) *The Postmodern Urban Condition*. Oxford: Blackwell.

Dear, M.J., Schockman, H.E. and Hise, G. (eds.) (1996) *Rethinking Los Angeles*. Thousand Oaks, Ca.: Sage.

Deb, S. (2004) 'Call me', *The Guardian Weekend*, 3 April: 14–23.

Dennis, N., Henriques, F. and Slaughter, C. (1956) *Coal is Our Life: An Analysis of a Yorkshire Mining Community*. London: Tavistock Publications.

Devine, F. (1992a) *Affluent Workers Revisited: Privatism and the Working Class*. Edinburgh: Edinburgh University Press.

Devine, F. (1992b) 'Social identities, class identity and political perspectives', *Sociological Review*, 40: 229–52.

Devine, F. (1997) *Social Class in America and Britain*. Edinburgh: Edinburgh University Press.

Devine, F. (2004a) *Class Practices: How Parents Help their Children Get Good Jobs*. Cambridge: Cambridge University Press.

Devine, F. (2004b) 'Talking about class in Britain', in F. Devine and M.C. Waters (eds.) *Social Inequalities in Comparative Perspective*. Oxford: Blackwell Publishing, pp. 191–213.

Devine, F. and Savage, M. (2005) 'The cultural turn, sociology and class analysis', in F. Devine, M. Savage, J. Scott and R. Crompton (eds.) *Rethinking Class: Culture, Identities and Lifestyles*. Basingstoke: Palgrave Macmillan, pp. 1–23.

Devine, F., Savage, M., Scott, J. and Crompton, R. (eds.) (2005) *Rethinking Class: Culture, Identities and Lifestyles*. Basingstoke: Palgrave Macmillan.

Dickens, C. (1994 [1854]) *Hard Times*. London: Penguin.

Dickens, R., Gregg, P. and Wadsworth, J. (2003) *The Labour Market under New Labour: The State of Working Britain*. Basingstoke: Palgrave Macmillan.

Dromey, J. and Taylor, G. (1978) *Grunwick: The Workers' Story*. London: Lawrence & Wishart.

Duke, V. and Edgell, S. (1987) 'The operationalisation of class in British sociology: theoretical and empirical considerations', *British Journal of Sociology*, 38(4): 445–63.

Durrschmidt, J. (2000) *Everyday Lives in the Global City*. London: Routledge.

Dutton, P. (2003) 'Leeds Calling: the influence of London on the gentrification of regional cities', *Urban Studies*, 40(12): 2557–72.

Dyos, H.J. (1961) *Victorian Suburb: A Study of the Growth of Camberwell*. Leicester: Leicester University Press.

Egerton, M. and Savage, M. (1997) 'Social mobility, individual mobility and the inheritance of class inequality', *Sociology*, 31(4): 645–72.

Ehrenreich, B. (2002) *Nickel and Dimed: Undercover in Low-wage USA*. London: Granta Books.

Ehrenreich, B. and Hochschild, A.R. (eds.) (2003) *Global Woman: Nannies, Maids and Sex Workers in the New Economy*. London: Granta Books.

Elliott, B. (1997) 'Migration, mobility and social process: Scottish migrants in Canada', in D. Bertaux and P. Thompson (eds.) *Pathways to Social Class*. Oxford: Clarendon Press.

Engels, F. (1987) *The Condition of the Working Class in England*. London: Penguin.

England, K. and Stiell, B. (1997) '"They think you're as stupid as your English is": constructing foreign domestic workers in Toronto', *Environment and Planning A*, 29(2): 195–215.

Erikson, R. and Goldthorpe, J.H. (1993) *The Constant Flux: A Study of Class Mobility in Industrial Societies*. Oxford: Clarendon Press.

Esping-Andersen, G. (1990) *The Three Worlds of Welfare Capitalism*. Cambridge: Polity Press.

Esping-Andersen, G. (ed.) (1993) *Changing Classes: Stratification and Mobility in Post-Industrial Societies*. London: Sage.

Esping-Andersen, G. (ed.) (1996) *Welfare States in Transition*. London: Sage Publications.

Esping-Andersen, G. (1999) *Social Foundations of Postindustrial Economies*. Oxford: Oxford University Press.

Esping-Andersen, G. (2002) 'Towards the Good Society, once again?' in G. Esping-Andersen (ed.) *Why We Need a New Welfare State*. Oxford: Oxford University Press, pp. 1–25.

Eurostat (2002) *Living Conditions in Europe: Statistical Pocketbook*. Luxembourg: Office for Official Publications of the European Communities.

Eurostat (2004) *European Social Statistics: Income, Poverty and Social Exclusion, 2nd Report*. Luxembourg: Office for Official Publications of the European Communities.

Fainstein, N. and Fainstein, S. (1996) 'Urban regimes and black citizens: the economic and social impacts of black political incorporation in US cities', *International Journal of Urban and Regional Research*, 20(1): 23–37.

Fainstein, S. (1998) 'Assimilation and exclusion in US cities: the treatment of African-Americans and immigrants', in S. Musterd and W. Ostendorf (eds.) *Urban Segregation and the Welfare State: Inequality and Exclusion in Western Cities*. London: Routledge, pp. 28–44.

Fainstein, S., Gordon, I. and Harloe, M. (eds.) (1992) *Divided Cities: New York and London in the Contemporary World*. Oxford: Blackwell.

Fantasia, R. (1988) *Cultures of Solidarity*. Berkeley: University of California Press.

Fernie, S. and Metcalf, D. (1998) *(Not) Hanging on the Telephone: Payment Systems in the New Sweatshops*. London: Centre for Economic Performance, London School of Economics.

Flaherty, J., Veit-Wilson, J. and Dornan, P. (2004) *Poverty: the Facts*, 5th edn. London: CPAG.

Florida, R. (2002) *The Rise of the Creative Class*. New York: Basic Books.

Ford, T. and Champion, T. (2000) 'Who moves into, out of and within London? An analysis based on the 1991 Census 2% Sample of Anonymised Records', *Area*, 32: 259–70.

Fouarge, D. and Layte, R. (2005) 'Welfare regimes and poverty dynamics: the duration and recurrence of poverty spells in Europe', *Journal of Social Policy*, 34(3): 407–26.

Frankenberg, R. (1966) *Communities in Britain*. Harmondsworth: Penguin.

Fraser, V. (2000) *Building the New World: Studies in the Modern Architecture of Latin America, 1930–60*. London: Verso.

Freedman, J. (ed.) (2003) *Gender and Insecurity: Migrant Women in Europe*. Aldershot: Ashgate.

Frenkel, S.J. et al. (1999) *On the Front Line: Organization of Work in the Information Economy*. Ithaca: Cornell University Press.

Friedman, A.L. (1977) *Industry and Labour: Class Struggle at Work and Monopoly Capitalism*. London: Macmillan.

Friedmann, J. (1986) 'The World City Hypothesis', *Development and Change*, 17: 69–83.

Friedmann, J. and Woolff, G. (1982) 'World city formation an agenda for research and action', *International Journal of Urban and Regional Research*, 6: 309–44.

Friedrichs, J., Galster, G. and Musterd, S. (eds.) (2005) *Life in Poverty Neighbourhoods: European and American Perspectives*. London: Routledge.

Furlong, A. (1992) *Growing Up in a Classless Society? School to Work Transitions*. Edinburgh: Edinburgh University Press.

Furlong, A. and Cartmel, F. (1997) *Young People and Social Change*. Buckingham: Open University Press.

Furlong, A. and Cartmel, F. (2003) 'Unemployment, integration and marginalisation: a comparative perspective on 18-to-24 year olds in Finland, Sweden, Scotland and Spain', in T. Hammer (ed.) *Youth Unemployment and Social Exclusion in Europe: A Comparative Study*. Bristol: The Policy Press, pp. 29–43.

Gall, G. (ed.) (2003) *Union Organizing: Campaigning for Trade Union Recognition*. London: Routledge.

Gallie, D., White, M., Cheng, Y. and Tomlinson, M. (1998) *Restructuring the Employment Relationship*. Oxford: Oxford University Press.

Gallie, D. (1978) *In Search of the New Working Class*. Cambridge: Cambridge University Press.

Gallie, D. (1994a) 'Social consequences of long-term unemployment in Britain', in O. Benoit-Guilbot and D. Gallie (eds.) *Long-term Unemployment*. London: Pinter Publishers, pp. 121–36.

Gallie, D. (1994b) 'Are the unemployed an underclass? Some evidence from the Social Change and Economic Life Initiative', *Sociology*, 28(3): 737–57.

Gallie, D. (1996) 'New technology and the class structure: the blue–collar/white-collar divide revisited', *British Journal of Sociology*, 47(3): 447–73.

Gallie, D. (ed.) (2004) *Resisting Marginalization: Unemployment Experience and Social Policy in the European Union*. Oxford: Oxford University Press.

Gallie, D. and Paugam, S. (eds.) (2000) *Welfare Regimes and the Experience of Unemployment in Europe*. Oxford: Oxford University Press.

Gallie, D. and Paugam, S. (2004) 'Unemployment, poverty and social exclusion: an assessment of the current state of social exclusion theory', in D. Gallie (ed.) *Resisting Marginalization: Unemployment Experience and Social Policy in the European Union*. Oxford: Oxford University Press, pp. 34–53.

Gans, H. (1967) *The Levittowners: Ways of Life and Politics in a New Suburban Community*. London: Allen Lane, The Penguin Press.

Gardiner, J. (1997) *Gender, Care and Economics*. Basingstoke: Macmillan Press.

Geddes, A. (2000) 'Denying access: asylum seekers and welfare benefits in the UK', in M. Bommes and A. Geddes (eds.) *Immigration and Welfare: Challenging the Borders of the Welfare State*. London: Routledge, pp. 134–47.

Geertz, C. (1993) *The Interpretation of Cultures*. London: Fontana.

Gibson, W. (1993) *Neuromancer*. London: Harper-Collins.

Gibson-Graham, J.K., Resnick, S.A. and Wolff, R.D. (eds.) (2000) *Class and Its Others*. Minneapolis: University of Minnesota Press.

Giddens, A. (1973) *The Class Structure of the Advanced Societies*. London: Hutchinson.

Giddens, A. (1976) *New Rules of Sociological Method*. London: Hutchinson.

Giddens, A. (1996) *In Defence of Sociology: Essays, Interpretations and Rejoinders*. Cambridge: Polity Press.

Giddens, A. (2000) *The Third Way and its Critics*. Cambridge: Polity Press.

Giddens, A. (2002) *Runaway World: How Globalization is Reshaping Our Lives*. London: Profile Books.

Ginsburg, N. (1992) *Divisions of Welfare*. London: Sage.

Ginsburg, N. (2001) 'Sweden: the social democratic case', in A. Cochrane, J. Clarke and S. Gewirtz (eds.) *Comparing Welfare States*, 2nd edn. London: Sage Publications, pp. 195–222.

Glass, R. (1964) *London: Aspects of Change*. Centre for Urban Studies. London: MacGibbon & Kee. Report No. 3.

Glendinning, C. and Millar, J. (eds.) (1992) *Women and Poverty in Britain: the 1990s*. Hemel Hempstead: Harvester Wheatsheaf.

Glucksmann, M.A. (2004) 'Call configurations: varieties of call centre and divisions of labour', *Work, Employment and Society*, 18(4): 795–811.

Golding, P. (1999) 'Thinking the unthinkable: welfare reform and the media', in B. Franklin (ed.) *Social Policy, the Media and Misrepresentation*. London: Routledge, pp. 146–56.

Goldthorpe, J.H. (1980) *Social Mobility and Class Structure in Modern Britain*. Oxford: Clarendon Press.

Goldthorpe, J.H. (1982) 'On the service class, its formation and future', in A. Giddens and G. Mackenzie (eds.) *Social Class and the Division of Labour*. Cambridge: Cambridge University Press, pp. 162–84.

Goldthorpe, J.H. (1987) *Social Mobility and Class Structure in Modern Britain*, 2nd edn. Oxford: Clarendon Press.

Goldthorpe, J.H. and Lockwood, D. (1963) 'Affluence and the British class structure', *Sociological Review*, 11: 133–63.

Goldthorpe, J.H., Lockwood, D., Bechhofer, B. and Platt, J. (1968a) *The Affluent Worker: Industrial Attitudes and Behaviour*. Cambridge: Cambridge University Press.

Goldthorpe, J.H., Lockwood, D., Bechhofer, B. and Platt, J. (1968b) *The Affluent Worker: Political Attitudes and Behaviour*. Cambridge: Cambridge University Press.

Goldthorpe, J.H., Lockwood, D., Bechhofer, B. and Platt, J. (1969) *The Affluent Worker in the Class Structure*. Cambridge: Cambridge University Press.

Goos, M. and Manning, A. (2003) 'McJobs and MacJobs: the growing polarisation of jobs in the UK', in R. Dickens, P. Gregg and J. Wadsworth (eds.) *The Labour Market Under New Labour: The State of Working Britain 2003*. Basingstoke: Palgrave Macmillan, pp. 70–85.

Gordon, D. et al. (2000) *Poverty and Social Exclusion in Britain*. York: Joseph Rowntree Foundation.

Gorz, A. (1985) *Paths to Paradise: On the Liberation from Work*. London: Pluto.

Gottdiener, M. (2002) 'Urban analysis as merchandising: the "LA School" and the understanding of metropolitan development', in J. Eade and C. Mele (eds.) *Understanding the City*. Oxford: Blackwell. pp. 159–80.

Gough, I. and Olofsson, G. (eds.) (1999) *Capitalism and Social Cohesion*. Basingstoke: Macmillan Press.

Graham, S. and Marvin, S. (2001) *Splintering Urbanism: Networked Infrastructure, Technological Mobilities and the Urban Condition*. London: Routledge.

Gray, A. (2004) *Unsocial Europe: Social Protection or Flexploitation?* London: Pluto Press.

Gray, R. (1976) *The Labour Aristocracy in Victorian Edinburgh*. Oxford: Oxford University Press.

Gregson, N. and Lowe, M. (1994) *Servicing the Middle Classes: Class, Gender and Waged Domestic Labour in Britain*. London: Routledge.

Hacker, L. (1947) *The Triumph of American Capitalism*. New York: Columbia University Press.

Halford, S., Savage, M. and Witz, A. (1997) *Gender, Careers and Organisations*. Basingstoke: Macmillan.

Hall, P. (1962) *The Industries of London Since 1861*. London: Hutchinson.

Hall, S. and Jefferson, T. (eds.) (1976) *Resistance Through Rituals*. London: Hutchinson.

Halsey, A.H., Heath, A. and Ridge, J.M. (1980) *Origins and Destinations*. Oxford: Clarendon Press.

Hamilton, M. and Hirszowicz, M. (1993) *Class and Inequality: Comparative Perspectives*. Hemel Hempstead: Harvester Wheatsheaf.

Hammer, T. (2003a) 'Introduction' in T. Hammer (ed.) *Youth Unemployment and Social Exclusion in Europe: A Comparative Study*. Bristol: The Policy Press, pp. 1–20.

Hammer, T. (ed.) (2003b) *Youth Unemployment and Social Exclusion in Europe: A Comparative Study*. Bristol: The Policy Press.

Hammer, T. (2003c) 'Concluding remarks', in T. Hammer (ed.) *Youth Unemployment and Social Exclusion in Europe: A Comparative Study*. Bristol: The Policy Press, pp. 207–11.

Hamnett, C. (1984) 'Gentrification and residential location theory: a review and assessment', in D. Herbert and R. Johnston (eds.) *Geography and the Urban Environment: Progress in Research and Applications*. London: Wiley. VI.

Hamnett, C. (1991) 'The blind man and the elephant: the explanation of gentrification', *Transactions of the Institute of British Geographers: New Series*, 16: 173–89.

Hamnett, C. (1994) 'Social polarisation in global cities: theory and evidence', *Urban Studies*, 31: 401–24.

Hamnett, C. (1996) 'Why Sassen is wrong: a response to Burgers', *Urban Studies*, 33(1): 107–10.

Hamnett, C. (1998) 'Social polarisation, economic restructuring and welfare state regimes', in S. Musterd and W. Ostendorf (eds.) *Urban Segregation and the Welfare State: Inequality and Exclusion in Western Cities*. London: Routledge, pp. 15–27.

Hamnett, C. (2003) *Unequal City: London in the Global Arena*. London: Routledge.

Hamnett, C. and Randolph, W. (1988) 'Labour and housing market changes in London – a longitudinal analysis', *Urban Studies*, 25: 380–98.

Hamnett, C., McDowell, L. and Sarre, P. (eds.) (1989) *The Changing Social Structure*. London: Sage.

Hardt, M. and Negri, A. (2000) *Empire*. London: Harvard University Press.

Hargreaves, A.G. (1996) 'A deviant construction: the French media and the Banlieues', *New Community*, 22(4): 607–18.

Harloe, M. (1995) *The People's Home? Social Rented Housing in Europe and America*. Oxford: Blackwell.

Harris, L. (1988) 'The UK economy at a crossroads' in J. Allen and D. Massey (eds) *The Economy in Question*. London: Sage, pp. 7–44.

Harris, R. (2004) *Creeping Conformity: How Canada Became Suburban, 1900–1960*. Toronto: University of Toronto Press.

Hart, N. (1989) 'Gender and the rise and fall of class politics', *New Left Review*, 175: 19–47.

Harvey, D. (1989) *The Condition of Postmodernity*. Oxford: Blackwell.

Hauser, R. and Nolan, B. (2000) 'Unemployment and poverty: change over time', in D. Gallie and S. Paugam (eds.) *Welfare Regimes and the Experience of Unemployment in Europe*. Oxford: Oxford University Press, pp. 25–46.

Heathcote, D. (2004) *Barbican: Penthouse over the City*. London: Wiley-Academy.

Held, D., McGrew, A., Goldblatt, D. and Perraton, J. (1999) *Global Transformations: Politics, Economics and Culture*. Cambridge: Polity Press.

Hemerijck, A. (2002) 'The self-transformation of the European social model', in G. Esping-Andersen (ed.) *Why We Need a New Welfare State*. Oxford: Oxford University Press, pp. 173–214.

Herkommer, S. and Koch, M. (1999) 'The "underclass": a misleading concept and a scientific myth?', in P. Littlewood (ed.) *Social Exclusion in Europe: Problems and Paradigms*. Aldershot: Ashgate, pp. 89–111.

Hills, J. (1995) *Joseph Rowntree Inquiry into Income and Wealth: Volume 2*. York: Joseph Rowntree Foundation.

Hills, J. and Stewart, K. (eds.) (2005) *A More Equal Society? New Labour, Poverty, Inequality and Exclusion*. Bristol: The Policy Press.

Hirst, P. and Thompson, G. (1999) *Globalization in Question*. Cambridge: Polity Press.

Hobsbawm, E. (1994) *Age of Extremes: The Short Twentieth Century 1914–1991*. London: Michael Joseph.

Hobsbawm, E. and Rudè, G. (1969) *Captain Swing*. London: Lawrence & Wishart.

Hoggart, K. and Hiscock, C. (2005) 'Occupational structures in service class households: comparisons of rural, suburban and inner city residential environments', *Environment and Planning A: Government and Planning*, 37: 63–80.

Hoggart, R. (1958) *The Uses of Literacy*. Harmondsworth: Penguin.

Holgate, J. (2005) 'Organizing migrant workers: a case study of working conditions and unionization in a London sandwich factory', *Work, Employment and Society*, 19(3): 463–80.

Hollands, R. (2002) 'Division in the dark: youth cultures, transitions and segmented consumption spaces in the night-time economy', *Journal of Youth Studies*, 5(2): 153–71.

Holston, J. (1989) *The Modernist City: An Anthropological Critique of Brasilia*. Chicago: University of Chicago Press.

Holtgrewe, U., Kerst, C. and Shire, K. (eds.) (2002) *Re-Organising Service Work: Call Centres in Germany and Britain*. Aldershot: Ashgate.

Hondagneu-Sotelo, P. (2001) *Domestica: Immigrant Workers Cleaning and Caring in the Shadows of Affluence*. Berkeley: University of California Press.

Howarth, M., Kenway, P., Palmer, G. and Street, C. (1998) *Monitoring Poverty and Social Exclusion: Labour's Inheritance*. York: Joseph Rowntree Foundation.

Hyman, J., Baldry, C., Scholarios, D. and Bunzel, D. (2003) 'Work-life imbalance in call centres and software development', *British Journal of Industrial Relations*, 41(2): 215–239.

Jackson, A (1973) *Semi-Detached London: Suburban Devcelopment, Life and Transport, 1900–39*. London: Allen & Unwin.

Jackson, B. and Marsden, D. (1962) *Education and the Working Class*. London: Routledge & Kegan Paul.

Jackson, J.L. (2001) *Harlemworld: Doing Race and Class in Contemporary Black America*. Chicago and London: University of Chicago Press.

Jackson, K.T. (1985) *Crabgrass Frontier: the Suburbanization of the United States*. New York: Oxford University Press.

Jacobs, J. (1962) *The Death and Life of Great American Cities*. London: Jonathan Cape.

Jenkins, C. and Sherman, B. (1979) *The Collapse of Work*. London: Eyre Methuen.

Jenkins, R. (1992) *Pierre Bourdieu*. London: Routledge.

Johnson, R. (1978) 'Thompson, Genovese, and Socialist-Humanist History', *History Workshop*, 6(Autumn): 79–100.

Johnston, L., MacDonald, R., Mason, P., Ridley, L. and Webster, C. (2000) *Snakes and Ladders: Young People, Transitions and Social Exclusion*. Bristol: The Policy Press.

Johnston, R. (1994). 'World cities in a world system.' *International Journal of Urban and Regional Research*, 18(1): 150–2.

Jones, G. (1995) *Leaving Home*. Buckingham: Open University Press.

Jonsson, I. (1999) 'Women, work and welfare', in P. Littlewood (ed.) *Social Exclusion in Europe: Problems and Paradigms*. Aldershot: Ashgate, pp. 113–32.

Jordan, B., James, S., Kay, H. and Redley, M. (1992) *Trapped in Poverty? Labour-market Decisions in Low-income Households*. London: Routledge.

Karazman-Morawetz, I. and Ronneling, A. (2003) 'Legal exclusion and social exclusion: legal and illegal migrants', in H. Steinert and A. Pilgrim (eds.) *Welfare Policy from Below: Struggles Against Social Exclusion in Europe*. Aldershot, Ashgate, pp. 229–40.

Kaufman, J.L. (1998) 'Chicago: segregation and the new urban poverty', in S. Musterd and W. Ostendorf (eds.) *Urban Segregation and the Welfare State: Inequality and Exclusion in Western Cities*. London: Routledge, pp. 45–63.

Kefalas, M. (2003) *Working-Class Heroes: Protecting Home, Community and Nation in a Chicago Neighborhood*. Berkeley: University of California Press.

Kellett, J.R. (1969) *The Impact of Railways on Victorian Cities*. London: Routledge & Kegan Paul.

Kelly, J. (1998) *Rethinking Industrial Relations: Mobilization, Collectivism and Long Waves*. London: Routledge.

Kennedy, P. (2005) 'Social policy, social exclusion and commodity fetishism', *Capital & Class*, 85: 91–114.

Kerbo, H.R. (2003) *Social Stratification and Inequality: Class Conflict in Historical and Comparative Perspective*, 5th edn. New York: McGraw-Hill.

Kerr, C. et al. (1973) *Industrialism and Industrial Man.* Harmondsworth: Penguin.

Klein, J. (1965) *Samples from English Cultures: Volume I.* London: Routledge & Kegan Paul.

Klein, N. (1999) *No Logo: Money, Marketing and the Growing Anti-Corporate Movement.* New York: Picador.

Kloosterman, R. (1996) 'Mixed experiences: post-industrial transition and ethnic minorities on the Amsterdam labour market', *New Community*, 22(4): 637–53.

Knocke, W. (1999) 'The labour market for immigrant women in Sweden: marginalized women in low-valued jobs', in J. Wrench, A. Rea and N. Ouali (eds.) *Migrants, Ethnic Minorities and the Labour Market: Integration and Exclusion in Europe.* Basingstoke: Macmillan, pp. 108–31.

Knox, P. and Pinch, S. (2000) *Urban Social Geography: An Introduction*, 4th edn. Harlow: Prentice Hall.

Knuth, M. and Kalina, T. (2002) 'Early exit from the labour force between exclusion and privilege: unemployment as a transition from employment to retirement in West Germany', *European Societies*, 4(4): 393–418.

Kofman, E., Phizacklea, A., Raghuram, P. and Sales, R. (2000) *Gender and International Migration in Europe.* London: Routledge.

Kwong, P. (1997) *Forbidden Workers: Illegal Chinese Immigrants and American Labor.* New York: The New Press.

Lambert, C. and Boddy, M. (2002) *Transforming the City: Post Recession Gentrification and Re-Urbanization.* Upward Neighbourhood Trajectories: Gentrification in a New Century, Glasgow.

Lamont, M. (2000) *The Dignity of Working Men.* New York: Russell Sage Foundation.

Lane, C. (1988) 'New technology and clerical work', in D. Gallie (ed.) *Employment in Britain.* Oxford: Basil Blackwell.

Lash, S. and Urry, J. (1987) *The End of Organised Capitalism.* Cambridge: Polity Press.

Lash, S. and Urry, J. (1994) *The Economies of Signs and Space.* London: Sage.

Layte, R. and Whelan, C.T. (2003) 'Moving in and out of poverty: the impact of welfare regimes on poverty dynamics in the EU', *European Societies*, 5(2): 167–91.

Lazarsfeld, P. and Rosenberg, M. (eds.) (1955) *The Language of Social Research.* Glencoe: The Free Press.

Lechner, F.J. and Boli, J. (eds.) (2000) *The Globalization Reader.* Oxford: Blackwell.

Lee, D.J. and Turner, B.S. (eds.) (1996) *Conflicts About Class: Debating Inequality in Late Industrialism.* Harlow: Longman.

Lee, P. and Murie, A. (1997) *Poverty, Housing Tenure and Social Exclusion.* Bristol: Policy Press.

Lees, L. (1994) 'Rethinking gentrification: beyond the positions of economics or culture, *Progress in Human Geography,* 18: 137–50.

Lees, L. (2000) 'A reappraisal of gentrification: towards a "geography of gentrification"', *Progress in Human Geography,* 24: 389–408.

Lees, L. (2003a) 'Super-gentrification: the case of Brooklyn Heights, New York City', *Urban Studies,* 40(12): 2487–510.

Lees, L. (2003b) 'Visions of "urban renaissance": the Urban Task Force report and the Urban White Paper, in R. Imrie and M. Raco (eds.) *Urban Renaissance? New Labour, Community and Urban Policy.* Bristol: The Policy Press, pp. 61–82.

Lees, L. and Slater, T. (forthcoming) *Gentrification.* New York: Routledge.

Leidner, R. (2002) 'Fast-food work in the United States', in T. Royle and B. Towers (eds.), *Labour Relations in the Global Fast-Food Industry.* London: Routledge, pp. 8–29.

Lenin, V.I. (1999 [1916]) *Imperialism, the Highest Stage of Capitalism.* Sydney: Resistance Books.

Leonard, M. (1998a) 'The long-term unemployed, informal economic activity and the "underclass" in Belfast: rejecting or reinstating the work ethic', *International Journal of Urban and Regional Research,* 22: 42–59.

Leonard, M. (1998b) *Invisible Work, Invisible Workers: The Informal Economy in Europe and the US.* Basingstoke: Macmillan Press.

Levitas, R. (1998) *The Inclusive Society? Social Exclusion and New Labour.* Basingstoke: Macmillan Press.

Lewis, J. (2002) 'Gender and welfare state change', *European Societies*, 4(4): 331–57.

Lewis, O. (1966) *La Vida: A Puerto Rican Family in the Culture of Poverty – San Juan and New York*. London: Secker & Warburg.

Ley, D. (1986) 'Alternative explanations for inner city gentrification: a Canadian assessment', *Annals of the Association of American Geographers*, 76(4): 521–35.

Ley, D. (1994) 'Gentrification and the cultural politics of 1968. Paper given to annual conference of the Association of American Geographers.'

Ley, D. (1996) *The New Middle Class and the Remaking of the Central City*. Oxford: Oxford University Press.

Ley, D. (2003) 'Artists, aestheticization and the field of gentrification', *Urban Studies*, 40(12): 2527–44.

Leyshon, A. and Thrift, N. (1997) *Money/Space: geographies of monetary transformation*. London: Routledge.

Lindblom, C.E. (1977) *Politics and Markets: The World's Political-Economic Systems*. New York: Basic Books.

Lister, R. (2004) *Poverty*. Polity Press.

Littlewood, P. and Herkommer, S. (1999) 'Identifying social exclusion: some problems of meaning', in P. Littlewood (ed.) *Social Exclusion in Europe: Problems and Paradigms*. Aldershot: Ashgate, pp. 1–21.

Lockwood, D. (1956) 'Some remarks on *The Social System*', *British Journal of Sociology*, 7(June): 134–46.

Lockwood, D. (1958) *The Blackcoated Worker*. London: Allen & Unwin.

Lockwood, D. (1964) 'Social Integration and System Integration'. In G.W. Zollschan and W. Hirsch (eds.) *Explorations in Social Change*. London: Routledge & Kegan Paul.

Lockwood, D. (1966) 'Sources of variation in working class images of society', *Sociological Review*, 14: 249–63.

Lockwood, D. (1995) 'Marking out the middle classes', in T. Butler and M. Savage (eds.) *Social Change and the Middle Classes*. London: UCL Press, pp. 1–12.

Longhurst, B. (1995) *Popular Music and Society*. Cambridge: Polity Press.

Longhurst, B. and Savage, M. (1996) 'Social class, consumption and the influence of Bourdieu: some critical issues', in S. Edgell, K. Hetherington and A. Warde (eds.) *Consumption Matters*. Oxford: Blackwell, pp. 274–301.

Low, S. (2004) *Behind the Gates: Life, Security and the Pursuit of Happiness in Fortress America*. New York and London: Routledge.

Lupton, R. and Power, A. (2002) 'Social exclusion and neighbourhoods', in J. Hills, J. Le Grand and D. Piachaud (eds.) *Understanding Social Exclusion*. Oxford: Oxford University Press, pp. 118–40.

Lyotard, J-F. (1984) *The Postmodern Condition: A report on knowledge*. Manchester: Manchester University Press.

MacDonald, R. (1994) 'Fiddly jobs, undeclared working and the something for nothing society', *Work, Employment and Society*, 8(4): 507–30.

MacDonald, R. (ed.) (1997) *Youth, the 'Underclass' and Social Exclusion*. London: Routledge.

MacDonald, R. and Coffield, F. (1991) *Risky Business? Youth and the Enterprise Culture*. Basingstoke: Falmer Press.

MacDonald, R. and Marsh, J. (2000) 'Employment, unemployment and social polarization: young people and cyclical transitions', in R. Crompton, F. Devine, M. Savage and J. Scott (eds.) *Renewing Class Analysis*. Oxford: Blackwell, pp. 120–40.

MacDonald, R. and Marsh, J. (2005) *Disconnected Youth: Growing up in Britain's Poor Neighbourhoods*. Basingstoke: Palgrave Macmillan.

MacDonald, R., Mason, P., Shildrick, T., Webster, C., Johnston, L. and Ridley, L. (2001) 'Snakes and ladders: in defence of studies of youth transition', *Sociological Research Online*, 5(4): <http:www.socresonline.org.uk/5/4/macdonald.html>.

Mackenzie, G. (1974) 'The "Affluent Worker" study: an evaluation and critique', in F. Parkin (ed.) *The Social Analysis of Class Structure*. London: Tavistock Publications, pp. 237–56.

Macrae, H. (2004) *London – The Resurgent City*. London: LSE.

Mallet, S. (1975) *The New Working Class*. Nottingham: Spokesman Books.

Mann, M. (1973) *Consciousness and Action among the Western Working Class*. London: Macmillan.

Mann, M. (ed.) (1983) *Macmillan Student Encyclopedia of Sociology*. London: Macmillan.

Mann, M. (1993) *The Sources of Social Power: Volume II – The Rise of Classes and Nation States, 1760–1914*. Cambridge: Cambridge University Press.

Marcuse, H. (1964) *One Dimensional Man*. London: Routledge & Kegan Paul.

Marcuse, P. and Van Kempen, R. (eds.) (2000a) *Globalizing Cities: A New Spatial Order?* Oxford: Blackwell.

Marcuse, P. and Van Kempen, R. (2000b) 'Conclusion: a changed spatial order', in P. Marcuse and R. Van Kempen (eds.) *Globalizing Cities: A New Spatial Order?* Oxford: Blackwell, pp. 249–75.

Marcuse, P. and Van Kempen, R. (2000c) 'Introduction', in P. Marcuse and R. Van Kempen (eds.), *Globalizing Cities: A New Spatial Order?* Oxford: Blackwell, pp. 1–21.

Marshall, G. (1988) 'Some remarks on the study of working-class consciousness', in D. Rose (ed.) *Social Stratification and Economic Change*. London: Hutchinson, pp. 98–126.

Marshall, G. (1990) *In Praise of Sociology*. London: Unwin Hyman.

Marshall, G. (1997) *Repositioning Class: Social Inequality in Industrial Societies*. London: Sage.

Marshall, G., Roberts, S. and Burgoyne, C. (1996) 'Social class and underclass in Britain and the USA', *British Journal of Sociology*, 47(1): 23–44.

Marshall, G., Rose, D., Newby, H. and Vogler, C. (1988) *Social Class in Modern Britain*. London: Unwin Hyman.

Martin, R. (1988) 'Industrial capitalism in transition: the contemporary reorganization of the British space-economy', in D. Massey and J. Allen (eds.) *Uneven Re-development: cities and regions in transition*. London: Hodder and Stoughton. pp. 202–31.

Marx, K. (1974) *Capital: Volume I*. London: Lawrence & Wishart.

Massey, D. (1984) *Spatial Divisions of Labour*. London: Macmillan.

Massey, D. (1988) 'Uneven development: social change and spatial divisions of labour', in D. Massey and J. Allen (eds.) *Uneven Development: cities and regions in transition*. London: Hodder and Stoughton. pp. 250–76.

Massey, D. and Allen, J. (eds.) (1988) *Uneven Redevelopment: Cities and Regions in Transition*. London: Hodder and Stoughton.

Massey, D.S. and Denton, N.A. (1993) *American Apartheid: Segregation and the Making of the Underclass*. Cambridge: Harvard University Press.

Mayo, E. (1949) *The Human Problems of an Industrial Civilization*. London: Routledge & Kegan Paul.

McDowell, L. (1997) *Capital Culture: Gender at Work in the City*. Oxford: Blackwell.

McDowell, L., Sarre, P. and Hamnett, C. (eds.) (1989) *Divided Nation: Social and Cultural Change in Britain*. Hodder & Stoughton.

McKenzie, R.T. and Silver, A. (1968) *Angels in Marble: Working Class Conservatives in Urban England*. London: Heinemann.

McKnight, A. (2002) 'Low-paid work: drip-feeding the poor', in J. Hills, J. Le Grand and D. Piachaud (eds.) *Understanding Social Exclusion*. Oxford: Oxford University Press, pp. 97–117.

McNeill, D. (2005) 'Skyscraper geography', *Progress in Human Geography*, 29(1): 41–55.

McRobbie, A. (2004) '"Everyone is creative"; artists as pioneers of the new economy?', in E.B. Silva and T. Bennett (eds.) *Contemporary Culture and Everyday Life*. Durham: Sociology Press, pp.186–202.

Metcalf, D. (2003) 'Trade unions', in R. Dickens, P. Gregg and J. Wadsworth (eds.) *The Labour Market Under New Labour: The State of Working Britain*. Basingstoke: Palgrave Macmillan, pp. 170–87.

Merton, R. K. (1957) *Social Theory and Social Structure*. Glencoe: The Free Press.

Miles, S. (1995) 'Towards an understanding of the relationship between youth identities and consumer culture', *Youth & Policy*, 51: 35–45.

Miles, S. (2000) *Youth Lifestyles in a Changing World*. Buckingham, Open University Press.

Miliband, R. (1969) *The State in Capitalist Society*. London: Weidenfeld & Nicholson.

Miliband, R. (1973) *Parliamentary Socialism*. London: The Merlin Press.

Milkman, R., Reese, E. and Roth, B. (1998) 'The macrosociology of paid domestic labour', *Work and Occupations*, 25(4): 483–510.

Milkman, R. (ed.) (2000) *Organizing Immigrants: The Challenge for Unions in Contemporary California*. Ithaca and London: ILR Press.

Millar, J. and Glendinning, C. (1989) 'Gender and poverty', *Journal of Social Policy* 18(3): 363–81.

Mills, C. (1995) 'Managerial and professional work histories', in T. Butler and M. Savage (eds.) *Social Change and the Middle Classes*. London: UCL Press, pp. 95–116.

Mills, C.W. (1951) *White Collar: The American Middle Classes*. New York: Oxford University Press.

Mills, C.W. (1970) *The Sociological Imagination*. Harmondsworth: Penguin.

Mingione, E. (ed.) (1996) *Urban Poverty and the Underclass*. Oxford: Blackwell.

Mishra, R. (1999) *Globalization and the Welfare State*. Cheltenham: Edward Elgar.

Monbiot, G. (2000) *Captive State: The Corporate Takeover of Britain*. London: Macmillan.

Monbiot, G. (2003) *The Age of Consent: A Manifesto for a New World Order*. London: Flamingo.

Moore, R. (1974) *Pit-Men, Preachers and Politics: The Effects of Methodism in a Durham Mining Community*. Cambridge: Cambridge University Press.

Moore, R. (2004) 'Researching race and housing in Sparkbrook'. Whither Community Studies, Institute of Community Studies, London.

Morlicchio, E. (1996) 'Exclusion from work and the impoverishment processes in Naples', in E. Mingione (ed.) *Urban Poverty and the Underclass*. Oxford: Blackwell, pp. 325–42.

Morris, L. (1994) *Dangerous Classes: The Underclass and Social Citizenship*. London: Routledge.

Morris, L. (1995) *Social Divisions: Economic Decline and Social Structural Change*. London: UCL Press.

Morissens, A. and Sainsbury, D. (2005) 'Migrants' social rights, ethnicity and welfare regimes', *Journal of Social Policy*, 34(4): 637–60.

Moulaert, F., Salin, E. and Werquin, T. (2001) 'Euralille: large-scale urban development and social polarization', *European Urban and Regional Studies*, 8(2): 145–60.

Mulholland, K. (2004) 'Workplace resistance in an Irish call centre: slammin', scammin', smokin' and leavin'', *Work, Employment and Society*, 18(4): 709–24.

Mumford, L. (1961) *The City in History*. New York: Harcourt Brace.

Munt, S.R. (2000) *Cultural Studies and the Working Class*. London: Cassell.

Murard, N. (2002) 'Guilty victims: social exclusion in contemporary France', in P. Chamberlayne, M. Rustin and T. Wengraf (eds.) *Biography and Social Exclusion in Europe: Experiences and Life Journeys*. Bristol: The Policy Press, pp. 41–60.

Murdie, R.A. (1998) 'The welfare state, economic restructuring and immigrant flows: impacts on socio-spatial segregation in Greater Toronto', in S. Musterd and W. Ostendorf (eds.) *Urban Segregation and the Welfare State: Inequality and Exclusion in Western Cities*. London: Routledge, pp. 64–93.

Murie, A. (1998) 'Segregation, exclusion and housing in the divided city', in S. Musterd and W. Ostendorf (eds.) *Urban Segregation and the Welfare State: Inequality and Exclusion in Western Cities*. London: Routledge, pp. 110–25.

Murie, A. (2005) 'The dynamics of social exclusion and neighbourhood decline: welfare regimes, decommodification, housing and urban inequality', in Y. Kazepov (ed.) *Cities of Europe*. Oxford: Blackwell, pp. 151–69.

Murray, C. (1984) *Losing Ground: American Social Policy, 1950–1980*. New York: Basic Books.

Murray, C. (1990) *The Emerging British Underclass*. London: IEA.

Musterd, S. (2003) 'Segregation and integration: a contested relationship'. *Journal of Ethnic and Migration Studies*, 29(4): 623–41.

Musterd, S. and Ostendorf, W. (eds.) (1998) *Urban Segregation and the Welfare State: Inequality and Exclusion in Western Cities*. London: Routledge.

Nayak, A. (2003) *Race, Place and Globalization: Youth Cultures in a Changing World*. Oxford: Berg.

Newby, H. (1977) *The Deferential Worker*. Harmondsworth: Penguin.

Newman, K.S. (1999) *No Shame in My Game: The Working Poor in the Inner City*. New York: Vintage Books & Russell Sage Foundation.

Newman, K. and Lennon, C. (2004) 'Working poor, working hard: trajectories at the bottom of the American labor market', in F. Devine and M.C. Waters (eds.) *Social Inequalities in Comparative Perspective*. Oxford: Blackwell Publishing, pp. 116–40.

Nichols, T. and Beynon, H. (1977) *Living with Capitalism: Class Relations and the Modern Factory*. London: Routledge & Kegan Paul.

Nickell, S. (2004) 'Poverty and worklessness in Britain', *The Economic Journal*, 114: C1–25.

O'Connor, J. (1973) *The Fiscal Crisis of the State*. New York: St. Martins Press.

O'Connor, J. (1993) 'Gender, class and citizenship in the comparative analysis of welfare regimes: theoretical and methodological issues', *British Journal of Sociology*, 44: 501–18.

Office of Population Censuses and Surveys [OPCS] (1991) *Standard Occupational Classification, Volume 3*. London: HMSO.

Olechnowicz, A. (1997) *Working-Class Housing in England between the Wars: The Becontree Estate*. Oxford: Clarendon Press.

Orwell, G. (1940) *Down and Out in Paris and London*. Harmondsworth: Penguin.

Orwell, G. (1962) *The Road to Wigan Pier*. Harmondsworth: Penguin.

Page, D. (2000) *Communities in the Balance: The Reality of Social Exclusion on Housing Estates*. York: Joseph Rowntree Foundation.

Pahl, R.E. (1965) *Urbs in Rure*. London: Weidenfeld & Nicholson.

Pahl, R.E. (1984) *Divisions of Labour*. Oxford: Basil Blackwell.

Pahl, R.E. (1989) 'Is the emperor naked? Some questions on the adequacy of sociological theory in urban and regional research', *International Journal of Urban and Regional Research*, 13: 709–20.

Pakulski, J. and Waters, M. (1996) *The Death of Class*. London: Sage.

Palme, J., Bergmark, A., Backman, O., Estrada, F., Fritzell, J., Lundberg, O., Sjoberg and Szebehely, M. (2002) 'Welfare trends in Sweden: balancing the books for the 1990s', *Journal of European Social Policy*, 12(4): 329–346.

Parker, S. (2004) *Urban Theory and the Urban Experience: Encountering the City*. London: Routledge.

Parkin, F. (1971) *Class Inequality and the Political Order*. London: McGibbon and Kee.

Parrenas, R.S. (2001) *Servants of Globalization: Women, Migration and Domestic Work*. Stanford: Stanford University Press.

Parsons, T. (1970) *The Social System*. London: Routledge & Kegan Paul.

Pascall, G. (1997) *Social Policy: A New Feminist Analysis*. London: Routledge.

Pattillo-McCoy, M. (1999) *Black Picket Fences: Privilege and Peril among the Black Middle Class*. Chicago: University of Chicago Press.

Payne, J. and Payne, C. (1994) 'Recession, restructuring and the fate of the unemployed: evidence in the underclass debate', *Sociology*, 28(1): 1–19.

Peach, C. (1996) 'Does Britain have ghettos?', *Transactions of the Institute of British Geographers New Series*, 21(1): 216–35.

Peck, J. and Ward, K. (eds.) (2002) *City of Revolution: Restructuring Manchester*. Manchester: Manchester University Press.

Perrons, D. (2004) *Globalization and Social Change: People and Places in a Divided World*. London: Routledge.

Peterson, M. (2002) 'Corporatist structures and cultural diversity in Sweden', in P. Chamberlayne, M. Rustin and T. Wengraf (eds.) *Biography and Social Exclusion in Europe: Experiences and Life Journeys*. Bristol, The Policy Press, pp. 193–212.

Phillips, M. (2004) 'Other geographies of gentrification', *Progress in Human Geography*, 28(1): 5–30.

Phillimore, A.J. (1989) 'Flexible specialisation, work organisation and skills: approaching the "second industrial divide"', *New Technology, Work and Employment*, 4(2): 79–91.

Pilkington, A. (2003) *Racial Disadvantage and Ethnic Diversity in Britain*. Basingstoke: Palgrave Macmillan.

Piore, M.J. and Sabel, C.F. (1984) *The Second Industrial Divide*. New York: Basic Books.

Platt, J. (1971) *Social Research in Bethnal Green: an evaluation of the work of the Institute of Community Studies*. London: Macmillan.

Pollert, A. (1991) (ed.) *Farewell to Flexibility?* Oxford: Basil Blackwell.

Pond, C. (1989) 'The changing distribution of income, wealth and poverty', in C. Hamnett, L. McDowell and P. Sarre (eds.) *The Changing Social Structure*. London: Sage, pp. 43–77.

Powell, M., Boyne, G. and Ashworth, R. (2001) 'Towards a geography of people poverty and place poverty', *Policy & Politics*, 29(3): 243–58.

Power, A. (1997) *Estates on the Edge*. Basingstoke: Macmillan.

Power, S. et al. (2003) *Education and the Middle Class*. Buckingham: Open University Press.

Proctor, B.D. and Dalaker, J. (2003) *Poverty in the United States: 2002*. Current Population Reports, P60–222. Washington, U.S. Census Bureau.

Puntenney, D.L. (2000) 'Working at the margins: poor women and survival in the inner city', in R. Hodson (ed.) *Marginal Employment*. Stamford, JAI Press, pp. 51–72.

Ransome, P. (2005) *Work, Consumption and Culture: Affluence and Social Change in the Twenty-First Century*. London: Sage Publications.

Ray, L. (2002) 'Crossing borders: sociology, globalization and immobility', *Sociological Research Online* 7(3): <http://www.socresonline.org.uk/7/3/ray.html>.

Reay, D. (1998a) 'Rethinking class and gender: qualitative perspectives on class and gender', *Sociology*, 32(2): 259–75.

Reay, D. (1998b) *Class Work: Mothers' Involvement in their Children's Primary Schooling*. London: UCL Press.

Redfern, P. (2003) 'What makes gentrification "gentrification"?', *Urban Studies*, 40(12): 2351–66.

Redhead, S. (ed.) (1993) *Rave Off: Politics and Deviance in Contemporary Youth Culture*. Aldershot, Avebury.

Reid, I. (1998) *Class in Britain*. Cambridge: Polity Press.

Renner, K. (1978) The Service Class. *Austro Marxism*. T. Bottomore and P. Goode. Oxford, Oxford University Press.

Rex, J. (1961) *Key Problems in Sociological Theory*. London: Routledge & Kegan Paul.

Rex, J. and R. Moore (1967) *Race, Community and Conflict: A Study of Sparkbrook*. Oxford: Oxford University Press.

Richards, A.J. (1996) *Miners on Strike: Class Solidarity and Division in Britain*. Oxford: Berg.

Richards, L. (1990) *Nobody's Home: Dreams and Realities in a New Suburb*. Melbourne: Oxford University Press.

Richardson, R., Belt, V. and Marshall, N. (2000) 'Taking calls to Newcastle: the regional implications of the growth in call centres', *Regional Studies*, 34(4): 357–69.

Roberts, H. (1993) 'The women and class debate', in D. Morgan and L. Stanley (eds.) *Debates in Sociology*. Manchester: Manchester University Press, pp. 52–70.

Roberts, I. (1993) *Craft, Class and Control: The Sociology of a Shipbuilding Community*. Edinburgh: Edinburgh University Press.

Roberts, K. (1997) 'Is there an emerging British underclass? The evidence from youth research', in R. MacDonald (ed.) *Youth, the 'Underclass' and Social Exclusion*. London: Routledge, pp. 39–54.

Roberts, K. (2001) *Class in Modern Britain*. Basingstoke: Palgrave.

Robson, G. (2000) *'No One Likes Us, We Don't Care': The Myth and Reality of Millwall Fandom*. Oxford: Berg.

Room, G. (1995) 'Poverty and social exclusion: the new European agenda for policy and research', in G. Room (ed.) *Beyond the Threshold: The Measurement and Analysis of Social Exclusion*. Bristol: The Policy Press, pp. 1–9.

Rose, D. and O'Reilly, K. (eds.) (1997) *Constructing Classes: Towards a New Social Classification for the UK*. Swindon: ESRC/ONS.

Rowntree, B.S. and Lavers, G.R. (1951) *Poverty and the Welfare State*. London: Longmans, Green & Co.

Royle, T. and Towers, B. (2002a) 'Introduction', in T. Royle and B. Towers (eds.) *Labour Relations in the Global Fast-Food Industry*. London: Routledge, pp. 1–7.

Royle, T. and Towers, B. (eds.) (2002b) *Labour Relations in the Global Fast-Food Industry*. London: Routledge.

Runciman, W.G. (1966) *Relative Deprivation and Social Justice*. London: Routledge & Kegan Paul.

Rupp, J.C.C. (1997) 'Rethinking cultural and economic capital', in J.H. Hall (ed.) *Reworking Class*. Ithaca & London: Cornell University Press, pp. 221–41.

Rustin, M. (1989) 'The politics of post-Fordism: or, the trouble with "new times"', *New Left Review*, 175: 54–78.

Sabour, M. (1999) 'The socio-cultural exclusion and self-exclusion of foreigners in Finland: the case of Joensuu', in P. Littlewood (ed.) *Social Exclusion in Europe: Problems and Paradigms*. Aldershot: Ashgate, pp. 219–47.

Sainsbury, D. (ed.) (1994) *Gendering Welfare States*. London: Sage.

Sassen, S. (1991) *The Global City*. Princeton: Princeton University Press.

Sassen, S. (1994) *Cities in a World Economy*. Thousand Oaks, CA: Pine Forge.

Sassen, S. (2001) *The Global City: London, New York, Tokyo*. Chichester: Princeton University Press.

Sassen, S. (2003) 'Global Cities and survival circuits', in B. Ehrenreich and A.R. Hochschild (eds.) *Global Woman: Nannies, Maids and Sex Workers in the New Economy*. London: Granta Books, pp. 254–74.

Saunders, P. (1986) *Social Theory and the Urban Question*, 2nd edn. London: Routledge.

Saunders, P. (1989) 'Left write in sociology', *Network*, 44: 3–4.

Saunders, P. (1990) *A Nation of Homeowners*. London: Unwin Hyman.

Savage, M. (1995) 'Class analysis and social research', in T. Butler and M. Savage (eds.) *Social Change and the Middle Classes*. London: UCL Press, pp. 15–25.

Savage, M. (2000) *Class Analysis and Social Transformation*. Buckingham: Open University Press.

Savage, M. (2003) 'Social exclusion and class analysis', in P. Braham and L. Janes (eds.) *Social Differences and Divisions*. Oxford: Blackwell Publishing, pp. 59–100.

Savage, M. (2005) 'Working-class identities in the 1960s: revisiting the Affluent Worker Study', *Sociology*, 39(5): 929–46.

Savage, M., Bagnall, G. and Longhurst, B. (2001) 'Ordinary, ambivalent and defensive: class identities in the Northwest of England', *Sociology* 35(4): 875–92.

Savage, M., Bagnall, G. and Longhurst, B. (2004) 'Place, belonging, and identity: globalisation and the Northern middle class', in E.B. Silva and T. Bennett (eds.) *Contemporary Culture and Everyday Life*. Durham: Sociology Press, pp. 166–85.

Savage, M., Bagnall, G. and Longhurst, B. (2005a) *Globalisation and Belonging*. London: Sage.

Savage, M., Bagnall, G. and Longhurst, B. (2005b) 'Local habitus and working-class culture', in F. Devine, M. Savage, J. Scott and R. Crompton (eds.) *Rethinking Class: Culture, Identities and Lifestyles*. Basingstoke: Palgrave Macmillan, pp. 95–122.

Savage, M., Barlow, J., Dickens, P. and Fielding, A. (1992) *Property Bureaucracy and Culture: Middle Class Formation in Contemporary Britain*. London: Routledge.

Savage, M., Warde, A. and Ward, K. (2003) *Urban Sociology, Capitalism and Modernity*. Basingstoke: Palgrave Macmillan.

Savage, M., Warde, A. and Devine, F. (2005) 'Capitals, assets, and resources: some critical issues', *The British Journal of Sociology*, 56(1): 31–47.

Savage, M., Watt, P. and Arber, S. (1990) 'The consumption sector debate and housing mobility', *Sociology*, 24: 97–117.

Saville, J. (2003) *Memoirs from the Left*. London: The Merlin Press.

Sayer, A. (2005) *The Moral Significance of Class*. Cambridge: Cambridge University Press.

Schlosser, E. (2004) *Reefer Madness and Other Tales from the American Underground*. Harmondsworth: Penguin.

Schumpeter, J. (1943) *Capitalism, Socialism and Democracy*. London: Allen & Unwin.

Scott, A. (1988) *Metropolis*. London: University of California Press.

Scott, A. (2000a) 'The cultural economy of Paris', *International Journal of Urban and Regional Research*, 24: 567–82.

Scott, A. (2000b) *The Cultural Economy of Cities*. London: Sage.

Scrinzi, F. (2003) 'The globalization of domestic work: women migrants and neo-domesticity' in J. Freedman (ed.) *Gender and Insecurity: Migrant Women in Europe*. Aldershot: Ashgate, pp. 77–90.

Sefton, T. and Sutherland, H. (2005) 'Inequality and poverty under New Labour', in J. Hills and K. Stewart (eds.) *A More Equal Society? New Labour, Poverty, Inequality and Exclusion*. Bristol: The Policy Press, pp. 231–49.

Sennett, R. (1998) *The Corrosion of Character*. New York: W.W. Norton.

Shire, K., Holtgrewe, U. and Kerst, C. (2002) 'Re-organising customer service work: an introduction', in U. Holtgrewe, C. Kerst and K. Shire (eds.) *Re-Organising Service Work: Call Centres in Germany and Britain*. Aldershot: Ashgate, pp. 1–16.

Shulman, B. (2003) *The Betrayal of Work: How Low-Wage Jobs Fail 30 Million Americans and their Families*. New York: The New Press.

Silver, H. (1994) 'Social exclusion and social solidarity: three paradigms', *International Labour Review*, 133: 531–78.

Silver, H. (1996) 'Culture, poverty and national discourses of the new urban poverty', in E. Mingione (ed.) *Urban Poverty and the Underclass: A Reader*. Oxford, Blackwell, pp. 105–38.

Silver, H. (ed.) (1973) *Equal Opportunity in Education*. London: Methuen.

Skeggs, B. (1994) 'Situating the production of feminist ethnography', in M. Maynard and J. Purvis (eds.) *Researching Women's Lives from a Feminist Perspective*. London: Taylor & Francis, pp. 72–92.

Skeggs, B. (1997) *Formations of Class and Gender*. London: Sage.

Skeggs, B. (2004) *Class, Self, Culture*. London: Routledge.

Slater, T., Curran, W. and Lees, L. (2004) 'Gentrification research: new directions and critical scholarship', *Environment and Planning A*, 36: 1141–50.

Smeeding, T.M., Rainwater, L. and Burtless, G. (2000) 'U.S. poverty in a cross-national context', in S.H. Danziger and R.H. Haveman (eds.) *Understanding Poverty*. Cambridge and New York: Harvard University Press and Russell Sage Foundation, pp. 162–89.

Smith, D.J. (ed.) (1992) *Understanding the Underclass*. London: Policy Studies Institute.

Smith, D.M. (2005) *On the Margins of Inclusion: Changing Labour Markets and Social Exclusion in London*. Bristol: The Policy Press.

Smith, N. (1979) 'Towards a theory of gentrification: a back to the city movement by capital, not people', *Journal of the American Planning Association*, 45: 538–48.

Smith, N. (1996) *The New Urban Frontier: Gentrification and the Revanchist City*. London: Routledge.

Smith, N. (2002) 'New globalism, new urbanism: gentrification as global urban strategy', *Antipode*, 34(3): 427–50.

Smith, V. (2001) *Crossing the Great Divide: Workers, Risk and Opportunity in the New Economy*. Ithaca and London: Cornell University Press.

Smith, Y. (1997) 'The household, women's employment and social exclusion', *Urban Studies*, 34: 1159–77.

Social Exclusion Unit (1998) *Bringing Britain Together: a National Strategy for Neighbourhood Renewal*. London: The Stationery Office.

Sociology (2005) 'Special Issue on Class, Culture and Identity', *Sociology*, 39(4).

Soja, E.W. (1989) *Postmodern Geographies*. London: Verso.

Soja, E.W. (1995) 'Postmodern urbanization: the six restructurings of Los Angeles', in S. Watson and K. Gibson (eds.) *Postmodern Cities and Spaces*. Oxford: Blackwell, pp. 125–37.

Southern, J. (2000) 'Blue collar, white collar: deconstructing classification', in J.K. Gibson-Graham, S.A. Resnick and R.D. Wolff (eds.) *Class and Its Others*. Minneapolis, University of Minnesota Press, pp. 191–224.

Spano, A. (2002) 'Premodernity and postmodernity in Southern Italy', in P. Chamberlayne, M. Rustin and T. Wengraf (eds.) *Biography and Social Exclusion in Europe: Experiences and Life Journeys*. Bristol: The Policy Press, pp. 61–75.

Spicker, P. (1993) *Poverty and Social Security*. London: Routledge.

Stacey, M. (1960) *Tradition and Change: A Study of Banbury*. London: Oxford University Press.

Stedman Jones, G. (1974) *Outcast London*. Harmondsworth: Penguin.

Steinert, H. (2003) 'Participation and social exclusion: a conceptual framework', in H. Steinert and A. Pilgrim (eds.) *Welfare Policy from Below: Struggles Against Social Exclusion in Europe*. Aldershot: Ashgate, pp. 45–59.

Steinert, H. and Pilgrim, A. (eds.) (2003) *Welfare Policy from Below: Struggles Against Social Exclusion in Europe*. Aldershot: Ashgate.

Stenson, K. and Watt, P. (1999) 'Governmentality and the death of the social? A discourse analysis of local government texts in the South East of England', *Urban Studies*, 36(1): 189–201.

Stewart, M.B. (1999) 'Low pay in Britain', in P. Gregg and J. Wadsworth (eds.) *The State of Working Britain*. Manchester: Manchester University Press, pp. 225–48.

Stewart, M.B. (2004) 'The inter-related dynamics of unemployment and low-wage employment'. Working Paper, University of Warwick.

Stiglitz, J. E. (2002) *Globalization and its Discontents*. London: Allen Lane.

Sugrue, T.J. (1996) *The Origins of the Urban Crisis: Race and Inequality in Post-War Detroit*. Princeton: Princeton University Press.

Swartz, D. (1997) *Culture and Power: The Sociology of Pierre Bourdieu*. Chicago: University of Chicago Press.

Talwar, J.P. (2001) 'Contradictory assumptions in the minimum-wage workplace'. *Journal of Contemporary Ethnography*, 30(1): 92–127.

Talwar, J.P. (2004) *Fast Food, Fast Track: Immigrants, Big Business and the American Dream*. Boulder: Westview Press.

Taylor, F. (1998) *The Principles of Scientific Management*. Mineola, NY: Dover Publications.

Taylor, I., Evans, K. and Fraser, P. (1996) *A Tale of Two Cities: A Study in Manchester and Sheffield*. London: Routledge.

Taylor, P. and Bain P. (1999) 'An assembly line in the head: work and employee relations in the call centre', *Industrial Relations Journal*, 30(2): 101–17.

Taylor, P. and Bain P. (2003) 'Call center organizing in adversity: from Excell to Vertex', in G. Gall (ed.) *Union Organizing: Campaigning for Trade Union Recognition*. London: Routledge, pp. 153–72.

Taylor, P. and Bain P. (2005) '"India calling to the far away towns": the call centre labour process and globalization', *Work, Employment and Society*, 19(2): 261–82.

Taylor, P., Hyman, J., Mulvey, G. and Bain, P. (2002) 'Work organization, control and the experience of work in call centres', *Work, Employment and Society*, 16(1): 133–50.

Taylor, P., Baldry, C., Bain, P. and Ellis, V. (2003) 'A unique working environment: health, sickness and absence management in UK call centres', *Work, Employment and Society*, 17(3): 435–58.

Thompson, E.P. (1968) *Making of the English Working Class*. Harmondsworth: Penguin.

Thompson, E.P. (1978) *The Poverty of Theory and Other Essays*. London: Merlin Press.

Thrift, N. (1988) 'The geography of economic international disorder', in D. Massey and J. Allen (eds.) *Uneven Development: Cities and Regions in Transition*. London: Hodder and Stoughton, pp. 6–46.

Touraine, A. (1971) *The Post Industrial Society*. New York: Random House.

Townsend, P. (1979) *Poverty in the United Kingdom*. London: Penguin.

Townsend, P., Davidson, N. and Whitehead, M. (1988) *Inequalities in Health: The Black Report and The Health Divide*. Harmondsworth: Penguin.

Toynbee, P. (2003) *Hard Work: Life in Low-pay Britain*. London: Bloomsbury.

Travers, M. (2001) *Qualitative Research Through Case Studies*. London: Sage.

Tufts, S. (2006) '"We make it work": the cultural transformation of hotel workers in the city', *Antipode*, 38(2): 350–373.

Turner, F. (1961) *Frontier and Section: Selected Essays of Frederick Jackson Turner*. Englewood Cliffts, NJ: Prentice Hall.

Urry, J. (2000) *Sociology Beyond Societies: Mobilities for the Twenty-first Century*. London: Routledge.

Van Gyes, G., De Witte, H. and Pasture, P. (eds.) (2001) *Can Class Still Unite? The Differentiated Workforce, Class Solidarity and Trade Unions*. Aldershot: Ashgate.

Venkatesh, S.A. (1994) 'Getting ahead: social mobility among the urban poor', *Sociological Perspectives*, 37(2): 157–82.

Venkatesh, S.A. (2000) *American Project: The Rise and Fall of a Modern Ghetto*. Cambridge and London: Harvard University Press.

Visser, J. (2002) 'Why fewer workers join unions in Europe: a social custom explanation of membership trends', *British Journal of Industrial Relations*, 40(3): 403–30.

Wacquant, L.J.D. (1996) 'Red belt, black belt: racial division, class inequality and the state in the French urban periphery and the American ghetto', in E. Mingione (ed.) *Urban Poverty and the Underclass: A Reader*. Oxford, Blackwell, pp. 234–74.

Wacquant, L.J.D. (1997) 'Three pernicious premises in the study of the American ghetto', *International Journal of Urban and Regional Research* 21(2): 341–53.

Wacquant, L.J.D. (1998) 'Pierre Bourdieu', in R. Stones (ed.) *Key Sociological Thinkers*. Basingstoke: Palgrave, pp. 215–29.

Wacquant, L.J.D. (1999) 'Urban marginality in the coming millennium', *Urban Studies* 36: 1639–47.

Walby, S. (1992) 'Post-post-modernism? Theorizing social complexity', in M. Barrett and A. Phillips (eds.) *Destabilizing Theory: Contemporary Feminist Debates*. Cambridge: Polity Press, pp. 31–52.

Waldinger, R., Erickson, C., Milkman, R., Mitchell, D.J.B., Valenzuela, A., Wong, K. and Zeitlin, M. (1998) 'Heltos no more: a case study of the Justice for Janitors Campaign in Los Angeles', in K. Bronfenbrenner, S. Friedman, R.W. Hurd, R.A. Oswald and R.L. Seeber (eds.), *Organizing to Win: New Research on Union Strategies*. Ithaca and London: ILR Press.

Waldinger, R. and Lichter, M.I. (2003) *How the Other Half Works: Immigration and the Social Organizaton of Labor*. Berkeley: University of California Press.

Walker, A. and Walker, C. (eds.) (1997) *Britain Divided: The Growth of Social Exclusion in the 1980s and 1990s*. London: CPAG.

Warhol, A. and J. Baudrillard (1995) *Andy Warhol: paintings 1960–1986* / mit Beitragen von: Jean Baudrillard. [et al.]; herausgegeben von Martin Schwander. Stuttgart, Hatje.

Watt, P. (1996) 'Social stratification and housing mobility', *Sociology*, 30(3): 533–50.

Watt, P. (1998) 'Going out of town: youth, race and place in the South East of England', *Environment & Planning D: Society and Space*, 16: 687–703.

Watt, P. (2001) 'The Dynamics of Social Class and Housing: A Study of Local Authority Tenants in the London Borough of Camden'. Unpublished PhD thesis, Department of Geography, King's College, University of London, London.

Watt, P. (2003) 'Urban marginality and labour market restructuring: local authority tenants and employment in an Inner London borough', *Urban Studies* 40(9): 1769–89.

Watt, P. (2004) 'Narratives of urban decline and ethnic diversity: white flight and the racialization of space in London and the south east of England', paper presented at the Countering Urban Segregation Conference, Free University of Amsterdam.

Watt, P. (2005) 'Housing histories and fragmented middle-class careers: the case of marginal professionals in London council housing', *Housing Studies*, 20(3): 359–81.

Watt, P. (forthcoming) 'Respectability, roughness and "race": neighbourhood place images and the making of working-class social distinctions in London, *International Journal of Urban & Regional Research*.

Watt, P. and Jacobs, K. (2000) 'Discourses of social exclusion: an analysis of Bringing Britain together: a national strategy for neighbourhood renewal', *Housing, Theory and Society*, 17: 14–26.

Watt, P. and Stenson, K. (1998) '"It's a bit dodgy around there": safety, danger, ethnicity and young people's use of public space', in T. Skelton and G. Valentine (eds.) *Cool Places: Geographies of Youth Cultures*. London: Routledge, pp. 249–65.

Webb, S. (1990) 'Counter-arguments: an ethnographic look at women and class', in L. Stanley (ed.) *Feminist Praxis: Research, Theory and Epistemology in Feminist Sociology*. London: Routledge.

Webster, C. (2003) 'Race, space and fear: imagined geographies of racism, violence and disorder in Northern England', *Capital & Class*, 80: 95–122.

Webster, F. (1995) *Theories of the Information Society*. London: Routledge.

Westergaard, J. and Resler, H. (1976) *Class in a Capitalist Society*. Harmondsworth: Penguin.

Westergaard, J., Noble, I. and Walker, A. (1989) *After Redundancy: the Experience of Economic Insecurity*. Cambridge: Polity Press.

Western, B. (1997) *Between Class and Market: Postwar Unionization in the Capitalist Democracies*. Princeton: Princeton University Press.

Whyte, W. (1956) *The Organization Man*. New York: Simon and Schuster.

Wilks, S. (1996) 'Class compromise and the international economy: the rise and fall of Swedish social democracy', *Capital & Class*, 58: 89–111.

Williams, C.C. and Windebank, J. (1998) *Informal Employment in the Advanced Economies*. London: Routledge.

Williams, C.C. and Windebank, J. (2002) 'The uneven geographies of informal economic activities: a case study of two British cities', *Work, Employment and Society* 16(2): 231–50.

Williams, C. (1988) *Blue, White and Pink Collar Workers in Australia*. Sydney: Allen & Unwin.

Willis, P. (1977) *Learning to Labour: How Working Class Kids Get Working Class Jobs*. Farnborough: Saxon House.

Willmott, P. and Young, M. (1960) *Family and Class in a London Suburb*. London: Routledge & Kegan Paul.

Wills, J. (2005a) 'The geography of union organizing in low-paid service industries in the UK: lessons from the T&G's campaign to unionise the Dorchester Hotel, London', *Antipode*, 37: 139–59.

Wills, J. (2005b) 'Work, identity and new rhetorics of mobilisation', paper presented at ESRC seminar series, Working Class Lives: Sociologies and Geographies (No. 6: New Workers, New Organising, New Working Class Studies), London.

Wilson, W.J. (1987) *The Truly Disadvantaged: the Inner City, the Underclass and Public Policy*. Chicago: University of Chicago Press.

Wilson, W.J. (1991) 'Studying inner-city social dislocations: the challenge of public agenda research', *American Sociological Review*, 56: 1–14.

Wilson, W.J. (1996) *When Work Disappears: the World of the New Urban Poor*. New York: Knopf.

Wirth, L. (1938) 'Urbanism as a way of life', *American Journal of Sociology*, XLIV: 1–24.

Wood, S. (ed.) (1982) *The Degradation of Work? Skill, Deskilling and the Labour Process*. London: Hutchinson.

Worth, S. (2005) 'Beating the "churning trap" in the youth labour market', *Work, Employment and Society*, 19(2): 403–14.

Wrench, J., Rea, A. and Ouali, N. (eds.) (1999) *Migrants, Ethnic Minorities and the Labour Market: Integration and Exclusion in Europe*. Basingstoke: Macmillan.

Wright, E.O. (1985) *Classes*. London: Verso.

Wright, E.O. (1997) *Class Counts: Comparative Studies in Class Analysis*. Cambridge: Cambridge University Press.

Wright, E.O. (ed.) (2005) *Approaches to Class Analysis*. Cambridge: Cambridge University Press.

Wynne, D. (1998) *Leisure, Lifestyle and the New Middle Class*. London: Routledge.

Young Jr., A.A. (2000) 'On the outside looking in: low-income black men's conceptions of work opportunity and the good job', in S. Danziger and A.C. Lin (eds.) *Coping With Poverty: The Social Contexts of Neighborhood, Work and Family in the African-American Community*. Ann Arbor: University of Michigan Press, pp. 141–71.

Young, M. and Willmott, P. (1957) *Family and Kinship in East London*. London: Routledge & Kegan Paul.

Zuberi, D. (2006) *Differences that Matter: Social Policy and the Working Poor in the United States and Canada*. Ithaca and London: Cornell University Press.

Zweig, F. (1952) *The British Worker*. Harmondsworth: Penguin.

Zweig, F. (1961) *The Worker in an Affluent Society*. London: Heinemann.

Zweig, M. (2000) *The Working Class Majority: America's Best Kept Secret*. Ithaca: Cornell University Press.

••••••••• Notes

1   These journalistic accounts follow in a long and honourable tradition of reporting about poverty and the working class; see George Orwell's *Down and Out in Paris and London* (Orwell, 1940) and *The Road to Wigan Pier* (Orwell, 1962).
2   We leave to one side the possibility that this maybe due to our own limitations as teachers.
3   The government has employed a version of the RG scheme since the 1911 Census; the class categories in use up until 2001 were originally devised to assist in measuring infant mortality (Crompton, 1998: 59). Until 1970, the RG scheme was based on clustering occupations by 'standing within the community', but this was changed in 1980 to reflect similar levels of occupational skill (Reid, 1998).
4   See Ray (2002) for an excellent discussion of the extent to which these embedded concepts articulated the process of economic globalization.
5   The popularity of 'reality' TV shows based around 'ordinary lives' is a further exemplar of this in ways which some might feel are empowering; it is not just the celebrity who can be 'gutted' at their latest failure.
6   The philosopher Immanuel Kant is said to have cancelled his 'regular as clockwork' afternoon walk when he received the news whilst the poet Wordsworth wrote that 'bliss was it to be alive that day'. The philosophical revolution, which became known as the Enlightenment, was already underway at the time of French Revolution of 1789.
7   As we shall see in Chapter 5, one explanation for the rise of gentrification is the search for a sense of belonging by today's disequilibriated members of the professional middle classes.
8   This built on earlier work (the so-called Hawthorne Electric studies) which had shown, also from a non-Marxist perspective, how different forms of managerial control influenced worker productivity and alienation; where an interest was taken in the workers, productivity tended to rise (Mayo, 1949).
9   This reflects the evocative description in D.H. Lawrence's *Sons and Lovers* of the way the miner divides his wage packet and gives the wife her wages whilst he keeps his for the pub and other such activities.
10 Robert Moore (2004) was an undergraduate student at the time and a later collaborator with Rex. He claimed that Rex's (1961) *Key Problems in Sociological Thought* was the only theory text that students had to bother with, although he concedes that the publication of *Classes in Modern Society* by Bottomore (1965) caused some anxiety as final examinations approached.
11 It is worth noting for students reading these accounts 40 or so years later that the pace of academic life was a little less frantic and publication dates of the books were often much later than the ideas themselves, which had been promulgated in seminars and conference papers. It might be argued that this allowed for them to be well-considered pieces which might be contrasted to the current rush to publish which is caused by the regular Research Assessment Exercises and the workings of the academic promotion system.

12 T.B. recalls as a student in the late 1960s trying to find a copy of Lockwood's article in the University of Essex library only to discover that it had been removed with a razor blade from the bound version of the *British Journal of Sociology*. When it was eventually tracked down, it was quite apparent from the physical state of the volume that it was probably the only set of pages that had been read.

13 Many of the contemporary novels of the time explored this theme, usually in terms of a Northern working class. Examples include Alan Sillitoe's *Saturday Night and Sunday Morning* and David Storey's *This Sporting Life* both of which were filmed.

14 For example, Edward Thompson never received a professorship and Eric Hobsbawm only got a chair towards the end of his academic career.

15 The racialized 'white flight' aspect of post-war working-class suburbanization in England was not as sharply crystallized as in the United States, but at the same time this was also a function of the class-dominated perspective that British sociologists used at the time (Watt, 2004).

16 Friedman's theories had their first outing in Chile under General Pinochet following the coup d'etat in 1973, which deposed and murdered the elected President Salvador Allende. They were brutally effective in cutting inflation and living standards and raising unemployment.

17 See Willis (1977) for a classic Marxist account of such transitions for young men.

18 It is towards this social exclusion resulting from industrial restructuring that the EU has directed its 'objective two' structural funding.

19 The Randstad is a collective term for the Dutch cities of Amsterdam, Rotterdam, Utrecht and The Hague; see Burgers (1996) for a critique of whether the Randstad is a credible geographical unit.

20 We should, however, bear in mind Smith's (2002) point that it is often the non-gentrified cities in Africa, Asia and Latin America which have borne most painfully and directly the costs of this process of global industrial change.

21 The term 'LA School' was then exported as a 'ready to use' concept to the rest of the academic world; see Gottdiener (2002) for a pointed critique.

22 A condition of the state-backed insurance policies is that you only get a payout if you rebuild in the same place, thus guaranteeing much of the lunacy will continue.

23 Confusingly, this would be termed a working-class household in the United Kingdom.

24 One could add a fifth aspect, political alienation, whereby the underclass is said to reject mainstream politics in either a radical or retreatist non-participation direction (Gallie, 1994b; Buckingham, 1999).

25 Although Murray (1984) is described as a 'conservative' by commentators in the United States, his approach shares a great deal with neo-liberal economists like Friedman who stress the negative effects of public services and policies as opposed to those supplied by the market.

26 Puntenney's study illustrates Wacquant's (1997) point that official statistics and other survey data provide a limited purchase on understanding certain aspects of the lives of the urban poor, notably those informal and illegal activities they use to 'get by' which necessitate the use of qualitative methods. Initially Puntenney (2000) used a survey of the mothers and then followed this up with semi-structured interviews. As she says, the women did not reveal their earnings from informal employment in the survey whereas 'the in-depth interviews elicited far more information about this type of employment' (2000: 70, note 3). A similar methodological discrepancy occurred in research undertaken in North London by Watt (2001, 2003) on council tenants; see also Bourgois, 1995: 2–8; Smith, 2005.

27 These labour market conditions cluster in 'labour market regimes' which are distributed according to the welfare state regimes in place (Esping-Andersen, 1990: 144–61).

28 Alesina and Glaeser (2004) provide a recent account of why the welfare state in the United States differs so markedly from those found in European societies.

29 The neglect of housing is arguably particularly detrimental to understanding the notion of decommodification given the way that housing plays such a significant role in the social and spatial distribution of resources (Murie, 1998; Harloe, 1995).

30 See Esping-Andersen (1996), Mishra (1999), Alcock and Craig (2001).

31 Our calculations are based on Enrenreich's (2002: 197–8) earnings. There is likely to be a slight discrepancy between the official figures we present, based on 2002 data, and Ehrenreich's wages earned during 1998–2000. However, she herself calculated that her wages in Portland as a cleaner were $43 a week above the poverty level (2002: 61).

32 Ehrenreich (2002: 213) cites data from the Economic Policy Institute that suggests that a 'living wage' for a family of one adult and two children was $30,000 annually or $14 an hour, around double the official poverty level.

33 This official 'claimant count' number is significantly less than the International Labour Organization figure of 1.46 million in June 2003 (Flaherty et al., 2004: 33).

34 See Watt and Jacobs (2000) for a critique of this report using Levitas' model of three discourses of social exclusion.

35 See Morlicchio (1996) for an overview of deteriorating labour market and social conditions in Naples.

36 The dire employment circumstances frequently faced by immigrants are highlighted by the drowning of 19 Chinese cockle pickers in 2004 in Morecambe Bay in the North of England. They were employed on an illegal basis by 'gangmasters' in a complex and shadowy world of sub-contracting. The cockle pickers lived, worked and died in appalling social conditions that make the term 'social exclusion' seem somewhat inadequate ('Cockler deaths', *The Guardian*, 9 February 2004: 4).

37 Karazman-Morawetz and Ronneling (2003: 239) comment that an irregular economic sector is 'apparently absent in Sweden'. See also Breckner (2002) and Peterson (2002) for case studies and discussion on how refugees have fared within the Swedish labour market and social democratic welfare state.

38 Although immigrants may not necessarily be poor income-wise in social democratic countries, their day-to-day mobility may be restricted by fears of racist attacks as in the case of Africans living in Finnish cities (Sabour, 1999).

39 Thanks to Loic Wacquant for his assistance in devising this table.

40 From the left, see Wilks' account of 'the Swedish model in ruins' (1996: 94) as a consequence of globalization.

41 Managers 'enforce flexibility' among their employees by basing work schedules according to their previous weeks' 'performance' (Talwar, 2004: 73). This means managers effectively determine who works and for how many hours on a week-by-week basis.

42 See Talwar (2001) for an extended discussion of this issue.

43 Taylor and Bain (2005) estimate that Indian call centres employed between 75,000–115,000 people in June 2003.

44 This commonality occurs despite the fact that the research has been undertaken from a variety of theoretical perspectives: Taylor and Bain write from a labour process perspective, Belt writes from a feminist perspective, while Hyman et al. (2003) use a Weberian action-centred approach.

45 Research on both paid domestic employers and employees has been undertaken by Hondagneu-Sotelo (2001) in Los Angeles and Scrinzi (2003) in Genoa. See also Andall (2000) for a black feminist analysis of African paid domestic service workers in Rome.

46 This area of South London was one of the five locations included by Zweig (1961) in his study of affluent industrial workers; he interviewed workers at an electrical assembly plant. Reading Smith's book alongside that of Zweig provides a stark illustration of the seismic shifts that have occurred in working-class neighbourhoods and employment patterns during the last four decades.

47 With apologies to Frankie Goes to Hollywood.

48 See I Roberts (1993) for a detailed account of the ship-building industry in Sunderland and the role of skilled craft workers.

49 Similar to the recent national 'chav' style.

50 Savage (2000) has made the point that individualism was a strong theme of manual working-class culture in the post-war period.

51 Florida (2002) makes a similar point; he claims that in casual conversations on aircraft, people used to tell you for whom they worked but now they tell you where they live.

52 Interestingly, he has had more influence in the United Kingdom in terms of thinking about class than in his native France; English language writers have been able to draw on his published work without committing to his overall institutional and intellectual position in ways that were not open to French sociologists.

53 The role of symbolic capital in Bourdieu's theoretical oeuvre is complex and it can be having a different status from that of the other three capitals (Swartz, 1997: 90–93).

54 Bourdieu's pictorial map of class positions in France only includes economic and cultural capital (1984: 128–9).

55 See Charlesworth (2000) for an illustration of this point.

56 See Skeggs (1994) for a detailed account of how she undertook this feminist ethnography and Travers (2001: 141–2) for a methodological critique.

57 A slight majority of manual home owners in suburban Woodford near London self-identified as middle class (Willmott and Young, 1960).

58 An examination of the Essex Class Survey questionnaire lends credence to Saunders' criticism, given that the first class-identity question was directly preceded by twelve other questions on class (Marshall et al., 1988: 295).

Index